THE
CELTIC DRUIDS'
YEAR

THE
CELTIC DRUIDS'
YEAR

Seasonal Cycles of the
· Ancient Celts ·

JOHN KING

BLANDFORD

A BLANDFORD BOOK
Paperback edition published 1995
Hardback first published in the UK 1994 by Blandford
A Cassell imprint
Cassell plc, Wellington House,
125 Strand, London WC2R OBB

Hardback reprinted 1994, 1995

Distributed in the United States by
Sterling Publishing Co., Inc.,
387 Park Avenue South, New York, NY 10016-8310

Distributed in Australia by
Capricorn Link (Australia) Pty Ltd
2/13 Carrington Road, Castle Hill, NSW 2154

British Library Cataloguing-in-Publication Data
*A catalogue entry for this title is available from
the British Library*
ISBN 0-7137 24617 (Hardback)
0-7137 24633 (Paperback)

Typeset in Litho Link Ltd, Welshpool, Powys, Wales
Printed and bound in Great Britain by
Hartnolls Limited, Bodmin, Cornwall

Rag ow mamm, Myghternes a Nev, neb a wra ow hembronk yn-mes ankow bys yn bywnans.
Rag ow gwreg, Mary Jane, an bennseviges neb a dheuth ha bos ow myghternes.
Rag ow mab, Gawan Ke, avel ro gwaytyans ha kevarwoedhyans.

For my mother, Queen of Heaven, who will lead me out of death and into life.
For my wife, Mary Jane, the princess who became my queen.
For my son, Gawan Ke, as a gift of hope and guidance.

CONTENTS

Acknowledgments

I am grateful to my wife, Mary Jane, for reading the first manuscript in draft and making many helpful suggestions and comments; to Frances Lynch of the University College of North Wales at Bangor and to Richard White of the Gwynedd Archaeological Trust, for their correspondence on Anglesey; and to the late Frank Baker, of Cornwall, for interesting correspondence and discussions about the Magi and other Biblical topics. I am also grateful to Dr Ken George of the University of Plymouth for his helpful corrections to some literally astronomical errors. Any remaining mistakes are, of course, my own responsibility.

Note on Time Measurement

All year dates are given using the Christian conventions AD (Anno Domini) and BC (Before Christ), simply for universality of understanding.

All times are given in Universal Time, also called Greenwich Mean Time. To convert to local times, the reader should subtract one hour for each 15° longitude west of the Greenwich meridian. Moon phases are sometimes listed on different calendar dates because of these time differences.

In Druidism, as in some other religions, a day means a night followed by a day, starting and ending with sunset.

Note on Languages

Greek, Latin, Persian, etc. are in italics. Breton, Irish, Welsh, Cornish, Middle English, etc. are in roman type between single quotation marks at the first mention; subsequent references are without the quotation marks.

INTRODUCTION

THE WESTERN MIND has been fascinated by the archetypal image of the noble savage for at least two centuries. The dramatic shift in perspective expressed in the writings of Rousseau is now deeply rooted in the Western psyche, and our opinion of primitive peoples – by which we usually mean races, tribes or nations living in smaller social units than ours and more closely and directly involved in their own food production – is now permanently coloured, usually in rose tints, by a vague but general perception that the modern world has gone astray by becoming too mechanized and impersonal, and that in primitive cultures we see the last remnants of a higher, purer state of being, an Eden, from which we are now irrevocably cast out.

This highly romantic view is paradoxically coupled with an understandable disdain for the harsh realities of a primitive life – the discomfort, disease, danger – and a peculiarly ambivalent attitude towards primitive religions and belief systems. Profoundly insecure in its theologies and moral philosophies, the Western mind is simultaneously fascinated and repelled by religions which seem to offer simpler, more certain and more complete views of the cosmos, yet, at the same time, are full of logical inconsistencies and beliefs which the modern, scientific mind rejects. At the core of the three most influential Western religions, namely Judaism, Christianity and Islam, lies a mystery which is beyond science; yet this mystery sits uncomfortably in a society which sees empirical, scientific observation as the foundation of truth. Despite Einstein and the principle of uncertainty, we remain fundamentally Newtonian in our outlook, and we have compartmentalized all our metaphysics into holding areas: we expect the mystery of the universe to unfold when our telescopes and measuring instruments are sufficiently capable, not when a single God or many gods choose to reveal it.

Druidism is a Western religion (the quintessential Western religion, it might be argued). However, it comes from a time before Newton – from before Christ and from before Homer, for that matter – which considerably distances its tenets from the modern Western mind. Druidism also has fundamental relations, and perhaps a shared provenance, with Eastern religions (for example, in the doctrine of karma) which further removes it. As a result, the prevailing modern attitude towards Druidism is a paradoxical combination of mystical admiration and thorough scepticism. We see both attitudes, for example, in John Milton, who wrote in his *Areopagitica* of 1644 agreeing with 'writers of good antiquity and ablest judgment' that 'ev'n the school of Pythagoras, and the Persian wisdom, took beginning from the old Philosophy of this Iland', yet who three years later, paraphrasing a passage in Tacitus's description of the Anglesey massacre of AD 60, described the Druids as 'a barbarous and lunatic rout'. In our own time, such views as there are also tend to the polar extremes. The scientific view, perhaps best exemplified by the eminent archaeologist Stuart Piggott, finds the ancient history of Druidism interesting enough, but goes to some lengths to dismiss the philosophical or religious tenets of Druidism as simple, fatuous, childish. In part, this sceptical attitude is a reaction to a long parade of zealots and fanatics who have made Druids exemplars of their own mystic beliefs. 'Nearly everyone who has written of them at length has written of Druids of his own making,' says A.L. Owen in *The Famous Druids*, 'and this can be said not only of Drayton, Pope, Carte and Stukeley, for example, but also of distinguished modern scholars.'

I will probably commit the same sin, but not with any proselytizing intention. To write about the religion of Druidism (as opposed to just the archaeology and history of Druidism) without any reference to the metaphysical, indeed with active antipathy towards anything not susceptible of 'scientific' proof, would be a relatively pointless exercise. On the other hand, to write about Druidism with the intention of conveying and proselytizing an essentially mystic view of the cosmos to the reader, as so many have done already, would be a disservice to whatever truth about Druidism can still be discerned. In short, this book attempts to tread its own straight path, eschewing mystic proselytizing on the left and scientific scepticism on the right.

To a very great extent, the problem is one of historical and cultural perspective, exactly the same as with any other historical subject. For example, anecdotes given by classical writers tell us that Celtic warriors frequently agreed to repay small cash debts in the next world, which they (the Roman authors) took as evidence that the Celts were convinced of an immediate, real and active life after death. The imaginative leap required of the modern reader is the attempt to understand that the other world was as real to the early Celts as, say, China is to us now: we may not have been there ourselves, but we would find anyone sceptical of our belief that such a place exists decidedly odd. Attempting to understand Druidism requires a number of imaginative leaps, some of considerable proportions to a modern sensibility: heads which talk after death, people who shift their shape into animals and back again, and so on. Even if we cannot accept such events as real or possible, we have to accept that the early Celt's belief in them was real, which requires of us at least an empathetic understanding – something like the theatre audience's willing suspension of disbelief – to make any sense of further study.

The cultural alienation is compounded by the distance modern Western society has moved away from the realities of the agricultural cycle. We are, by and large, so far removed from direct involvement in the production of our own food, from wind, tide, spraint and track, that the routines of earth, sea, moon, sun and stars are foreign and mechanical to us. We no longer meet the cyclic changes of the year organically, instinctively, spiritually; we simply turn the heating or the air-conditioning up or down. It requires a considerable effort of imagination to go back to a time when the changes in the seasons and the changes in our own bodies felt intimately and irrevocably connected, and the tides and stations of the year demanded a physical response through ritual acknowledgment.

To an even greater extent, especially by comparison with other historical subjects, the problem is one of sources and interpretation. Because the Druidic tradition was oral, our written evidence is *about* Druids, not *by* Druids (with the possible exception of a few monumental inscriptions). There is a comparative abundance of archaeological evidence, all of which is subject to possible misinterpretation.

The archaeological evidence, which has quantitatively increased dramatically in this century, is almost entirely 'text-free', to use archaeological jargon; in other words, it is not accompanied directly by inscriptions or other written evidence which might help corroborate inferences. The Druids certainly had writing. We have inscriptions in Ogham, we have classical references to their use of Greek letters, we have a few actual inscriptions in Romanized Celtic, using the Roman alphabet; yet, by and large, the archaeological evidence stands alone. The problem of misinterpreting text-free archaeological evidence can be described quite simply. Suppose we find evidence of a large, rectangular wooden building. We can immediately infer, or speculate, that such a building would have had some use other than just basic shelter. It might have been a meeting hall, or a temple perhaps, but we have no evidence to prove that. Then, on the same site, we have the good fortune to find evidence of a burial site, containing both animal and human bones, and, a day or two later, to discover a well-preserved cauldron, extensively and lavishly decorated. We can make some logical inferences: the animals and humans probably died fairly close to the site; the animals were probably eaten, and so on. However, inference becomes speculation, and then invention, very quickly. We are strongly tempted to assume that the cauldron had some ritual or religious significance (particularly since magic cauldrons figure frequently in medieval Celtic literature), but we have no definitive proof. It may be that this particular tribe just happened to boil its porridge in highly elaborate cookware. The ground shakes even more when we begin thinking about the nature of the ritual, or the possible philosophical beliefs motivating it. There is a grey area between inference and assumption which is a trap for the unwary; it is all to easy to seize on unclear evidence and rush on to a preconceived conclusion.

At a certain point, the sceptic and the believer must part company. I have read the New Testament closely, with what I believe is a good deal of sympathy, empathy and understanding, but I am not a Christian, so the resonances of that text in me must be different from those experienced by someone who is. From the Renaissance onwards, too many scholars, authors, antiquarians and prophets have roped in and saddled Druidic lore, then, to borrow Stephen Leacock's witticism, ridden madly off in all directions. From Aubrey, Stukeley, Rowlands, Wood and Iolo Morganwg through to the modern practitioners of the religion, Druidism has become a hotchpotch of taboos, moral and even political strictures, vague theories of the cosmos, interpretations, conjectures, eccentricities and plain inventions, until whatever remains of original and ancient Druidic lore is very difficult to discern. We are looking at a muddy river and trying to form a true picture of the clear stream from which it sprang. The believer, or at least the reader who is willing to suspend disbelief, may finally gain the better view; the sceptic will continue to see nothing but mud.

The accounts of Druidism in classical and medieval literature must all be considered as distorted in one way or another. Rome, which provides many of our earliest descriptions of the Celts, was utterly different in character from the peoples its authors described. The Roman Empire was urbane, organized, politically centralized, literary, cultured and militaristic. The Celts had no (or at least very few) organized political alliances, no concept of empire, no written literary tradition, no centralized military system. Where Rome had soldiers, the Celts had warriors. Naturally, when we read a Roman account of the battle of Arausio in 105 BC in which the Celts slaughtered more than 80,000 Roman soldiers, we expect the author to accentuate the barbaric, bellicose and bizarre aspects of his Celtic subjects. Often, the Celts were indiscriminately lumped together with Germans and Scythians, even with Parthians – the point being that they were all barbarians living beyond the civilizing influence of Rome. Caesar and, later, Strabo, both attribute to the Celts a form of human sacrifice in which great numbers of victims, animal and human, were supposedly imprisoned in a huge wickerwork figure (Strabo uses the Greek word *kolosson*, Caesar writes of *immani magnitudine simulacra*) and burned alive. Two separate authors give us similar accounts: that sounds convincing. Yet Strabo also describes execution by arrows, and we have good evidence that the early Celts never used archery in warfare. We know that bows and arrows are not mentioned anywhere in the earliest Celtic texts, and even the words for bow and arrow in Goidelic are late loan-words. Similarly, Pliny's famous account of the Druidic mistletoe ritual is full of implausible details. So, we must accept classical written evidence with caution.

There is a similar antipathy between describers and described in the Christian literature of the Romanesque period and the early Middle Ages. Much of the history and mythology of the early insular Celts survives only through the writings of monks in the early Celtic Christian Church. Slap in the middle of a clearly pagan text, we find sudden interpolations of Christian nomenclature or ideology. For example, a very early Welsh chronicle has the following entry for the year AD 516 or 518 (the exact date is disputed): 'The battle of Badon in which Arthur carried the cross of Our Lord Jesus Christ, for three days and nights, on his shoulders, and the Britons were victorious.' What does this text tell us? Arthur was victorious – that seems acceptable without too much dispute. Arthur was a Christian? Well, perhaps he was; his enemies, after all, were pagan Saxons who still worshipped Frey and Woden. He was an important military leader (only much later was he elevated to the status of king) in a nation now largely converted to Roman Christianity. He literally carried a cross for three days and nights? Perhaps he did, but why? To give thanks for his victory? To seek divine intervention in a ritual practised before the battle? Or even, to take the phrase literally, Arthur carried the cross *during* three days and nights of battle: it was his only weapon, and gave him divine protection. Or perhaps the chronicler is using the phrase metaphorically, to express the notion that Arthur represented the Christian force ('carried the cross') against the pagan? We will never know.

In any case, all of the early texts were written centuries after the period in which Druidism flourished untrammelled by Christian influence. In the Irish texts, for example, the earliest complete version of *The Wooing of Etain* appears in the fourteenth-century *Yellow Book of Lecan*. An earlier, partial version is to be found in the twelfth-century *Lebor Na Huidre*. The contents list of *The Book of Druimm Snechtai* suggests that the tale existed in written form as early as the eighth century. Even so, that still means the earliest possible written version dates from at least 500 years after the Christianization of Britain.

The Druids functioned in a real society. They were the priests, judges and diplomats of a complex ancient culture, and however dimly they themselves may be remembered, the Celtic society to which they belonged is at least to some extent known to us. The Druids were profoundly respected both by their own people and by Greek and Roman authors who considered themselves civilized commentators on an uncivilized pagan enemy. The Druids are mentioned by name by Aristotle, Sotion, Posidonius, Julius Caesar, Cicero, Diodorus of Sicily and Timageneus; in the Christian era, by Strabo, Pomponius Mela, Lucian, Pliny, Tacitus, Suetonius, Dion Chrysostom and Clement of Alexandria. Most of these writers, and many of the later Christian commentators, discussed a system of belief sufficiently organized to be dignified by the term 'philosophy', a body of belief which probably existed before the time of Homer and which was still actively followed until at least the Middle Ages in Europe. Its moral precepts, converted and absorbed in the medieval code of chivalry, are deeply embedded in Western culture and affect us to this day. Despite the paucity of historical evidence, despite the unreliability and bias of our acknowledged sources, despite the layer upon layer of invention and historical reconstruction, our effort to discover and understand ancient Druidic beliefs will be rewarded if it sheds some further light, however small, on the reality of the human condition in our own age, and on the correlation between the tides, seasons and stations of the year and our own interaction with the divine.

CHAPTER ONE

RELATIONS AND ORIGINS

IT IS A FAIRLY SIMPLE TASK to plot similarities of belief and practice between Druidism and other religions. Far more difficult – in fact, more or less impossible – is the task of making a convincing demonstration that any of these similarities might represent an actual relationship, or, even more significantly, a common origin. None the less, several writers have attempted it, which in part accounts for the poor reputation Druidic scholarship has acquired.

All human beings, whatever their culture, follow a basic pattern of life so obviously universal it seems hardly worth describing: we are born, we grow, we find food, we make war and peace, we raise children, we experience pleasure and pain, we grow old, we die. Out of that common experience grow archetypal images and symbols of different aspects of the human condition. Jung argues that these symbols are, in fact, available to all of us through a 'collective unconscious' intelligence.[1] The gods who emerge from these common experiences will often be very similar in aspect, even though they are culturally quite distinct. For example, Mars is the Roman god of war, Ares is his Greek counterpart, Thor is his Teutonic name, to the Irish he is Lug or Lugh, to Slavs he is Pyerun and to the Chinese he is Kuan-ti. We know that there are cultural connections between the Greek pantheon and the Roman pantheon, but it would be an obvious mistake to assume that, say, the Chinese and Slavic pantheons are culturally related merely because they share some gods with very similar characteristics.

Druidism is a primitive religion (primitive does not mean simple, however) in the sense that its precepts spring from close observation of the natural world and an intimate connection with the rhythms of the annual agricultural cycle. It shares many symbols, and some ritual practices, with other primitive and early religions. In two vital aspects, namely its doctrine of metempsychosis and its emphasis on mathematics and calendrical propriety, it seems closely related to the philosophy of Pythagoras. None of the apparent relationships emerging from these similarities can be proven beyond doubt, although some long-held convictions about the origins of Druidism can certainly be disproved. The rest of this chapter describes the apparent relationships with other early religions and peoples, among which it is possible there may be some common origins, although that cannot be proven; briefly examines the question of Pythagoras, metempsychosis and karma; and looks at the etymology of the word 'druid' itself, for further evidence of possible origins.

The Persians

Fire, which plays an important role in Druidism, was directly worshipped in ancient Persia (modern Iran). It was a symbol of purification, personified in Persian mythology by Atar – the name itself means fire – who was the son of the highest god, Ahura Mazda. Mazdaians were also known as *ateshperest*, which means fire-worshippers, and several early Parthian or Persian princes took the honorific title *fratakara*, meaning fire-maker. Both Druids and ancient Persians used fire for ritual purification and as a prophylactic against disease, as well as an antidote. The Persians placed anyone who was wounded or sick close to a fire, which may also have been a Druidic practice. There are one or two instances of wounded heroes lying close by a fire in the early Irish texts, and quite frequently in later Arthurian literature, but whether it was for comfort, for physical healing or for spiritual healing, it is difficult to say: indeed, it may well have been for all three reasons.

Ancient Persians worshipped in the open air, as did the Druids. There were certainly dedicated Druid temples by Roman times, some with icons or statues of deities, but it seems that early Druids avoided buildings and representational icons of the Godhead. Most of the surviving Druidic icons and statues come from Gaul, which fell under Roman influence much earlier and more thoroughly than Britain, where such images are far rarer. For Mazdaians and for Druids (as for many American native peoples), features of geography held deep religious significance. Springs, wells, streams, rivers, lakes, rocks, mountains, groves, and even individual trees, were not only sites of worship but sacred in themselves. The Greek word *nemeton* (its precise derivation is unclear) is used by classical writers to describe the sacred grove, usually a circular clearing or glade in an oak forest, or mixed forest of oak, ash and beech, in which Druidic ceremonies took place. The Druids certainly also used stone circles under an open sky, including Stonehenge, although it is important to point out that the vast majority of such sites in the British Isles were built by the long-headed peoples who preceded the Celts, and any links between their practices and beliefs and the tenets of Druidism are extremely tenuous.

The Persians practised an ambrosial rite with a fermented liquor known as *haoma*, which was supposed to confer immortality. The early Celts seem to have believed that immortality was universally available in any event, although they were also inveterate and lusty users of fermented liquors. The Welsh legend of Gwion, found in *The Mabinogion*, inclues the episode of the boy Gwion tending a magic cauldron, licking from his fingers three drops of liquid which accidentally splash on them, and becoming instantly filled with the knowledge of all things present, past and future. The ritual cauldron figures strongly in early Celtic myth and remains a potent symbol of magical power.

To ancient Persia belong the Magi, originally a separate Medean priest cult. The word *magus* has since come to have a much wider significance for the Western world. It is the root of magic and magician, but its best-known application is to the 'wise men'[2] or 'astrologers'[3] who brought gifts of gold, frankincense and myrrh to the Christ Child at Bethlehem. Strabo, and the later English antiquarian, Borlase, noted a similarity between the Druids and the Magi in ceremonial practice, namely the carrying of sacred plants. The Persian equivalent of the sacred mistletoe is supposed to be the parastic *barsum*, which Stukeley associates with the 'teil' mentioned in Isaiah 6:13: 'But yet in it shall be a tenth, and it shall return, and shall be eaten: as a teil tree, and as an oak, whose substance is in them, when they cast their leaves: so the holy seed shall be the substance thereof.' O'Curry makes a specific claim (without any available proof) of the connection with the Magi:

It must occur to everyone who has read of Zoroaster, or of the Magi of Persia, and of the sorcerers of Egypt mentioned in the seventh chapter of Exodus, that Druids and Druidism did not originate in Britain any more than in Gaul or Erin. It is indeed probable that, notwithstanding

Pliny's high opinion of the power of the British Druids, the European Druidical system was but the offspring of the eastern augury, somewhat less complete, perhaps, when transplanted to a new soil than in its ancient home.[4]

The Egyptians

There are two obvious similarities between the religion of ancient Egypt and Druidism. The first is the shared notion of many gods, goddesses and spirits (over 3,000 of them in Egypt), all of whom are none the less inadequate representations, or subservient lesser gods, of a single deity beyond name, beyond representation. In addition to Osiris and Isis, the Egyptians worshipped separate gods named after the moon, the elements and the River Nile. They even combined gods, as occasion required: for example, the god Apis, son of Osiris and Ptah (supposedly begotten by a ray of moonlight falling on his mother) was later amalgamated with Osiris and became Osiris-Apis, or Asar-Hepi; he was eventually Graecized as Serapis and worshipped by both Egyptians and Greeks. Yet, beyond and above all these gods, beyond even Osiris, was the deity mentioned very infrequently and only by the name Neter, meaning God, who parthenogenetically brought forth the two eldest gods, Shu and Tefnut, through whom in turn all creation came about.[5] This concept, similar in some ways to the Christian one of the Logos or the Holy Spirit, is also found in Pythagorean number mysticism (obviously related to the number one, or unity), and it is also found in Druidism. It is a doctrine quite alien to the straightforward pantheons of Greece and Rome, but it is very similar to Hinduism, and close in pattern to the Christian model of a single God manifest in a mystic Trinity and surrounded by archangels, angels, cherubim and seraphim. The most obviously different element in Druidism is that the figure of the immutable deity is female, rather than male or neuter.

Secondly, the Egyptian deities were frequently associated with animals and animal cults, or represented as having animal heads on human bodies, as were some Celtic deities. Osiris the bull-headed, Anubis the jackal-headed and Horus the falcon-headed have an almost identical counterpart in form in Cernunnos, the stag-headed Celtic god widely worshipped in Gaul and universally represented as having a human body and an antlered head. This stag-king, probably shamanistic in origin, is a figure of great antiquity: he, or a god of the

Horus, son of Isis, a falcon-headed god from the Egyptian pantheon.

An image of the horned god Cernunnos, from the cauldron found at Gundestrup, Jutland. The creature in the god's left hand is a ram-headed serpent. In his right hand he holds a gold torque, or necklace.

same aspect, even appears in palaeolithic cave paintings over 20,000 years old. Stag-mummers, who dance in antlers, still survive in European folk-tradition. It is possible that the image of horns on the head of a defeated king (later, cuckolded husband) is related to ritual king-making practices using the god's image. Like Egyptian gods, Celtic gods frequently shapeshifted into animal form, the most frequent appearances being in the guise of bears, birds, or wolves. Unlike the Egyptians, however, the Celts also had a very important horse cult, the most powerful representation of which was the goddess Epona, who was depicted as a sacred white mare. The serpent was sacred to the Egyptians and frequently used, in exactly the same way as by the Druids, as a potent symbol for healing. Hippocrates, sometimes called the Father of Medicine and the originator of the Hippocratic oath, was born in Asia Minor in about 460 BC, and he had as his sign a rod or staff entwined with serpents. It is similar to the herald's *caduceus* associated with Hermes or, later, Mercury, also used as a wand or symbol of authority by Druids, which is used to this day as a universally recognized symbol for medicine or medical practice. At Dendera, the temple of Isis contains a frieze representing Isis and Osiris being presented with gifts of bulls, horns and mitred snakes. The winged snake, or dragon, figures in early Celtic mythology, as well as in later Arthurian and medieval romance.

According to *Lebor Gabala*, the Irish *Book of Invasions*, the earliest copy of which dates from the twelfth century, Ireland was populated before the Celts by waves of successive invasions, the invading tribes or nations being, in succession: the Cessair, the Partholon, the Nemed, the Fir Bolg, the Tuatha de Danaan and, lastly, the sons of Mil Espane. Of these, the earliest were Africans – that is, Egyptians – later defeated by Lugh the long-handed.

It has been suggested that the figure through whom Egyptian ideology came into the West, and therefore into Druidism, was Moses, who returned to Israel from Egypt, bringing with him the teachings of the god Ptah.

The Phoenicians

The Phoenicians, along with the Babylonians and Chaldeans, are credited with the earliest (Western) study of astronomy, principally on account of their manifest skill in maritime navigation. While no Phoenician sextant has been found, Phoenician sailors are thought to have had at least some practice in dead reckoning. Their ancient harbours, with the notable exception of present-day Beirut, are largely silted up and unusable now by maritime traffic, but there was a time when Phoenician captains were considered the ablest in the world. It is reasonable to assume that at least some mathematical and calendrical skill must have contributed towards this reputation.

The Phoenician language, descended from ancient Canaanite and related to Hebrew and Moab (the Phoenicians are called both

Canaanites and Sidonians in the Old Testament) is significant to us because the Phoenicians played an important role in developing and diffusing the alphabet which forms the foundation of Greek and, subsequently, all European writing. The Druids were certainly familiar with Greek letters, as well as with the distinctively Celtic Ogham script. The influence of the Phoenician language and culture was also long lasting. From a beginning somewhere around the fifteenth century BC, the language, later known as Punic, still survived as a rustic dialect in North Africa as late as the fifth century AD. Or, to make the same point more forcibly, Phoenician culture flourished before, during and even long after the advent of Druidism.

Like the early Celts, the Phoenicians believed that geographical features, such as headlands, mountains, springs, wells, even individual trees, were inhabited by different divinities. The god or goddess of such a site was generally called the Ba'al (master or owner) or Ba'alath (mistress) of the sacred site. This title (given in the form of the name 'Baal' in the Old Testament) was used by the Aramaeans (Be'el) and Babylonians (Bel) also, and there is strong support among several authors for the theory that the name is somehow directly related to that of the Celtic sun-god Bel, also known as Belinus.

The Phoenicians worshipped in the open air as well as in temples and placed pillars and conical standing stones, particularly meteoric stones (usually called by the Greek name *baetylia*), prominently in their sanctuaries, a practice which has obvious similarities to Druidism. They also followed the practice of inscribing wishes, messages or curses on small rolls of lead, which were then thrown into graves or wells to reach the spirits of the underworld, a similar practice to that of the Celts, Greeks and Romans.

Pinkarton argues that Druidism was patently directly descended from the Phoenicians, probably through Phoenician sailing expeditions to the Iberian peninsula, Gaul and Britain,[6] while Samnes states equally dogmatically that 'the customs, religion, idols, offices and dignities of the ancient Britons are all clearly Phoenician.'[7]

The Greeks

There are some observable similarities between early Greek religious practices and Druidic practices.

The Greeks worshipped on mountain tops, and in sacred clearings or groves in the forest. Strabo says that all sacred places, even those without trees, were called by the name *nemeton*, which has since come to refer specifically to the Druidic sacred grove.

The number three, or trinity, was especially significant to the Greeks, as well as to the Druids. The Greek practice of dividing sacred hymns into three stanzas (strophe, antistrophe and epode) is reminiscent of the Celtic practice of uttering mysteries, or even recording historical events, in triads or triple-phrases, often to the extent that content or meaning was distorted to make it conform to the pattern of coming in threes.

The oak, famously venerated by Druids, was looked upon as the oldest tree by the Greeks, and the most ancient Hellenic oracle was said to be sited by the oak of Dordona, the leaves of which were used to wrap and conceal the oracular declarations.

The Israelites

The antiquarian Stukeley argued that Druidism stemmed directly from Abraham, whom he called the 'Father of the Druids.'[8] There is little, if any, evidence to support his view. There are several Old Testament references to oaks which seem to imply some special mystical attribute to that particular tree. For example, Abraham's altar, for the ritual sacrifice of Isaac, was built 'by the oak of Moreh'. Hosea 4:13 tells us that the Israelites 'sacrifice upon the tops of mountains, and burn incense upon the hills, under oaks and poplars and elms, because the shadow thereof is good.' The Hebrew word for oak also means oath, and there is evidence that the oak signified a burial place.[9] The golden calf or bull worshipped as an idol by the Israelites has its counterpart in the Druidical image of the god Hu Gadarn, or Hu the Mighty, who, like Noah, survived the deluge and first brought the skill of ploughing to mankind. Dibbuks, demons and lesser deities, some of which might seem to correlate to Celtic spiritual figures, have been pushed into the background by contemporary Judaism. Generally, despite Stukeley's clear assertion, the connections between Judaism and Druidism seem very tenuous.

Other relations and possible origins

The Orient has suggested itself as a candidate to many writers. Bertrand claims parallels between Druidic rituals and religious practice in Tibetan lamaseries.[10] Maurice claims the Druids to be direct descendants of Brahmans living in the Caucasus.[11]

Other views tend towards the fanciful, even the absurd. There have been claims that the Druids came originally from the Moon – a literally lunatic view. Christine Hartley claims the Druids as Atlanteans:

> Schrader in his work 'Reallexicon' says that the Keltic Druids were quite different from any other priesthoods of western Europe and that it has never been known from where their origin sprang; we, with our perhaps great inner knowledge, are content to take it that their wisdom came with the basis of our mysteries from the great Temples of Atlantis.[12]

That offensive phrase 'our perhaps great inner knowledge' typifies much of the New Age romantic mysticism which muddies our view of real Druidism.

Pythagoras

The principle Druidic doctrine cited in evidence of the origin of Druidism is that of metempsychosis, or the transmigration of souls, also associated with the Eastern doctrine of karma. The classical philosopher with whom this doctrine is most closely identified is Pythagoras (he of the right-angled triangle theorem which every school student encounters in geometry). Western tradition has garbled and simplified the doctrine into the notion of weak or sinful humans returning to the world after death in the form of an animal, as in this exchange from Shakespeare's *Twelfth Night*:

> CLOWN: What is the opinion of Pythagoras concerning wildfowl?
> MALVOLIO: That the soul of our grandam might haply inhabit a bird.
> CLOWN: What thinkest thou of his opinion?
> MALVOLIO: I think nobly of the soul, and no way approve his opinion.

Many writers have suggested that the Druids derived the doctrine of metempsychosis directly from Pythagoras; that is certainly possible, as is the reverse view that it was Pythagoras who learned the doctrine from the Druids. Pythagoras was a native of the Greek island of Samos, and flourished about 530 BC. He moved from Samos to Croton, in southern Italy, a city famous for its medicine. Croton's main source of wealth was the importation of Ionian wares for resale in Spain and in Gaul. It is quite possible that Pythagoras travelled to those countries, and to Egypt and the British Isles. While both the latter would have been at the periphery of the known world, what we now know about, for example, the Brendan voyage and the arduous journeys of saints in the early Celtic church reminds us that we should not underestimate the nautical capabilities of earlier peoples. It is equally possible that British Druids visited Pythagoras in the Mediterranean, or in Egypt. From unrecorded antiquity, Britain exported tin (which is how it acquired the classical name Cassiterides) in exchange for Mediterranean wine and amber, and while all such commercial voyages would have been hazardous, they were by no means impossible. The legend that Jesus's uncle, Joseph of Arimathea, landed in Britain and stayed at Glastonbury, bringing the boy Jesus with him on at least one occasion, stems from the fact that Joseph was a seafaring merchant who would have frequently undertaken such voyages. The trade routes overland through Gaul were well established, which would require the briefest of passages across the English Channel; but there is also convincing evidence of maritime traffic all along the Atlantic seaboard, from the Mediterranean out into the Bay of Biscay and beyond.

Stuart Piggott, probably the greatest authority to date on the archaeology and history of Druidism, is highly sceptical of claims (and principally the claim made by Clement of Alexandria in the first century AD) that Pythagoras may have learned from the Druids. He is at pains to point out that over-enthusiasm has made more of Druidic philosophy than it deserves, and concludes that the legendary conversation between Pythagoras and Abaris the Hyperborean (that is Briton, one living beyond Boreas, or the home of the North Wind) can never have taken place, or, if it did, Abaris must have been a central Asian shaman.[13]

Piggott reaches this conclusion in defiance of the following evidence, which is Diodorus's quotation from the historian Hecateus, who was a contemporary of Pythagoras in the sixth century BC:

Opposite to the coast of Celtic Gaul there is an island in the ocean, not smaller than Sicily, lying to the north, which is inhabited by the Hyperboreans, who are so named because they dwell beyond the North Wind. This island is of a happy temperature, rich in soil and fruitful in everything, yielding its produce twice in the year. Tradition says that Latona was born there, and for that reason, the inhabitants venerate Apollo more than any other god. They are, in a manner, his priests, for they daily celebrate him with continual songs of praise and pay him abundant honours. In this island there is a magnificent grove, or precinct, of Apollo, and a remarkable temple, of a round form, adorned with many consecrated gifts. There is also a city, sacred to the same god, most of the inhabitants of which are harpers, who continually play upon their harps in the temple, and sing hymns to the god, extolling his actions.

The island is clearly Britain, not central Asia, and the 'remarkable temple' is obviously Stonehenge. The sacred city may be Avebury, or a site now lost to us. The same passage continues:

The Hyperboreans use a peculiar dialect, and have a remarkable attachment to the Greeks, especially to the Athenians and the Delians, deducing their friendship from remote periods. It is related that some Greeks formerly visited the Hyperboreans, with whom they left consecrated gifts of great value, and also that in ancient times Abaris, coming from the Hyperboreans into Greece, renewed their family intercourse with the Delians. It is also said that in this island the Moon appears very near to the Earth, that certain eminences of a terrestrial form are plainly seen in it, that Apollo visits the island once in a course of nineteen years, in which period the stars complete their revolutions, and that for this reason the Greeks distinguish the cycle of nineteen years by the name of 'the great year'. During the season of his appearance the god plays upon the harp and dances every night, from the vernal equinox until the rising of the Pleiades, pleased with his own successes. The supreme authority in that city and the sacred precinct is vested in those who are called Boreadae, being the descendants of Boreas, and their governments have been uninter-ruptedly transmitted in this line.

The most convincing evidence that it is Druidism being described here is the reference to the 19-year cycle, or 'great year', which will be discussed at length in Chapter Ten. This period – actually a little less than 19 years – is the rotation period required for the lunar and solar calendars to coincide exactly. Calculating the intermesh of the two systems requires fairly sophisticated mathematical, astronomical and calendrical skills. It is almost certainly related to the period of 19 years which Julius Caesar informs us was the statutory study period for any acolyte wanting to train for the Druidic priesthood. As Robert Graves points out, this cycle was not publicly accepted in Greece until about a century after Hecateus's time. Graves also explains the apparent anomaly of the two harvests in the year:

Since, according to Pliny, the Celtic year began in his day in July (as the Athenian also did) the statement about the country producing two harvests, one at the beginning and one at the end of the year, is understandable. The hay harvest would fall in the old year, the corn harvest in the new.[14]

The doctrine of metempsychosis, or reincarnation, has become better known more recently in the West through the influence of Eastern religions. The Sanskrit term karma is frequently used, although its precise meaning has been garbled and altered in much New Age mysticism. Christmas Humphreys gives us a good working definition of the original term:

> *Karma*: root meaning 'action'; derived meaning 'action and the appropriate result of action'; the law of cause and effect. As applied to the moral sphere it is the law of ethical causation, through the operation of which a man 'reaps what he sows', builds his character, makes his destiny, and works out his salvation. *Karma* is not limited by time or space, and is not strictly individual; there is group *karma*, family, national, etc. The doctrine of rebirth is an essential corollary to that of *karma*, the individual coming into physical life with a character and environment resulting from his actions in the past.[15]

That helpful definition might be applied almost verbatim to the Druidic concept of 'geis' (an Irish term, difficult to translate exactly, but implying both 'taboo, forbidden action' and 'predetermined fate') and more generally to the important Druidic concept, most fully expressed in the Irish law tracts, of the 'fitness of things', all of which will be discussed in more detail later. Whatever the difficulties of comparative origin, it is obvious that there is at least some correspondence between these Druidic beliefs and the doctrines of Pythagoras and of karma.

Russell, in a loose attempt at humour, describes Pythagoras as 'a combination of Einstein and Mrs Eddy.'[16] The Mrs Eddy, or ludicrous, aspect of Pythagoras's character he observes in the primitive taboos of the Pythagorean order: for example, the prohibition on eating beans (since, as Pliny points out, beans produce wind and wind is the expression of a departed soul or spirit escaping from the body). The Einstein reference – Einstein's name is used as a metaphor for mathematical genius – expresses admiration for

Pythagoras's mathematics, although Russell later goes on to summarize some of the mathematical difficulties and inconsistencies in Pythagoras's theories.

The famous theorem of Pythagoras, namely that in a right-angled triangle the sum of the squares on the sides adjoining the right angle is equal to the square on the third side, or hypotenuse, is probably familiar to the general reader. It is based, however, on a philosophical view of the cosmos which may not be so familiar. For Pythagoras, the entirety of the universe is charged with number; number is everywhere observable, 'all things are assimilated in number'. He speaks of oblong numbers, pyramidal numbers, in the same way that we still use the graphic terms square and cube, for example, to describe the relationships between 4 and 16, or 3 and 27. Number, shape, harmony and function are related.

Far more significantly, in number, and its associated science of geometry, there is a truth which is ineffable, transcendental. We know what a circle is, and can define it in mathematical terms; but a perfect circle, with no irregularity, however infinitesimal, cannot be drawn or observed. The circle (or square, or straight line) is a concept, not an empirically observable fact. Every line, no matter how finely drawn, has dimension, and is therefore not a line at all, strictly speaking, only the representation of the concept of a line. This is a simple enough observation, but one which has profound philosophical implications, all the way through Euclid, Plato, Leibnitz, Kant and the gamut of Western thought, as Russell points out:

Mathematics is, I believe, the chief source of the belief in eternal and exact truth, as well as in a super-sensible intelligible world. Geometry deals with exact circles, but no sensible object is exactly circular; however carefully we may use our compasses, there will be some imperfections and irregularities. This suggests the view that all exact reasoning applies to ideal as opposed to sensible objects; it is natural to go further, and argue that thought is nobler than sense, and the objects of thought more real than those of sense perception. Mystical doctrines as to the relation of time to eternity are also reinforced by pure mathematics, for mathematical objects, such as numbers, if real at all, are eternal and not in time. Such eternal objects can be conceived as God's thoughts. Hence Plato's doctrine that God is a geometer, and Sir James Jeans' belief that He is addicted to arithmetic. Rationalistic as opposed to apocalyptic religion has been, ever since Pythagoras, and notably ever since Plato, very completely dominated by mathematics and mathematical method.[17]

The origin of the name 'Druid'

In Old Irish, 'druid' is the plural form, 'drui' being the singular. There is a modern Irish word druid, which is a noun meaning starling or a verb meaning to close – both meanings seem totally unrelated to 'drui'. In the classical texts the form of the name is *druidai* in Greek, and *druidae* or *druides* in Latin. It occurs only in the plural. *Dryades* in Latin are water-nymphs, which may account for Lucan's variant spelling of *dryadae*. Other variants, such as *drysidae* or *drasidae* are assumed to be corruptions or the result of miscopying from manuscripts. Pliny correctly recognized the Greek *drus*, meaning oak, as related. The proto-Indo-European (i.e., reconstructed) original word element is given as 'deru-', from which root come many important words, including tree, truce, true, truth, trust, endure and druid.[18] Several authors suggest that the second syllable may be related to Indo-European 'wid' meaning know, as in Old English 'witan' and modern English wit – the derived meaning would be 'knower of the oak' or 'oak knowledge', which is attractively poetic but linguistically unlikely. More plausibly, the second syllable may be a Celtic terminal ('-ath' is an example in Cornish), which tends to extend and make more abstract a word's meaning. (For example, Cornish 'kov' means memory, the extended 'kovath' means remembrance.) Thus, 'derwydd' (Welsh for druid) would be from 'derw' (oak) and a terminal – 'ydd'. It has been suggested that bard ('bardd' in Welsh, 'bardh' in Cornish) might be formed similarly from the word 'barr', meaning branch. Some writers have tried to relate druid to dervish etymologically, to emphasize a mystical connection, but dervish is from the Turkish *dervis*, meaning mendicant, which in turn was derived from the Persian word *darvesh*, meaning poor.

Summary

There are clear parallels between Druidism and other early religions, although none of the evidence is sufficient to form any definite conclusions about relations and origins. My own view is that the similarities between Druidism and Pythagoreanism are so marked, and so abundant, that the likelihood of there being a direct relation between the two is very high, although the mechanisms and logistics through which such a relationship might have been established and maintained remain extremely unclear. This topic will be discussed in more detail in Chapter Seven.

What is clear is that the Druids functioned significantly within the context of early Celtic society, which is the subject matter of the next chapter.

Notes

1. Carl Jung, *Man and his Symbols*.
2. & 3. Gospel of St Matthew, King James or *Authorized Version of the Bible* (1604) and *New English Bible* (1961).
4. Eugene O'Curry, *The Manners and Customs of the Ancient Irish*.
5. E.A. Willis Budge, *Osiris and the Egyptian Resurrection*.
6. F. Pinkarton, *An Enquiry into the History of Scotland*.
7. Quoted in Dudley Wright, *Druidism, The Ancient Faith of Britain*.
8. William Stukeley, *Stonehenge*.
9. Genesis 25:8: 'But Deborah Rebeka's nurse died, and she was buried beneath Bethel under an oak: and the name of it was called Allon-ba-chuth.' And 1 Chronicles 10:12: 'They arose, all the valiant men, and took away the body of Saul, and the bodies of his sons, and brought them to Jabesh, and buried their bones under the oak in Jabesh, and fasted seven days.'
10. Bertrand, A., *Archéologie Celtique et Gauloise*.
11. Maurice, *Ancient History of Hindoostan*.
12. Christine Hartley, *The Western Mystery Tradition*.
13. Stuart Piggott, *The Druids*.
14. Robert Graves, *The White Goddess*.
15. Christmas Humphreys, *A Popular Dictionary of Buddhism*.
16. & 17. Bertrand Russell, *History of Western Philosophy*.
18. Calvert Watkins, 'Indo-European Roots', appendix to *The American Heritage Dictionary of the English Language*. Third edition, 1992.

· CHAPTER TWO ·

THE EARLY CELTS

GERHARD HERM DESCRIBES THE CELTS as 'the people who came out of the darkness.'[1] His figurative expression neatly describes our ignorance of the origins of the Celts. As I explained in the Introduction, our written evidence begins with the classical authors of Greece and Rome, who were neither reliable, nor objective, in their descriptions; they emphasized the exotic, the barbaric, the bellicose aspects of their subjects. Before them, we have only archaeological evidence, which is subject to misinterpretation. We can make some reasonable inferences, and by the time we reach the Hallstatt and La Tène periods, the number and complexity of discovered artefacts makes interpretation much easier and more reliable. However, the overall problem of insufficient evidence remains, and part of our reconstruction of earliest Celtic history has to be founded on conjecture.

Origins of the earliest Celts

A cave painting of the late Palaeolithic age (about 25,000 years ago), known as the Dead Man composition, is to be found at Lascaux in the Dordogne. The figure has been variously interpreted as a dead warrior, a sleeping hunter, or a shaman in a state of trance. It is painted on rock in a secret site, very difficult to reach, at the bottom of a steep shaft. We might take the known Druidic and early Celtic practice of shaft burial, and throwing votive and sacrificial objects down shafts, as evidence of a relationship with the Dead Man of Lascaux, but there is no direct link beyond that apparent similarity.

Equally uncertain is the Celtic connection with the taming of the horse during the Bronze Age. We are reasonably sure that the horse was first tamed by Asiatic peoples, whose nomadic drifts brought

34

The Dead Man composition found on a cave wall at Lascaux, France. At the bottom of a deep shaft, the figures are difficult to reach.

them westwards into the plains and steppes of central Europe somewhere around 3000 BC. The Celts were renowned horsemen from earliest times, and the cult of the mare-goddess Epona gives further evidence of the significance of the horse in Celtic culture. Even as late as in the fourteenth-century Welsh stories collected in *The Mabinogion*, we find a magical interchange between a new-cast colt and Gwri of the Golden Hair, later called Pryderi, son of Pwyll the ruler of the underworld. To this day, the Celts, particularly in Ireland, are famed for their skill with horses.

The earliest significant archaeological evidence dates from around 700 BC, in what is now known as the Hallstatt period, after the region near Salzburg in Austria where the evidence was found. The main technological feature of the period is the substitution of iron for bronze in weapons and tools.

A new cultural phase, known as the La Tène period, and characterized by extraordinarily complex and beautiful decoration on artefacts, begins around 500 BC. Just to put these dates in a global perspective, it is worth noting that at about this time the classical Greek alphabet is just beginning to emerge, iron is being used for the first time in Egypt, and the classical age of highest Chinese civilization has not yet begun. The opening of the La Tène phase also coincides with the life of Pythagoras, if we accept the date of his death as 497 BC, as has been suggested. This means that any religious concepts shared by Druidism and Pythagoreanism, if there is any real relation between them, must date from at least a full century before any Celtic contact with Rome.

There is no clear date for the arrival of the first Goidelic-speaking Celts in Britain, although any date earlier than 900 BC (about 600 years after the completion of Stonehenge) seems very unlikely. Some time between 500 and 250 BC, during the La Tène phase, occurred the arrival, or separation, of the Brythonic-speaking Celts. These two different groups are sometimes referred to as the Q-Celts and P-Celts.

The linguistic separation is marked by several features, the most obvious of which is the Brythonic (that is, British) substitution of p or b for the Goidelic (that is, Gaelic) q or k sound. The modern Gaelic languages are Irish, Scots Gaelic and Manx; the Brythonic languages are Welsh, Cornish and Breton. All six are sister languages, but where the Goidelic group has a k sound, as in, for example, the well known 'mac', meaning son, the Brythonic has a p or b, as in the Breton, Cornish and Welsh 'mab'. The Welsh word later appeared as 'map', shortened to 'ap', from which a name like Davydd ap (son of) Howell would eventually emerge as David Powell. Similarly, the Irish saint's name Kieran became Pyran (later, Perran) in Cornish.

On the mainland of Europe, the Celts began expanding southwards and westwards during the La Tène period. The first Celtic invasions of Italy took place before 400 BC, when Celtic tribes drove the Etruscans out of the Po valley. Interestingly, it is from the Etruscans that the later Romans borrowed many religious beliefs and practices, including the priestly sanctification of the foundations and outer bounds of a city. It is quite likely that the early Celts found the rigid fatalism of the Etruscans as antipathetic as they later found the rigid authoritarianism of the Romans.[2]

The rise of Rome

The first Celtic encounter with Rome was in 390 BC, at Clusium. The battle is described in detail by Livy (300 years after the event, it should be noted), who tells us that the Celts seized all of Rome except for the Capitol, sacked the city and then withdrew northwards again.

By 380 BC, Rome was rebuilt under an alliance with the Samnites, Rome's former enemy. This date effectively marks the beginning of the rise of the Roman Empire. For the next 400 years, Rome was intermittently at war with the world, including the Celts of Gaul and of Britain. Many of the classical accounts and descriptions of Druidism date from this period.

In 285 BC, Celtic hostilities against Rome began again. The Senones, a Celtic tribe, were exterminated by Roman forces under Dolabella. In retaliation, all the other Celtic tribes in the region rose to attack, but they were crushingly defeated on the banks of the Tiber. The carnage was reputed to be so great that the waters of the river ran red as far as Rome itself. In the following years, the Celts in Italy suffered further defeats, culminating in the Battle of Telemon, or Teleman, in 225 BC, when all the Celtic tribes south of the River Po were destroyed.

It would be natural to follow the story of Celts v. Romans further here, but, to keep events in roughly the right chronological order, we need to make two brief geographical excursions, one to Britain, the other to Asia Minor.

Some time between 500 and 250 BC, the La Tène culture gained predominance in Britain. No one is quite sure why. Rome had not yet expanded into Gaul, so any Gaulish or Belgian Celtic tribes crossing to Britain were not driven there by Romans. There seems to have been a general urge among Celtic tribes of this period to expand into new territory, as happened at approximately the same time in Greece and Asia Minor.

Climatic change would not account for such a sudden expansion, particularly one to the north and west and one to the south and east simultaneously, so there may have been some cultural or even political event or pressure: perhaps a change in hunting, herding or agricultural method, which is now lost to us. In any event, at about the same time, from 280 BC onwards, the Celts began their first invasions of the empire of Alexander the Great. After prolonged power struggles and inter-tribal conflicts, a permanent Celtic presence was established east of the Bosphorus, in the area subsequently known to the ancient world as Galatia, the land of the Gaels.

According to Strabo, the three main tribes involved, who presumably came originally from somewhere north of the Danube, were called Tolistoagii, Trocmi and Tectosages. Galatia was divided between them, each tribe taking responsibility for an area subsequently divided into four parts. These regions were ruled by men whom Strabo called *tetrarchs*, which simply means ruler of a fourth part, each of them answerable to a council of 300 members. If Strabo is right, this would have been a new and distinctly different system of Celtic government, in which democracy and councils or parliaments normally played no part (although there may well have been non-representative councils of warriors or petty chieftains). It may be that Strabo, for some unknown reason, is romanticizing or idealizing his description of the Celts in Asia Minor, or, either by accident or by design, associating them with Attic democracy as practised in Greece. More likely, he is garbling a description of some settlement of power distribution made internally by the Celts to minimize further tribal conflict. The significance of Strabo's attribution lies in the fact that settling tribal disputes was essentially a Druidic function, the Druids being powerful ambassadors, usually independent of any one king or chief.

By the Romans, Celts were most frequently called *Galli*, meaning Gauls, or by individual tribal names; but to the Greeks they were *keltoi* or *Galatai*, which confirms that the proper pronunciation of the word Celt should always be with a hard [k] sound, the Boston Celtics and others notwithstanding. The Romans developed the term *Celtae* from the Greek *keltoi*, and it was only centuries later when the Roman hard c became softened in popular pronunciation, that the soft c 'Selts' first appeared.

Back in Rome, the Battle at Telemon was closely followed in 219 BC by Hannibal's march from Carthage to begin the Second Punic, or Phoenician, War. Hannibal and his elephants were joined by some Celtic tribes, possibly as mercenaries, while other Celtic tribes, like the Allobroges and the Ceutrones, sided against him, despite the fact that Rome was their common enemy. Again according to Livy, Hannibal won the support of those Celtic tribes siding with him by offering to release some captured warriors of the Taurini tribe, after personal combat. (We cannot be sure whether this really happened, or whether Livy is painting us a picture of barbaric Celts casually indifferent to the dangers of trial by the sword.) In the event, Hannibal was defeated by Scipio at Zama in 202 BC, and with that defeat the extensive Romanization of many Celtic tribes began. Warriors became farmers and inn-keepers (very good ones, according to Pliny) as the Roman Empire began to grow. For the moment, Roman influence was confined to what the Romans called 'Gallia Cisalpina', meaning Gaul this side of the Alps. 'Gallia Transalpina', or 'Gaul beyond the Alps', remained relatively free of direct Rome influence.

While this was happening, Galatia in the east was being absorbed in the expansion of the Pergamon Empire, culminating in the defeat of the Celts by Eumenes II in 166 BC. In 133 BC Galatia was bequeathed as a semi-autonomous province to the Romans, who completed their conquest of the rest of Asia Minor by 47 BC. The Galatians continued to exist as an integral, Celtic community, the same community to which St Paul would later address his Epistles.

In the first century BC, the historian Diodorus Siculus wrote the following description of the Celtic peoples who were now succumbing to Roman rule:

> They are very tall in stature, with rippling muscles under clear white skin. Their hair is blond, but not naturally so: they bleach it, to this day, artificially, washing it in lime and combing it back from their foreheads. They look like wood-demons, their hair thick and shaggy like a horse's mane. Some of them are clean-shaven, but others – particularly those of high rank – shave their cheeks but leave a moustache that covers the whole mouth . . .. They wear brightly coloured and embroidered shirts, with trousers called 'bracae' and cloaks fastened at the shoulder with a brooch, heavy in winter, light in summer. These cloaks are striped or chequered in design, with the separate checks close together and in various colours.

We recognize in this ancient description some distinctively Celtic styles of appearance: the long moustache, the dyed and abundant hair, the 'bracae' (breeks, breeches or trousers), the plaid of the tartan or 'fileadh-mor' (the Scots Gaelic term, meaning the great wrap). We also know from modern tradition that individual plaid designs signified tribe or clan allegiance, as they do to this day in Scotland, and it seems reasonable to suppose that they may have had the same significance in Diodorus Siculus's time.[3] There is no mention of plant badges, such as, for example, the sprig of oak signifying the clan Macduff, which may be an omission on the historian's part, or may indicate that plant badges were a later development.

In the same year that Galatia became part of Rome, another Scipio conquered the Iberian Celtic province of Numantia in the west.[4] If the historical accounts are accurate, the Celts resisted the Romans with extraordinary courage and resolve. For 16 months a Celtic garrison of 4,000 held off 60,000 Roman legionaries; then, when all was clearly lost, burned what remained of their buildings and possessions and took their own lives rather than submit to Roman rule. Scipio's conquest was followed by that of Gaius Julius Caesar in 61 BC. Caesar drove the remaining Iberian Celts north and west, where they were finally defeated in their capital of Brigantium. (This north-western corner of Spain, still very Celtic in character, is called Galicia, and has a dialect, *Gallego*, whose name is clearly related to Gaelic).

By the time Caesar returned to Rome to be created consul in 59 BC, the known world south of the Alps, east to west from Galatia to Galicia, was under Roman rule. From here, Caesar's intentions and ambitions turned northwards, to Germany, Gaul and Britain. There followed a crucial period in Celtic history which is very short – a matter of only ten years or so – yet a period in which the entire pattern of the known world was dramatically and irrevocably altered.

The conquest of Gaul

If we suppose, as there seems good evidence for doing so, that Druidism was especially important in the British Isles, then the year 55 BC marks a definite boundary between one phase and the next in our history of Druidic thought and practice. Before then, Druidism flourished in the British Isles free of outside influence, from a beginning lost in the mists of antiquity. After that date, when Caesar sent the first punitive Roman expeditions to discourage the British Celtic mercenaries who had been supporting the resistance in Gaul, British Druidism found itself in contact with, and to a varying and uncertain degree in conflict with, the ideology of Rome, a contact that was destined to last for 500 years (see map).

We know Gaius Julius Caesar well. His own lengthy and detailed accounts of the Gallic Wars are very entertaining as well as informative. He stresses the military and political imperatives which necessitated his advances; but in those sober, relatively unassuming accounts, a monstrous personality is revealed: a genius of extra-ordinary ambition. Rex Warner, speaking in Caesar's voice, paraphrases his achievement:

> Now, at the age of forty-three, I had only a fraction of the military experience which had been possessed at this time of life by Lucullus or Pompey or even Crassus. I believed myself, however, to have no less

[Caledonia]

[Hibernia]

BRITANNIA

Germania
Inferior

Belgica

GERMANIA

Lugdunensis

Germania
Superior

GALLIA

Aquitania

Narbonensis

ITALIA

Carraconensis

HISPANIA

Lusitania

Baetica

Mauretania

Africa

Rome in the time of Augustus: the western provinces (adapted from R.F. Treharne and Harold Fuller (eds.), *Muir's Historical Atlas*).

ability than they, and I knew that, in these years during which I had struggled upwards from the status of a youth hunted by Sulla's executioners to that of a consul of the Roman people, I had acquired a rather exceptional knowledge of politics and of human nature . . .. I did not know that in the course of the next ten years I was to take by storm more than eight hundred cities, to subdue three hundred nations and to fight at various times pitched battles with three million men. Nor did I know that these achievements were only to be the prelude to a still more desperate struggle. All I knew was the strong invitation of a greater future.[5]

Caesar's personality, especially his reliability as a reporter and historian, is of particular interest to our purpose in this book because, of all the classical accounts of Druidism, Caesar's is reputedly the most reliable first-hand one. It is reasonable to conjecture that Caesar may have met Druids face to face: they were, after all, lawgivers and ambassadors among their own people, and they would almost certainly have been involved in any political or military negotiations or treaties. It is Caesar who first indicates the rank or importance of Druids in Celtic society; he uses the term *equites*, meaning literally horsemen, but usually translated as knights, a now archaic term which is overloaded with other subsequent connotations. However, it is clear that, in the vernacular of Caesar's time, the Druids were men of noble rank. Legend has it that Caesar held several lengthy conversations – presumably through an interpreter – with a Druid named Diviaticus or Diviacicus (not a very convincing Celtic name), in the course of which the Druid gave Caesar an outline of Celtic religious belief and practice. Piggott, with some justification, is sceptical of the relationship, attributing the account to 'stock-in-trade of ancient historiography.'[6]

The essential springboard for Caesar's northward advance was control of the broad strip of land known to the Romans as 'Gallia Narbonensis' (see map on page 41; now Languedoc and Provence) which ensured safe passage between the plains of northern Italy and the Iberian peninsula. In a protracted series of campaigns, begun a year after receiving his consulship, Caesar moved northwards to secure the upper and middle Rhine frontier. His enemies were Germans, not Celts, and it is clear from his accounts that he, at least, recognized the difference, although some other classical writers did not. In 54 BC, Caesar invaded Britain again, this time establishing a beach-head by defeating and subjugating Cassivelaunus, king of southern Britain, who thenceforth had to pay tribute to Rome. A Celtic revolt in central Gaul, led by the legendary Vercingetorix, was crushed in 53 BC. By 50 BC, Britain was partly conquered and the Romanization of defeated Gaul was firmly under way. Caesar sat down and wrote his account of the campaigns, *De Bello Gallico*.

During the final conquest of Gaul, it is possible that some Druids fled the mainland and escaped to Britain, although Caesar does not report it. (Even if he knew about it at the time, it would not have seemed historically significant to him.) Gaulish Druids might well have found a way to live in Britain. Their language and culture would certainly have been very close and similar to that of the Britons. Druids and their retinues were also free agents in early Celtic society, certainly by comparison with the warrior aristocracy tied to clan or tribal lands, and the agricultural peasantry bound in allegiance to them. Druids moved like petty kings, assigning themselves to the service of kings and chieftains without any necessary territorial commitment. The Celtic texts inform us that some Druids even had their own small armies.

Cultural assimilation

With Caesar's conquest of Gaul begins the second great phase of the history of the Celts. Druidism in unconquered Ireland and the furthest reaches of the Scottish highlands and islands remained unaffected by Rome. Brythonic Druidism, in what is now England, Cornwall and Wales (and, subsequently, Brittany) was affected by Roman influence, but to varying degree. Very often, indigenous Celtic gods continued to be worshipped alongside imported Roman gods, with little apparent difficulty. The cult of the sun god Mithras, immensely popular among Roman soldiers, spread widely. In Gaul, the Roman conquest had a greater and more complete social consequence; patterns of behaviour, civil government, commerce, transport, coinage, culture, art, and – undoubtedly – religious belief and practice were significantly altered. Even the Gaulish languages were replaced by Latin, which soon became the lingua franca of the entire civilized world.

Artefacts which have survived from this period of cultural assimilation indicate the diversity of influences, particularly in art and sculpture, on the Gaulish Celts. Uninfluenced Celtic art, as exemplified in the astonishingly powerful and distinctive Celtic art of Ireland, is basically of two kinds. The first is crudely and strikingly representational, primal in its impact, represented by the staring stone heads found in Ireland, or figures like the Sheila-na-gig, a grinning figure of the goddess, holding open the labia of her grotesquely large, all-devouring vulva. There is nothing delicate or refined about such images. On the other hand, the second type, as typified by a bronze and iron helmet of the fourth century BC from Amfreville, dredged up from an old channel of the Seine and now displayed at the Louvre in Paris, shows a remarkable subtlety of line, with natural objects like animals or plants flowing and melting seamlessly into intricate whorls, trefoils, spirals and geometric patterns of wonderful complexity, culminating in the knotwork which is now the metaphorical trademark of Celtic art.

However, Gaulish art, as distinct from British and Irish, reveals how other influences broke down these traditions. A limestone sculpture, known as 'The Man-Eating Monster' (page 46), which now stands in the Musée Lapidaire at Avignon, is indisputably Celtic in theme and treatment: a monster with one arm growing from its chin holds aloft in each hand a severed head. The crude representationalism of the piece is absolutely Celtic, the very opposite of classical style. But even as early as the third century BC, some signs of classical influence begin to reveal themselves. A human figure from

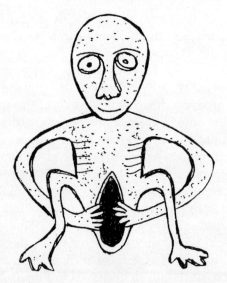

The Sheila-na-gig, a crude representation of the mother-goddess. Most examples are found on Irish stone carvings.

A bronze and iron helmet with gilt decoration, found in a former channel of the River Seine, near Amfreville-sous-les-Monts, Eure, France.

Roquepertuse (page 47), now in the Musée Archéologique in Marseilles, depicts another figure in limestone, but the modelling of the anatomy is more delicate, and the addition of a plinth shows a clear Greek influence, although the overall style of the piece is still distinctly Celtic. By the first century AD, the influences are much more obvious, and even the viewpoint or subject matter has become Romanized. At the Palais de Justice in Carpentras, an arch in the courtyard depicts captive Gauls chained to a tree; the bold outlines of the figures and the abstract patterning of the folds in the clothing suggest that this is the work of a Celtic sculptor, but the theme and treatment suggest a Roman influence, or, even more likely, that the work was sculpted by a Gaulish artist under Roman direction.

From 50 BC, however, Rome had internal struggles with which to occupy itself, culminating in the civil war between Caesar and Pompey which ended in 45 BC with Caesar's defeat of the final Pompeian revolt at Mundi. A year later, Caesar was assassinated by conspirators, led by Brutus and Cassius. His adopted heir, Octavius Caesar, found himself confronted with revolt in Egypt, led by Mark Antony and Cleopatra, and it was not until 27 BC that full internal order was restored to Rome. Octavius declared himself divine and took upon himself the title Augustus, the same Augustus Caesar whose imperial decree, as described in the second chapter of St Luke's Gospel, sent Joseph and Mary out of Nazareth and into Bethlehem. Roman preoccupations at this time were with Judaea in the east, and, to a lesser extent, with Germans in the north. The Celts of Gaul were thoroughly subjugated, and the Celts of Britain were at the periphery of the known world, offering no threat to Rome, and of no importance whatsoever to the emperor or to the Roman people.

The birth and life of Christ is, of course, an immensely significant event in any world view of this chronological account, but it is only of incidental significance to the history of the early Celts. There is a legend that an Irish Druid, Bachrach of Leinster, foretold Christ's birth, and the long-held notion of a direct relation between Druids and the Persian Magi, or Wise Men, who attended the event, was mentioned in the previous chapter. Centuries later, Druidism and Christianity apparently coexisted with remarkable ease, leading many subsequent commentators to draw all kinds of links, parallels, analogies and conclusions about the nature and interrelation of the two religions.

The 'Man-Eating Monster' found at Noves in the Rhône valley. The style and theme are unmistakably Celtic.

The 'Janus' head from Roquepertuse. While still clearly Celtic in style and theme, the treatment is more classical, including a shaped plinth which may show Greek influence.

To pick up the Celtic thread of this brief chronology again, the year AD 5 saw Cunobelinus or Cymbeline, chief of the Catuvellauni tribe, recognized by Rome as King of Britain.[7] Augustus died and was succeeded by Tiberius in AD 14, who in turn was succeeded in AD 37 by the mad Gaius, nicknamed Caligula (meaning little boot) by the soldiers who, when he was a child, adopted him as their mascot in the German wars. In AD 40, tribal wars in Britain led Aminius, son of Cunobelinus, to flee to Rome. Caligula promptly announced the conquest of Britain, and the right of Aminius to the royal title; but it was an empty gesture, since no Roman troops were sent to enforce the pronouncement.

Caligula lasted only four years. His insane excesses led to his assassination by the Praetorian Guard in AD 41, and a most unlikely candidate, his aged and scholarly uncle Claudius (the *I, Claudius* of Robert Graves's outstanding reconstruction) became emperor. Crippled, half-deaf, and deemed half-witted by most of Rome, Claudius nevertheless turned out to be more than Rome had bargained for. Among other signal achievements, he determined to make real the conquest of Britain and secure genuine Roman rule there.

The Roman occupation of Britain

In AD 43, an invasion force led by Aulus Plautius landed in Kent and the British of the south-east, led by Caractacus, were defeated at the Battle of the Medway. Thus the first incursion of Gaius Julius Caesar, almost a century previously, was finally consolidated into a real Roman occupation, made permanent by the vigorous expeditions led by Ostorius Scapula, who was subsequently appointed as the first Roman Governor of Britain in AD 47 (see map opposite).

The Caractacus defeated at the Battle of Medway (whose name would be far better Romanized as Caradocus, since the Celtic original is Caradoc) has since become a figure of high romance in Celtic literature. He was captured and brought to Rome, where, by various accounts, he made an eloquent plea for his family to be spared their lives. The eighteenth-century antiquarian Rowlands puts this version of the speech in Caradoc's mouth:

> If the moderation of my mind in prosperity had been answerable to my quality and fortune, I might have come a friend rather than a captive into this city, and you without dishonour might have confederated with me, royally descended, and then at the head of many nations. As my state at present is disgraceful, so yours is honourable and glorious. I had horses, men, arms and riches; why then is it strange I should unwillingly part with them? But since your power and empire must be universal, we, of course, among all others, must be subject. If I had forthwith yielded, neither my fortune nor your glory had been so eminent in the world – my grave would have buried the memory of it, as well as me – whereas if you suffer me to live now, your clemency will live in me for ever, as an example to after ages.[8]

Whether Caradoc made this speech in Celtic or in Latin is not told. One can easily observe that an imaginative reconstruction of Caradoc's speech would be a favourite literary pastime for Celtophile antiquarians, and there are probably several other windbag variants lying about. However, no matter what Caradoc really did or did not say, the historical fact is that Claudius authorized his release, and he and his immediate family lived out the rest of their natural lives in reasonably comfortable captivity in Rome. (It is interesting to speculate how long it took him to grow tired of the stares at his chequered plaid clothing and white, lime-washed spikes of hair, before he decided to adopt a more Roman style of dress and appearance.)

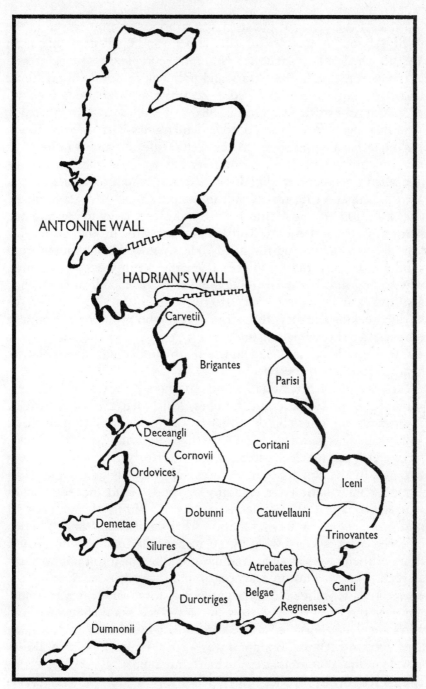

The administrative divisions of Roman Britain by tribal area (adapted from M. Falkus and J. Gillingham (eds.), *Kingfisher Historical Atlas of Britain*).

Some of the detail of the story of Caradoc's capture, given in the twelfth book of the *Annals* of the outstanding Roman historian Tacitus, sheds an informative light on the complexity of Roman and Celtic interaction, both military and political, in Britain at this time. Ostorius Scapula had advanced as far north as present-day Lincoln. Among the British tribe called Brigantes was a warrior chief, Venutius, who was married to a 'chieftainess' of great renown, Cartimandua ('pennseviges' is the Celtic title, usually translated as princess, but these ladies were no fairy-tale waifs). Tribal wars broke out when Cartimandua abandoned Venutius and took as her lover a warrior called Vellocatus. Ostorius Scapula took advantage of the disintegration of the Celtic forces and stepped in to declare the Brigantes' tribal lands a Roman protectorate. In the meantime, Caradoc was mustering his forces. He summoned the Silures from south Wales and the Ordovices from the north-west to join him, which they did. News of the combined force inexplicably reached Ostorius Scapula, who moved effectively against it. Caradoc fled for his life, seeking refuge with Cartimandua, who promptly announced that it was she who had informed Ostorius Scapula, then threw Caradoc in chains and had him sent to the Roman commander's headquarters at Colchester.

Mention of Cartimandua reminds us that women, as well as men, could head the aristocratic families which led the Celtic tribes. Women also fought in battle, either as warriors alongside the men, or as leaders. Best known of these, perhaps, is Boudicca, or Bodicea, *pennseviges* of the Iceni tribe, whose territory lay in the eastern flatlands by the North Sea now known as East Anglia. It requires an effort of imagination, or empathy, to understand the position of women in early Celtic society: we have to shrug off centuries of misogyny heaped on us by Judaism, Christianity and Islam. Women in early Celtic society were by no means inferior to men, did not think of themselves as such, and did not allow men to think of them as such. This was not in reaction to male subjugation, which is the perspective our modern feminism tends to force on us: it was simply the way things were. The Romans, far more male chauvinist and patrician, were horrified to be confronted by women in battle, as their accounts tell us.[9] Boudicca was a royal figure, a political leader and a military commander-in-chief; quite possibly she was also considered divine by her tribe, or at least endowed with divine attributes. She is romantically depicted riding full gallop in a war chariot, blades fixed to the wheel hubs flashing in the sun, her long red hair and blue robes streaming in the wind, a spear held aloft in her hand, the reins of the chariot in the other. The picture is appealing, and may be correct in spirit, but the likelihood is greater that she surveyed her battles as a general usually does, from a higher and safer position to the rear.

Caradoc's capture was in AD 51. Nine years later follows an event which is still difficult to understand in plain historical terms, and which is directly relevant to our theme: the destruction of the Druid settlement on Mona.

The bare facts (in so far as they can be ascertained) are these. In AD 60, the Roman general Suetonius Paulinus marched his forces to the extreme north-western corner of the land we now call Wales, and assembled them opposite the island of Anglesey, known as Mona in classical times (see also page 53). His forces crossed the Menai Strait and completely destroyed a vast encampment of Druids and their retinues who had assembled there. Druidic ritual sites and artefacts were also destroyed.

Again, it is Tacitus who gives us the most detailed account of the event. Tacitus is an impressive and convincing historian, but he did not witness the massacre first hand (he was only five years old when it took place), so we cannot be certain what exactly his sources were, nor how much of the detail is fabricated, either by Tacitus or by the sources. Nevertheless, his description is graphic. He tells us that Suetonius Paulinus first gathered his troops on the mainland, and observed the Druids across the 400 yards (366 metres) of the strait. The Druids clustered in groups, holding their arms up to the sky in prayer, offering 'fearful curses' against the Roman horde. Their women, in mourning, long hair flying in the wind, screamed and lamented with such vehemence that the Roman troops were unsettled and had to be brought back to order. The Roman army crossed the strait, and, after prolonged and bitter fighting, defeated and slaughtered the Druids and their followers, after which 'the groves sacred to savage rites were cut down.'[10]

The difficulty in explaining this event lies in finding, firstly a motive for the Druids assembling on Mona and, secondly, a motive for the Romans wanting to destroy them. It was the Roman custom, acquired through long practice in Gaul and elsewhere, to absorb and gradually assimilate alien religions in conquered territory. As long as the religious beliefs or practices of the local peoples had no direct political consequence, Rome learned that benign toleration of non-Roman religions was by far the most secure method of maintaining a successful occupation. One convincing piece of evidence for this assumption is the great number of religious sites which had dual or parallel dedications, one to a local or tribal Celtic god, the other to the nearest Roman counterpart. For example, at Bath, with its healing springs, the original Celtic deity, Sulis, was honoured in the Roman name for the place (Aquae Sulis), but the site was also dedicated to Minerva, and votive offerings have been found with both names inscribed on them. There were certainly many religious sites with dual dedications in Gaul and in Britain.

Then why did the Romans attack the Druids of Mona with such ferocity? There is no clear answer, but one possible inference is that the Druids represented far more of a political force than simply a religious force, a notion which is very much in accord with our other information, chiefly from Irish sources, about Druids as diplomats, ambassadors, lawmakers and lawgivers. It has been suggested that Mona was the collective granary of all the Celtic tribes of Britain, the distribution of the grain being supervised by Druids, and that the destruction of the granary was decided as a simple military

An altarpiece discovered at Reims, in France. The Celtic god Cernunnos, in the centre, is flanked by the Roman gods, Apollo and Mercury. It was common for Celtic and Roman gods to be worshipped at the same site.

expediency to weaken the enemy's strength. The theory is plausible, but it seems insufficient. The gathering of Druids in large numbers, coupled with our knowledge of the sanctity of geographical locations in Druidism, suggests very strongly that Mona was an especially sacred place, although that in itself would not fully account for the Roman destruction either.

Frances Lynch, the authority on Anglesey, writes about Tacitus's description in the following way:

> He nowhere actually states that Anglesey was a noted centre of Druidic power, though the political refugees that he mentions more than once may have included many Druids. The description of Anglesey as the main seat of the British Druidic Order is that of commentators influenced by the large part played by the Druids in the battle to defend the island (actual involvement in warfare was exceptional among Druids) and the unusually determined effort made by the Romans to wipe out the Order and prevent their sacrifices after their victory. Recent commentators have pointed to the finds at Llyn Cerrig Bach in support of their view . . ... Although it is worth pointing out that Tacitus does not actually say that Anglesey was a renowned religious centre, the implications and conclusions drawn by most commentators are probably true: the island may well have contained an exceptionally large and influential community of Druids.[11]

Druids did maintain retinues which sometimes included warriors, even small armies, but the vernacular texts in particular give us a very clear picture of Druids as essentially non-belligerent, at least in directly military operations. Their weapons, if they had any, were satire and malevolent utterance.

Llyn Cerrig Bach (meaning 'lake of the small rock' in Welsh) is a small pool, close by Traeth Cymyran, on Anglesey, in which many remains of votive offerings have been found, some of them apparently originating hundreds of miles away, suggesting perhaps further evidence of the transcendence of Druidic authority over tribal boundaries.

Richard White, Director of the Gwynedd Archaeological Trust, reminded me that the Isle of Man and Manaw Gododdin are also associated with the classical name Mona, and that Ptolemy registers Mona as an offshore island of Hibernia. However, the research of his own Trust in discovering the auxiliary fort attested by Tacitus at Aberffraw seems to confirm that Anglesey was, indeed, the Mona on which the massacre occurred.

The pattern on a shield-boss found at Llyn Cerrig Bach, on the island of Anglesey, off the Welsh coast.

The massacre on Mona in AD 60 marks the end of a very short but highly significant period in the history of the British Druids. If we take the first phase, the phase of Druidism unaffected by Rome previously described, as being from undefined date, but perhaps even as early as approximately 900 BC, up to the first Roman landings in Britain in the first century BC, the second phase is a much shorter period – the 115 years from 55 BC to AD 60, which point we have just reached. The third phase, from AD 60 to the present day, when outside influences, and especially Christianity, increasingly affect, distort, diminish and marginalize Druidism, is less significant to the purpose of this book, and so will be summarized more briefly.

The Roman occupation of Britain, with the exception of Ireland and central and northern Scotland, continued for the next 400 years. The Roman armies used Celtic tribes as mercenaries, intermingled with them and absorbed them, until eventually almost whole legions of men originally of Celtic stock fought as soldiers in the name of Rome. Through intermarriage and the introduction of Roman ways of life – particularly commerce – Celtic attitudes were modified, and gradually Celtic culture and religion were absorbed into a broader Romano-British structure. New words came with new ideas. The Latin *fenestra*, meaning window, is 'fenester' in Cornish, 'ffenestr' in Welsh. Similarly, *pons* (bridge) is 'pont' in Welsh. Even the word for a church or temple, the Latin *ecclesia*, was adopted: the modern Cornish is 'eglos'.

During this 400-year period, Rome itself became Christian, and the new religion spread to all parts of the empire. The Celts, although numerically superior to any settlers of purely Roman stock, became so extensively Romanized that many aspects of earlier Celtic culture were transformed or lost. The schools of the 'filid', or seers, supposedly Druidic, are said to have survived in the Scottish Highlands until the eighteenth century. It is certainly true that Ireland and parts of Scotland escaped Roman influence, but the mainstream Druidism of mainland Britain must have undergone either extensive moderation or extensive decline during this period. As was mentioned earlier in this chapter, the advent of Christianity did not seem to precipitate any particular friction. It seems reasonable to suggest that the centres of strongest Roman influence, the south and east, the military settlements, where Mithras, Mars and Jupiter had earlier held sway, probably converted soonest to Christianity, while the peripheral and rural communities, particularly in Cornwall and Wales and along the Atlantic seaboard, probably remained more actively involved in Druidism.

Around AD 285 the Emperor Diocletian partitioned the Roman Empire into two separate empires, the western centered on Rome, the eastern on Byzantium. Way up north, at the edge of the known world, the Roman commander of the British fleet, named Marcus Aurelius Carausius, took advantage of the imperial power shifts and declared himself Emperor of Britain. Diocletian, busily engaged in trying to check Rome's decline, had neither the political will nor the resources to challenge the claim, in such an unimportant corner of the world.

Direct Roman rule was eventually restored by the Emperor Constantius, who had commemorative medallions struck portraying London at his feet, with the legend 'Restorer of the Eternal Light' (page 56). His son, Constantine the Great, semi-mythologized as Costentyn in early Celtic literature and still commemorated in place-names like Constantine, near Helston in Cornwall, reunited the two empires under Rome in 312 and he was baptized a Christian on his death-bed in 337.

About AD 360, Picts and Scots crossed Hadrian's Wall to invade northern Britain, and they were finally repulsed by Theodosius in 369. The fourth century also saw a series of raids and incursions into Romano-Celtic Britain by Irish tribes. In 395, Niall of the Nine Hostages, High King of Ireland, raided Chester and Caerleon, and a series of pirate wars continued for ten years until Niall's death in a sea battle in 405.

In 436, Roman troops left Britain for good. Almost immediately, new raids on Britain began from the east, led by Germanic tribes of the peoples known as Angles, Saxons and Jutes. The name of one of

The Arras medallion, struck about AD 296, depicts Emperor Constantius as the saviour of Britain and the 'Restorer of Eternal Light'.

their languages, Anglish (later English) came to signify the whole group. This new enemy worshipped neither Christ, nor the older gods of Rome, nor the earliest gods worshipped by Druids: they worshipped Frey, Thor and Woden, and believed in an abode of the gods called Valhalla. They were as ferocious and undisciplined in their warfare as the Celts had been before Roman influence, and they swept the Romano-British westwards before them to the mouth of the River Severn, thus dividing the western Brythonic Celts into two groups: those who fled into what is now Wales and those who fled into the south-western peninsula, modern-day Cornwall, Devon and Somerset. It was at this point that the languages now known as Welsh and Cornish began to develop separately. Indeed, the whole of the south-western peninsula was usually called West Wales, the name Wales itself being derived from the Saxon word *weahlas*, meaning foreigners. (Centuries later, further migrations across the Channel to Armorica established the Breton language. To this day, Welsh, Cornish and Breton are such close sister languages that much of their vocabulary is mutually intelligible.)

An interesting comparison in the chronology suggests that Druidism flourished longer and more securely in Wales than anywhere else. At about the same time as the leader Arthur, later romanticized to King Arthur, almost certainly by now a Christian leader against the heathen invaders, was killed at the Battle of Camlann, St David was only just converting Wales to Christianity: both events are given as taking place around AD 540 to 550.

While the heathen Angles, Saxons and Jutes controlled most of the central and southern mainland of Britain, communication between the northern and western Celtic peoples, pagan and Christian, did not cease entirely. Indeed, Christianity was kept alive in Britain by the missionaries of the Celtic Church, until, in 597, Augustine landed in Kent and began the conversion of the Angles, Saxons and Jutes themselves. Many Celtic saints' legends, and place-names, are derived from this period: St Pyran of Cornwall, for example, sailed from Ireland (where his name was Kieran) on a millstone, to a spot near where Perranporth now stands. The millstone was probably a romanticization or exaggeration of the small, dedicated altar stone which the saint may have worn tied to a cord around his neck, although it is also possible that a real millstone was used as ballast in a wooden boat. Some of the miracles, such as St Meryasek of Britanny striking bare rock with his staff to bring forth a fresh spring of water, or many dedications of holy wells, are so close to Druidic belief and practice, that, cumulatively, the evidence overwhelmingly suggests that many miracles and feats of magic attributed to saints are Druidic magic in different clothing. These early saints wrestle dragons and shapeshift, too. Some are so nebulous as to suggest that they are simply abstractions of earlier Celtic deities.

St Madron, for example, is portrayed in his dedicatory church in western Cornwall as a middle-aged man with robes, beard and staff – a patriarch whose real, historical origins and life are extremely vague. His name is pronounced Maddern by local people. However, no more than 100 paces from the site of his original baptistery, lies an ancient well, much older than the baptistery and, indeed, feeding water to it, dedicated to the pagan mother-goddess Madron. (Madron and Mabon, Mother or Matron and Son, are frequently found pagan names to represent the mother-goddess, son-god axis). It takes a very determined effort of will, or imagination, to believe wholeheartedly in the bearded Christian saint Madron and deny entirely the pagan mother-goddess whose very name is still evident in the place where the supposed saint's church stands.[12]

During this period, memorial inscriptions begin to appear in Latin script. Earlier stones use Ogham, a script almost certainly devised in Ireland and imported via Wales, but, during the sixth and seventh centuries, Latin script becomes more frequent on memorial stones.

One such stone, the Men Skrifa (meaning stone of writing) standing on the bleak moors of Penwith between Morvah and Zennor in western Cornwall, is dedicated to *Rialobranus fili[us] Cunomor[i]*. The text means Royal Crow, son of Great Hound (or Sea-Hound), and it is almost certainly dedicatory to a local chieftain, whose name in Celtic would have been Ryalbran or Ryalvran.[13] Again in Cornwall, two stones at Lewannick are inscribed both in Ogham and in Latin.

The Norman Conquest

The invasion which was to establish the foundation and subsequent division of Britain more or less as we now know it, was the Norman Conquest which began in 1066. By 1068, William's men had reached as far west as Exeter. Within a very short period, the remaining Celts became isolated groups on the fringes of Anglo-Norman society. Scotland, which had become one realm with the coalition of Picts and Scots against invading Danes in 843, succumbed to William in 1072. Ireland, still independent of Britain, but greatly altered in character, and even in language, by successive Viking raids, had long since adopted Christianity under St Padraig, although the great sagas and literary epics through which we learn so much about earlier Celtic society and the Druids were only just beginning to be committed to parchment.

Memories of the Druids, and probably some isolated Druidic practice, may well have persisted in the more isolated Brythonic settlements along the Atlantic seaboard. The scattered remnants of the tradition, particularly the legends, began to be recorded, most notably in the Welsh *Mabinogion*. Eventually, some of this material, greatly altered, was transmogrified by medieval romance into the tales of chivalry and high endeavour known as the Matter of Britain, the saga of King Arthur and his knights and followers, including that most patently Druidic figure, Merlin.

However, the Druids themselves were no longer to be found. They, and the Celtic tribal society within which they flourished, had disappeared into history. Because their tradition was oral, much of their knowledge, which took so many years to acquire and which commanded such respect from the classical authors of the ancient world, went with them. Druidism, as an active, participatory religion untrammelled by outside influence, no longer existed.

Summary of important dates and events

	*c.*900 BC	Celtic peoples invade British Isles.
	*c.*700	Hallstatt period.
	*c.*500	Separation of Goidelic (Q) and Brythonic (P) Celts in Britain.
	497	Death of Pythagoras.
	*c.*450	First Celtic invasions of Italy.
	390	Battle of Clusium; Celts sack all Rome except Capitol.
	380	Rome rebuilt under alliance with Samnites.
	285	Further Celtic hostilities against Rome; massacre on the River Tiber.
	*c.*280	Celtic tribes advance into Galatia in Asia Minor.
Celts in Italy and Asia Minor	*c.*250	La Tène culture gains predominance in Britain.
	225	Battle of Telemon; all Celtic tribes south of River Po destroyed.
	219	Second Punic War; Hannibal marches on Rome from Carthage.
	202	Hannibal defeated at Zama by Scipio; extensive Romanization of Celtic tribes begins.
	133	Galatia bequeathed to Rome as a semi-autonomous Celtic province.
	133	Scipio Aemilianus conquers Iberian Celtic province of Numantia.
	61	Gaius Julius Caesar conquers remaining Iberian Celts at Brigantium.
	59	Caesar created consul.
	55	First Roman invasion of Britain; Caesar sends punitive expeditions to discourage Celtic mercenaries from supporting resistance in Gaul.
	54	Second Roman invasion of Britain; Cassivelaunus subjugated and required to pay tribute.
British Celts and Druids resist Roman rule	53	Rome crushes Gaulish revolt led by Vercingetorix.
	50–45	Civil war in Rome; revolts led by Pompey against Caesar.
	47	Rome completes conquest of Asia Minor.
	44	Julius Caesar assassinated, succeeded by Octavius.
	27	Octavius declares himself divine and assumes title Augustus.
	AD 5	Cunobelinus (Cymbeline) recognized by Rome as King of Britain.

British Celts and Druids resist Roman rule	37	Caligula succeeds Tiberius as Roman emperor.
	40	Tribal wars in Britain; Aminius, son of Cunobelinus, flees to Rome, where Caligula confirms him as King of Britain.
	41	Caligula succeeded as emperor by Claudius.
	43	Aulus Plautius lands Roman troops in Kent; permanent Roman occupation of Britain begins.
	47	Ostorius Scapula appointed first Roman Governor of Britain.
	51	Caractacus (Caradoc) captured and sent to Rome.
	60	Roman forces, led by Suetonius Paulinus, attack and massacre a Celtic settlement on Mona (Anglesey), destroying sacred sites and artefacts. Druids participate in the battle.
Decline of Roman Empire	285	Emperor Diocletian partitions empire. Roman fleet commander, Marcus Aurelius Carausius, declares himself Emperor of Britain.
	293	Carausius defeated and killed by Alectus.
	296	Alectus defeated by Emperor Constantius; direct Roman rule restored; commemorative medals struck.
	312	Constantine, son of Constantius, reunites Roman Empire.
	337	Constantine given Christian baptism on his death-bed.
	c.360	Picts and Scots cross Hadrian's Wall.
	395–405	Irish raids on northern and western British coast.
	436	Roman troops leave Britain
	c.450–850	Successive waves of invasion begin from the east, led by the Angles, Saxons and Jutes.
	c.540–550	St David converts Wales to Christianity.
	c.540–550	Arthur, British military leader against the eastern heathens, finally defeated and killed at battle of Camlann.
	597	St Augustine lands in Kent to begin conversion of Angles, Saxons and Jutes (the 'English') to Christianity.
	1066	Norman invasion of Britain. Saxons and others subjugated to Norman French rule. Celts dispersed into isolated groups on Atlantic seaboard.
	c.1100–1300	Earliest written texts of Celtic literature.

Notes

1. Gerhard Herm, *The Celts*.
2. Werner Keller, *The Etruscans*.
3. Acts of the English Parliament following the Jacobite rising of 1715 and 1745 made the wearing of clan plaids illegal for a period, during which the significance of the tartan as a symbol of the Celtic spirit, of anti-English sentiment, as well as of clan allegiance, increased greatly.
4. The conqueror of the Carthaginians in the Second Punic War was Publius Cornelius Scipio Africanus major, and Publius Cornelius Scipio Africanus minor in the Third Punic War. The conqueror of Numantia was Publius Cornelius Scipio Aemilianus. The family Scipio, of the *gens* Cornelia, became renowned for generations of military and public leaders, to the extent that a generic noun, *Scipiades*, was coined, meaning a Scipio, one of the Scipio family, and was used in poetry as a metaphor for hero or leader.
5. Rex Warner, *The Young Caesar*.
6. Stuart Piggott, *The Druids*.
7. The name Cunobelinus seems to contain two elements. The first, 'cun', could mean hound or dog – it was very common for Celtic nobles to include animal elements, probably totemic, in their names. The second element, 'belinus', is frequently found standing alone as an alternative name for the Celtic sun god Bel. The name was later anglicized to Cymbeline, as in Shakespeare's play of the same name.
8. Henry Rowlands, *Mona Antiqua Restaurata*.
9. Notably Tacitus and Agricola.
10. Tacitus *Annals xiv, xxix, xxx* and *Agricola xiv, xviii*.
11. Frances Lynch, *Prehistoric Anglesey*.
12. The mother-goddess is still worshipped at her original well. Thousands of people, mostly local, still follow the practice of tying dedicatory strips of cloth to trees above the well.
13. 'Rial' is a loan-word, meaning royal; 'Bran', also the name of a Celtic god, means raven. The father's name begins with 'Cun', meaning hound (similar to Cunobelinus or Cymbeline), followed either by 'mor', meaning sea, or, far more likely, by 'mor' ('meur' in modern Cornish) meaning great.

· CHAPTER THREE ·

EARLY CELTIC
SOCIETY

CHAPTER FOUR WILL EXAMINE the Druids' role and functions in more detail, but the purpose of this chapter is to describe briefly early Celtic tribal society in order to lay a foundation for the next chapter. To understand Druidic practice in its context, we need to take a broader look at the society within which the Druids operated. There are several authoritative works on this topic, the best of which is Anne Ross's *Everyday Life of the Pagan Celts*, from which some of the material of this chapter is summarized, and to which the reader is unhesitatingly recommended for further information.

It is worth reminding ourselves of the difficulty of sources. Our picture of early Celtic society emerges from: archaeological evidence; descriptions by classical authors; descriptions in the vernacular literature of the insular Celts, particularly of Ireland and, to a lesser extent, Wales. While each of these source areas is independently suspect, we do find a considerable body of evidence which is corroborated by more than one source. Obviously, we can be more confident about accepting as true a practice or event described by a Greek or Roman writer if we have archaeological evidence to support it, or confirmation in the later Celtic texts. Even so, the problem of interpretation still arises.

We can use inference and deduction without stretching credibility too far. For example, without any direct evidence, I feel confident in asserting that the early Celts used trained sheepdogs. What basis is there for the assertion? Well, we know that the Celts wore heavy woollen cloaks, so we can reasonably deduce that they kept domesticated sheep as well as cattle and that they ate mutton as well as beef. We note the Irish legend of Cu Chulainn, the hero who takes his very name (it means Culainn's Hound) from the dog he killed, and who is ordered by Cathbad the Druid to guard Culainn's flocks and herds. We note the archaeological evidence of a dog cult associated with the semi-deity Nodens, Lludd or Lear. We note how, to this day, skill in using dogs to control sheep is concentrated in Ireland, Wales, Scotland and the earlier Celtic regions of north-western England. Cumulatively, the inference that early Celts most probably used trained dogs to help herd their sheep is, I believe, very persuasive.

The classical texts inform us that the Celts were distinctive in appearance, both in physique and in dress. Even allowing for some confusion with Germans, the classical texts tell us that the Celts were tall and fair. In the Irish vernacular texts, also, the aristocracy is always described as having fair, or red hair, oval faces and light skin. In addition to this apparently Nordic type, however, there seems also to have been an Alpine type of Celt, especially in Gaul, who was rather stockier, with mousy hair and brown or grey eyes (but still taller and fairer than the Mediterranean type). A further complication is that an early Celtic migration into the Iberian peninsula produced a group, sometimes referred to as Celtiberians, whose small stature and darkness of skin were much closer to the Mediterranean type. The later intermingling of Celts and Romans had a similar effect.

Personal appearance

The early Celts were preoccupied obsessively with their personal appearance, particularly with their hair, as Strabo describes:

> Their hair is not only naturally blond, but they also use artificial means to increase this natural quality of colour, for they continually wash their hair with lime-wash and draw it from the forehead to the crown and to the nape of the neck, with the result that their appearance resembles that of Satyrs or of Pans, for the hair is so thickened by this treatment that it differs in no way from a horse's mane.

This description, even to the mention of the horse's mane, is very similar to that of Diodorus Siculus: we might guess that one description is an uninformed copy of the other, were it not for the very similar descriptions we also find in the vernacular texts. Cu Chulainn, hero of the *Tain Bo Cuailnge* (Cattle-raid of Cooley), is described as having three shades of hair: dark at the roots, brown in the middle and fair at the ends, which suggests very strongly that it was dyed. The descriptive passage from the *Tain* continues:

> His hair curled about his head like branches of red hawthorn used to refence the gap in a hedge. Though a noble apple tree weighed down with fruit had been shaken about his hair, scarcely one apple would have reached the ground through it, but an apple would have stayed impaled on each single hair, because of the fierce bristling of his hair above him.

For both men and women, the hair was the first attribute of beauty. Constantly in the vernacular texts, and even in much later Celtic tales, the hair is the first element of description to be mentioned. The prophetess Fedelm is described in the *Tain* as having 'long, fair-yellow, golden hair', of which three tresses were wound about her head and the fourth cascaded down her back to her calves. The Roman author Dio Cassius describes Boudicca, Queen of the Iceni, as having 'a great mass of bright red hair' which fell to her knees.

As well as washing their hair frequently, the Celts were unusual in also often washing their bodies. They made soap from fat, but later, especially in Gaul, also used body oils, after the Roman fashion. In the vernacular texts, aristocrats are found bathing in milk (and at least one description of ritual practice involved bathing in the blood of a slaughtered mare – obviously not an everyday ablution). Washing, bathing and shaving (of the chin and cheeks – the moustache was usually left luxuriant) were common practice, at least among the wealthy, and probably among all Celts – many fine and ornate mirrors and razors have been found by archaeologists.

As well as using dyes for their hair, women (and perhaps some men, too) used a herb called 'ruam' to heighten the colour of their cheeks, and they dyed their brows black with berry juice. Deidre, in the Irish tales, is so consumed by sorrow, and therefore unconcerned with her personal appearance, that, as she says: 'I do not redden my finger-nails.' Celtic women in Gaul certainly used cosmetics: the Roman poet Propertius reviles his mistress for 'making up like the Celts.'

As we noted in the last chapter, the Celts were also easily recognized by their distinctive mode of dress. The men typically wore *bracae* (breeches made of wool), with a short woollen cloak. The toga-wearing Romans were impressed by the strangeness of trousers, but soon came to see the advantages of wearing them on horseback, and, in due course, trousers became standard wear in the Roman cavalry, which in any case was often supplied by soldiers of Celtic or Scythian stock. Short tunics and short leather coats, particularly for charioteers, are also mentioned. The great cloak, lightweight in summer and heavy in winter, fastened by an elaborately decorated brooch, was so famous a Celtic garment that some were even exported from the provinces to Rome, where they were highly valued. Again, as has been mentioned, these woollen garments were woven in many colours, often in a plaid or tartan pattern.

The Celts also loved jewellery, as might be expected. Many fine rings, torques, brooches, necklaces and ear-rings have been found. The intricate whorls, spirals, trefoils and zoomorphics found in early Celtic jewellery are reproduced to this day, and they are still immensely popular.

Apart from appearance, there are three areas in which the early Celts are clearly distinguishable from other early tribal societies. Firstly, there is a distinctively Celtic attitude towards warfare, individual combat and death. Secondly, a widespread religious influence deeply affected the Celts in every aspect of their lives. Thirdly, the Celts had an unusual respect for, and obedience to, observed and interpreted law. In all three areas, the Druids played significant roles.

The back of the bronze mirror unearthed at Birdlip, Gloucestershire.

Warfare and weapons

The most obvious and immediate aspect of early Celtic culture, confirmed by all our sources, is the hegemony of warfare. Fighting seems to have been a primary, frequent and honourable occupation. Cu Chulainn, mentioned above, demands a set of weapons from his uncle King Conchobar mac Nessa with these words: 'It is a wonderful thing, if I am but one day and one night in the world, provided that my fame and my deeds live after me.' This sentiment was common in other early societies, too. We find in an early Old English poem, *The Seafarer*, a virtually identical declaration: 'Therefore it is best for any lord to have his deeds quoted after him, the praise of those who survive him, lasting words, which he earned before setting out on his way, good actions on earth against the violence of enemies.'[1]

However, the anonymous *Seafarer* poet also gives us detailed and moving accounts of the hardship of life at sea, the bitter cold and loneliness, sentiments which are distinctly un-Celtic. The Celts, even among warrior societies, seem to have been especially renowned for their savagery in warfare, their apparent indifference to pain and to violent death, and their quick, quarrelsome character. Classical writers asserted that the Celts' apparent contempt for death sprang from their absolute conviction that an immediate, real and full afterlife follows this one. The archaeological evidence, particularly funerary offerings, seems to confirm the idea that the Celts believed in a literal, material life after death (like many other early peoples, including the Egyptians). Graves of the aristocracy are furnished with weapons, clothing and provisions, including whole joints of salt pork. Mention has already been made of the Celtic habit of offering to settle debts in the next world.

Classical authors were at pains to point out both how belligerent and how unorganized their barbarian enemies were. Strabo's description of the Celts is typical:

> The whole race, which is called Celtic or Galatic, is madly fond of war, high-spirited and quick to battle, but otherwise straightforward and not of evil character. And so when they are stirred up they assemble in their bands for battle, quite openly and without forethought; so that they are easily handled by those who desire to outwit them. For at any time or place, and on whatever pretext you stir them up, you will have them ready to face danger, even if they have nothing on their side but their own strength and courage.

The British tribes, at least, seem to have had better military organization than Strabo's description suggests. In any event, while a cool-headed Roman commander might well have been able to use the Celts' impetuosity to his advantage, he still had to lead troops who may have been sorely demoralized by confronting such terrifying, lusty abandonment and joy in facing violent death. Polybius tells us, in his account of the Battle of Telemon (mentioned on page 37), that while the Insubres and Boii wore their trousers and light cloaks in the battle, the Gaesatae fought stark naked in the front line.[2] The Roman troops, confronted by these tall, strongly built men, laughing maniacally and advancing naked upon them with absolute and contemptuous disregard for their own safety, were apparently filled with dismay and had to be disciplined sternly to come back into rank.

Celtic women, as well as men, fought in the front line of battle. Cartimandua and Boudicca have already been mentioned in this context. The Roman historian Ammianus Marcellinus informs us:

> Almost all the Gauls are of tall stature, fair and ruddy, terrible for the fierceness of their eyes, fond of quarreling, and of overbearing insolence. In fact, a whole band of foreigners will be unable to cope with one of them in a fight, if he calls in his wife, stronger than he by far and with flashing eyes; least of all when she swells her neck and gnashes her teeth, and poising her huge white arms, begins to rain blows mingled with kicks like shots discharged by the twisted cords of a catapult.

Dio Cassius, whose description of Boudicca was mentioned a moment ago, describes her as being 'huge of frame and terrifying of aspect and with a harsh voice.'

The Celts had (and still have) great faith in the efficacy of words and music to affect the human spirit. Tacitus described the Druids at the Mona massacre uttering 'dreadful imprecations' and curses against the Romans, with the Celtic women (almost certainly including priestesses) shrieking and wailing until the Roman troops were so disheartened that they broke ranks (see page 51). It was typical of Celtic warriors to shout and ululate, proclaiming their own lineage and valour and deprecating the puny strength of the opposition. They used a war trumpet, called a 'carnyx' (page 68), which was often decorated with a bronze depiction of an animal's head, perhaps totemic of the tribe or chief. The carnyx also frequently had a wooden tongue attached, which served as a clapper.

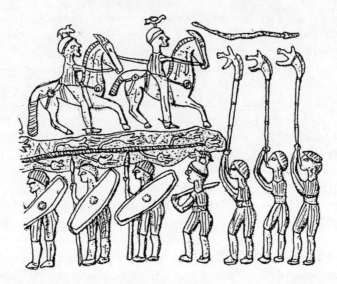

Celtic warriors, from the Gundestrup cauldron. The three warriors on the right are sounding 'carnyxes', or battle-horns. Although all the figures are helmeted, actual helmets are rarely found by archaeologists. Top right is a ram-headed serpent. The horizontal material below the horsemen may be a sacred tree.

Bagpipes were used by the Scots and the Irish from early medieval times as battle instruments, and it may be that the early Celts used something similar, although we have no descriptions. There is also no mention of drums, although they, too, may well have been used. However produced, this combined battle tumult was highly effective, as Polybius again reminds us:

> The Romans were terrified by the fine order of the Celtic host, and the dreadful din, for there were innumerable horn-blowers and trumpeters and, as the whole army were shouting their war-cries at the same time, there was such a tumult of sound that it seemed that not only the trumpets and the soldiers but all the country round had got a voice and caught up the cry.

The weapons used by the Celts in war were many and varied. The most distinctively Celtic, although it may not be thought of immediately as a weapon, was the two-wheeled war chariot. Chariot warfare died out in Gaul by the time of Caesar's campaigns, but in the British campaigns, the speed and skill of the British charioteers made a great impression on the invading Romans. Boudicca is often depicted in her chariot, long curving blades attached to the wheels, charging wildly through the enemy, ecstatic in battle, her blood-red hair flowing wild and free behind her. In fact, chariot warfare was highly organized, and very effective. The chariots were very light, no more than wickerwork over a tight frame, and the small, sure-footed horses pulling them could gallop almost as fast as if ridden by a single rider. Each chariot was usually occupied by two riders. One was the warrior proper, the other his charioteer. Sometimes they were kinsmen, or, as the Irish texts inform us, the charioteer might be a freeman who was the warrior's friend or confidant. As the charioteer drove headlong into the enemy, too quickly for immediate retaliation, the warrior could hurl spears while on the move, leap from the chariot to inflict blows or engage in hand-to-hand combat, then leap swiftly aboard the chariot again on a return pass. A slow-moving or static infantry, such as the Romans used, was quickly decimated by such tactics, even when the chariot forces were numerically inferior.

The hand weapons used are mentioned frequently in the classical and vernacular texts, and many of the descriptions have been verified by archaeological finds. Early bronze swords were bent easily in battle: Polybius describes swords being straightened by the foot and the Irish texts (naturally more melodramatic), swords being gripped for straightening in the teeth. They were replaced from about 700 BC by more durable iron swords. Daggers were used for close fighting. Both swords and daggers were carried in decorated scabbards. Shields were generally made of alder or oak wood, edged with metal, or of leather, sometimes even of wickerwork. Spears were of two distinct types. The first was long and broad-bladed for thrusting (the word lance is Celtic in origin). The second was short and meant to be thrown. Strabo uses the word *madaris* to describe it. The common Latin word for a throwing spear or javelin was *alia*, which suggests that *madaris* may be a coining by Strabo, or (more likely) a Celtic word originally, although its etymology is uncertain.

One spear of the first, or thrusting type, deserves special mention. It is called the 'ga bulga' in the Irish texts, where it is imbued with mysterious and ritual properties. It was a barbed spear, which may have been used ritually, perhaps in sacrificial divination, but it also appears to have been used in ordinary warfare, as Diodorus Siculus informs us: 'Some of their javelins are forged with a straight head, while some are spiral with breaks throughout their entire length so that the blow not only cuts but also tears the flesh, and the recovery of the spear tears open the wound'. The classical description of the spear with spiral flanges seems to accord with the vernacular descriptions of the 'ga bulga', but, unfortunately, there is no archaeological evidence to cement the proof.

A type of sling was used, and a small wooden club thrown by hand. Classical writers tell us these weapons were also used for bird hunting, although we learn elsewhere that there was a taboo against eating the flesh of any winged creature, since it was in the form of a bird that many spirits passed to and fro between this world and the other world.

Strabo describes the Celts using bows and arrows, but this seems almost certain to be wrong, as has been mentioned. There are no bows or arrows in the vernacular texts, no archaeological finds, and the very words bow and arrow are late loan-words in the Celtic languages. Perhaps Strabo is casually throwing in descriptions of Parthian or Scythian practice – whether unintentionally, or by design, is not clear.

Personal armour is also very rare. Some helmets have been found, but in such small numbers as to suggest that generally the Celts went into battle at least bare-headed, if not always entirely naked.

Druids, generally speaking, did not take part in battle. Some appear to have had a personal retinue large enough to be called an army, or at least a bodyguard, but there are very few descriptions or instances of Druids actually fighting. They were, however, supposed to be so articulate that they could destroy a man merely by uttering a satire or curse against him. Whenever Druids appear in tales of battle or warfare, their role is diplomatic. They give judgements, approve or disapprove terms of settlement, and so on.

Fortifications, natural concomitants of a warrior society, played an important part in Celtic tribal life. It seems that the Celts, unlike their Mediterranean neighbours, were rarely concerned with permanent settlements, urban development or architectural elaboration. We have to imagine a Celtic settlement as more or less permanently on the move within the confines of its tribal areas (which themselves would shift as a result of tribal warfare), driving flocks and herds from one stockade to another. In such circumstances, cattle-raids would be common, and we are not surprised to find one of the important Irish vernacular texts, the *Tain Bo Cuailnge*, taking as its starting-point precisely such a raid. Classical descriptions inform us that the Celts frequently came to battle with their womenfolk and children, their cattle, sheep and other belongings, all in tow. They used hilltops (which would also have been sacred sites) as natural defences, reinforcing them with ditching and banking. They were skilled weavers, and they could throw together a light but effective stockade of wickerwork and sharpened stakes at very short notice. In more permanent encampments, drystone walls were sometimes reinforced with internal timbers, a style of defence which Caesar called *murus gallicus*, meaning the Gallic wall. Many Celtic fortified enclosures have been excavated by archaeologists, and some of the later examples are very large, by classical standards. At Bibracte on Mont Beuvray, near Autun, France, a Celtic fortification encloses an area of some 335 acres (136 hectares), which, as Anne Ross points out,[3] compares with approximately 5 acres (2 hectares) for Homeric Troy.

One distinctive, and notorious, Celtic battle practice needs special mention: the Celts were head-hunters. The heads of important enemies were cut off after battle and displayed as trophies of war. Several sanctuary finds have included skull-niches (page 73) in the walls for the display of human heads, as well as representations of severed heads carved in stone. The Romans regarded decapitation (and human sacrifice, although they practised that themselves earlier) as utterly barbaric and depraved. To the Celts, the human head was obviously especially significant. In the context of an unshakable belief in a real and immediate afterlife, it is reasonable to infer that the purpose of the decapitation was effectively to capture the spirit of the defeated enemy and to prevent him emerging from the other world to wreak revenge or further havoc, as well as to provide a boastful display. (Some writers have made comparison with the native American practice of scalp-hunting, but that was a practice introduced by Europeans, calculated and cynical, to ensure that tribal mercenaries were actually killing the numbers they claimed.)

One of the tales of *The Mabinogion* explicitly deals with the power of the decapitated head after battle. Bendigeidfran is mortally wounded in battle. (The name means Bran the Blessed. 'Bran', met already in the Cornish standing-stone dedication to the chieftain Rialobranus, or Ryalbran, means crow, and it was the name of a Celtic god of sufficient importance to be worshipped by several tribes. He is related, according to Robert Graves,[4] to the Pelasgian hero, Aesculapius, a king of the tribe of Lapiths in Thessaly, whose totem was also a crow.) Fast approaching death, Bran orders his men to strike off his head and carry it to 'the White Mount in London.' This they do, subsequently spending a strange and enchanted period in the mysterious head's company:

And that night they were there without stint, and were joyful. And notwithstanding all the sorrows they had seen before their eyes, and notwithstanding that they themselves had suffered, there came to them no remembrance either of that, or of any sorrow in the world. And there they passed the fourscore years so that they were not aware of having ever spent a time more joyous and delightful than that. It was not more irksome, nor could any tell of his fellow that he was older during that time, than when they came there. Nor was it more irksome having the head with them then than when Bendigeidfran had been with them alive. And because of those fourscore years it was called the Assembly of the Wondrous Head.

Clearly, these men, and the talking severed head which continues to guide them and provide them good company, are temporarily stationed in the timeless joy of the afterlife. Only when one of them forgets Bran's command not to look towards Cornwall is the spell broken. The head, beginning to decay, commands the men to bury it on White Hill, now Tower Hill in London. To this day, there persists a legend that if the ravens who live around the Tower ever fly away, London will die. The ravens, unknown even to many who are familiar with the legend, are totems of the mysterious buried head of Bran, the raven-god.

Diodorus Siculus tells us that captured heads were embalmed in cedar oil and displayed, some of them being of such value that 'some of them boast that they refused the weight of the head in gold.'

Cu Chulainn, attacked by Ferchu Loingseach and his followers, kills them all and then ritually displays their severed heads:

And they came forward to the place where Cu Chulainn was, and when they came they did not grant him fair play or single combat, but all twelve of them attacked him straightway. However, Cu Chulainn fell upon them, and forthwith struck off their twelve heads. And he planted twelve stones for them in the ground, and put a head of each one of them on the stone, and also put Ferchu Loingseach's head on its stone. So that the spot where Ferchu Loingseach left his head is called Cinnit Ferchou, that is Cennait Ferchou ('the head-place of Ferchu').[5]

The 'fair play' mentioned above was one of the main guiding principles of Druidic law, along with the utterance of truth (even in such a vain and boastful people) and 'the fitness of things', to which we shall return later. 'Fir fer', or 'fair play', was very important in individual combat. The implication in the Cennait Ferchou incident described above is that, by denying Cu Chulainn the right of 'fir fer',

A skull-niche found at Roquepertuse, in Provence, southern France, dating from the third century BC.

Ferchu more or less automatically condemned himself and his followers to defeat and death, because they were violating a natural, spiritual law. The notion that a warrior offering single combat should, in fairness, only be met by a single opponent, is distinctively Celtic. This concept was quite alien to the Romans – despite their experience with gladiators – and it was almost certainly modified extensively in conquered Gaul. But in Britain, and particularly in Ireland, the 'fir fer' concept remained very strong, to the extent that centuries later it re-emerges in the chivalric code of medieval romance: there are countless examples of individual combat in the Arthurian legends (and the basic notion survives even in our own troubled times as the exemplar of honourable combat). Arthur gives a judgement in 'Culhwch and Olwen'[6] which requires Gwyn, son of Nudd to fight in individual combat with Gwythyr, son of Greidawl, until Doomsday.[7] Individual combat trysts are common in the vernacular literature, suggesting they may also have been common in actual practice. In 'Pwyll, Prince of Dyfed'[8], the hero, Pwyll, meets Arawn Pen Annwn ('Arawn Head, or King, of the Underworld'), who asks Pwyll to take his place at a combat tryst set for a year ahead.

A particular kind of tryst, the tryst of the returned blow, persists in the literature through centuries. The theme of the beheading match, in which the hero faces the challenge of beheading a superhuman opponent on condition that he submit himself to a return blow the next day (or after a year and a day, the significance of that period will be discussed later) first appears in 'Fled Bricreud' (Bricreud's Feast), in the Irish texts dating from about AD 1100, although the story itself is evidently much older. It reappears in different forms (mostly in French) through the next 300 years, until, in about 1400, it reappears as the great classic of Middle English literature, *Sir Gawain and the Green Knight*.

Religion

Religion was as significant in Celtic tribal life as warfare, if not more so. Anne Ross expresses the point succinctly:

> Religion and superstition . . . played a fundamental and profound role in the *everyday* life of the Celts. This is, in fact, the key to any understanding of their distinctive character. Caesar says: 'The whole Gallic people is exceedingly given to religious superstition.' All the evidence supports his statement, and we have little need to seek for underlying political bias here. Perhaps even more than other ancient peoples, the Celts were so engrossed with, and preoccupied by, their religion and its expression that it was constantly and positively to the forefront of their lives. The deities and the Otherworld in which they were believed to reside – when they were not intruding upon the world of men as they frequently did – were not mere academic concepts to be remembered at convenient intervals, on feast-days, or when a great victory was to be celebrated, at times of national sacrifice, or distress, either tribal or personal, or when something special was desired. They were ever-present, sometimes menacing, always dangerous. When placated, helpful and generous; when offended, vengeful and without mercy. The everyday life of the Celts included the supernatural equally with the natural, the divine with the mundane; for them the Otherworld was as real as the tangible physical world and as ever-present.[9]

The religious functions supplied by the Druids will be discussed more fully in the next chapter, but it is important to note the significance of religion to every member of early Celtic tribal society and, accordingly, the importance and significance of rank which would accrue to its principal guides and practitioners, the Druidic priesthood.

The extent to which any buildings were dedicated to religious functions, either as meeting-houses, temples or palaces (not necessarily too opulent a word) for Druids and their retinues, remains very unclear. Most building remains examined through archaeology have been small. The impression given is that domestic buildings were rather crude, although there is some evidence that in Ireland they may have reached two storeys. A form of balcony, for which we have the Gaelic word 'grianan', literally meaning sun room, is thought to have projected outwards above the main living area and seems to have been used mainly by women. In eastern and central Europe, the houses were rectangular in plan: a Gaulish hut would not have looked very different from the crude shelters used in Alpine regions to this day. In Spain, Portugal and Britain, the buildings are mainly circular, although a few larger, rectangular halls have also been found, which might conceivably have been temples or meeting-houses. The circular houses appear to have been constructed around a principal timber supporting a roof of thatch or turf which sloped down steeply towards a low enclosing dry wall. The interiors were divided into small compartments, some obviously intended for sleeping, with a main fire in the centre of the structure under the highest part of the roof. One house, even though fairly small, could have accommodated several families. Diodorus Siculus tells us that the Celtic custom was 'to sleep on the ground upon the skins of wild animals and to wallow among bed-fellows on either side'. The houses were built close together in patterns defining areas of space between them, which may have been used as communal areas, or courtyards. Outstanding examples of the remains of such construction, open and easily accessible to the public, are to be found at Chysauster and Carn Euny in western Cornwall.

Also in Cornwall are several outstanding examples of the construction kown as a 'fogo' or 'fogou'. This Cornish word was permanently lenited in Late Cornish from the earlier word 'mogow', which means cave (the Breton cognate is 'mougev'). However, these constructions are not caves in the normal sense: they are more like tunnels. A hollow, either natural or constructed, is lined and roofed with slabs of granite to form a low tunnel. Sometimes the tunnel is one-ended only, sometimes it opens to ground at both ends. The Carn Euny fogou, still quite solid in its construction, travels a gloomy

40 feet (12 metres) or so before it turns and opens into a special, circular chamber with a gabled roof of granite slabs. I can testify from personal experience that it is an awe-inspiring place. However, the function of the fogou in Druidic times is still unclear. Suggestions range from the prosaic (it was a grain store, or a sheltering place from wild animals) to the mystic (it was a site for worship or meditation, a physical representation of the womb of Mother Earth, and so on). We can never be certain which interpretation is correct. The Cornish periodical 'Meyn Mamvro' (Stones of the Motherland) carries regular investigative features and articles on Cornish fogous. The only thing which can be said with confidence is that the remaining examples indicate clearly that the fogou was a very important part of the domestic settlement. It would have taken as much physical effort to construct as several of the main dwelling structures combined, so it must have been sufficiently important to the whole community to justify such effort and expenditure of materials.

If one function of the fogou was to act as some kind of gateway to the other world, that interpretation, however fanciful, would accord with the very common Celtic theme of the gatekeeper, watchman or porter. This role was so significant in Celtic society that echoes of it survive well into modern times. The porter in Shakespeare's *Macbeth*, a comic character nevertheless closely associated with the dark, mystic themes of fate and witchcraft in the play, is a stock Celtic figure. In the vernacular literature, the porter or gatekeeper is a figure of great significance. In 'Culhwch and Olwen', already mentioned, the hero Culhwch demands entrance to (King) Arthur's court. The porter, Glewlwyd (the name means Grey Hero, telling us immediately that he is old and of high rank) refuses him entrance because 'knife has gone into meat, and drink into horn, and a thronging in Arthur's hall. Save the son of a king of a rightful dominion, or a craftsman who brings his craft, none may enter.' There is more than simple social etiquette at stake here. What Glewlwyd is articulating has a mystic significance: he is describing a fit or proper state of affairs, and clarifying to the supplicant that the fitness of things must not lightly be disturbed, or there will be serious consequences. The same text confirms Glewlwyd's high rank by giving us a long account of all the battles across the world (some obviously invented) in which he has served Arthur. While none of the archaeological remains suggests a regular pattern of guarded entrances in Celtic defensive formations, and certainly nothing as formalized as the gates in walled Roman cities, it is clear that the gatekeeper or porter played an important role in the real world, as well as a symbolic role. To this day, various forms of the Wiccan religion still attach great significance to the role of gatekeeper, or watchtower, usually stationed at the four cardinal points: a practice which may be related to earlier Druidism.

Social hierarchy

The general social hierarchy is described by the classical authors and revealed to us in the vernacular texts. The pattern is similar to many other early tribal societies. The basic social unit was the tribe, or clan. Probably no more than an extended family unit in origin, but capable of considerable expansion through marriage, fosterage, conquest, assimilation and so on, the tribe or clan was usually associated with a specific tribal area. Some of these areas would have expanded or contracted through conquest, but the geographical area was contiguous with an area of spiritual significance, whose borders would not be so susceptible to quick or easy change – like many native American peoples, early Celtic tribes bonded closely with the sacred places and geographical features of their tribal area. The head of the tribal unit was the chief, king or queen, who often adopted the role of direct descendant, or representative, of the eponymous tribal god or goddess. As we have already seen in the examples of Cartimandua and Boudicca, it was quite common for a woman to be the head of the tribal unit. Right of inheritance was both patrilinear and matrilinear, but, in the specific question of royal succession, there is a strong suggestion that religious considerations – fitness, appropriateness, augury of greatness or prosperity, and so on – would have been at least as important as, if not more important than political considerations. In which case, it is reasonable to conjecture that Druids may have had an important role in the king-making or queen-making process. The story of Merlin being instrumental not only in Arthur's conception, but also in his accession to the throne, may derive from a memory of this important social role.

Below the king or queen was a hierarchy of nobles, some of them direct blood relatives of the royal line, but others promoted to the nobility either by marriage, by fosterage or by merit, usually in battle. Attached to the nobles were retinues of landed freemen and craftsmen, who in turn were superior to the general populace, many of whom, according to Caesar, were 'nearly regarded as slaves.' The slavery, however, would have been of a distinctively Celtic type. Individual peasants would not be bought and sold (as slaves were in Rome), but they would be inextricably bound to a specific tribal area and to allegiance to the freeman above them and the noble lord or lady served by the freeman. In return for the portion of tribal land on which they were allowed to live and raise their crops and a few animals, they were required to fight in the freeman's or noble's service, either in small cattle-raids, internal tribal disputes, disputes with other tribes, or even full-scale wars of resistance against Romans or invading Anglo-Saxons. The tribal or clan name, its gods and goddesses, its animal and plant totems, were all great unifying forces. We can see to this day in the strong emotional ties still associated with the Scottish clans, scattered and dispersed all across the world as they are, a faint echo of the pattern of tribal allegiance which was so central to the organization of early Celtic tribal society.

The Druids and their retinues were not tied into these geographical and tribal allegiances. In fact, there is strong evidence to infer that Druids must have gone to considerable lengths to preserve their independence of individual kings and chieftains. Druids were ambassadors, lawgivers and judges, and, although there is evidence that a few Druids were directly retained, the more likely pattern is that of Druids maintaining themselves and their retinues independently. They received precious metals, jewellery and other valuables, cattle, sheep, horses and agricultural produce in payment for their services, rather than gifts of tribal land to which they would become bound through allegiance. Caesar states explicitly that Druids were exempt from taxes and from military service.

The Roman conquest of Gaul saw the gradual erosion of petty kingship there, the kings being replaced by chief magistrates, known by the Celtic title 'vergobretos'. To what extent these magistrates altered or replaced Druidic functions – some of them may even have been Druids – it is difficult to ascertain. The rank of Druids was unquestionably a high rank. As has been mentioned, Caesar equated them with the rank he called *equites*, literally meaning horse-riders and most commonly translated nowadays as knights. We should be careful, however, not to associate Druids with the medieval concept of a knight: Druids rarely fought in battle, and were not warriors. The vernacular texts also attest to their importance and high social rank. In Ireland, no one, not even the king, was allowed to speak before the Druid had spoken, since the power of correct utterance was a mystical power. Conchobar mac Nessa, High King of Ulster, retained Cathbad as his chief Druid; Cathbad was also the king's father.

The noble clansmen, whom Caesar calls *equites*, maintained and improved their social and political status by the system of clientship, in a manner very similar to that employed in Scottish Gaelic society down to the eighteenth century. The pattern is also very familiar in the Arthurian legends. A freeman could bind himself as client to another noble, offering his service in arms and attendance on important political and religious occasions. In return for his clientship, the lesser noble received his greater lord's protection and concern, and he could borrow capital from him to be returned with interest, or he could take stewardship of a particular tract of land and its agricultural revenues. Thus, strong bonds could be created between nobles who were not directly related by blood, and a freeman could, by enterprise, become a powerful noble through the acquisition and skilful manipulation of client relationships. In early Irish law, clientship is known by the Gaelic term 'ceilsine'. Client bonds could be dissolved by mutual agreement, or at the end of a specified time period. Again, there is strong evidence to infer a specific Druidical function here: it is highly likely that such bonds and agreements of clientship were written, authorized, administered and adjudicated by Druids.

Fosterage, like clientship, is an early Celtic tribal custom which survived in practice in Scotland into the eighteenth century. It is widely attested in the vernacular texts, reappearing in the later Arthurian stories, indeed in the traditional legend of Arthur himself being raised and tutored by the unrelated Sir Ector, in place of his natural father, Uther Pendragon. Sons of lesser nobles were sent to be reared, and trained in arms, in the households of richer and more powerful nobles. The advantage to the lesser noble was that his son would be taught warfare in mighty company and, through natural foster-parent and foster-brother bonds of affection, would become closely allied to the interests of a powerful family. The advantage to the greater noble, perhaps not so immediately obvious, was that possession of, or at least dominion over, his client's sons gave him additional power over the client, especially reinforcing the client's loyal service in warfare. From the abundant references in the vernacular texts, it is clear that both blood relationships and relationships in fosterage had more than just legal or political significance: there was a deep spiritual or religious aspect to them, to the extent that kinship and fosterage allegiances imposed obligations which were spiritually, as well as legally, binding. The medieval chivalric code, under which, among other things, a word of honour given must not in any circumstances be broken, has its foundations in this strict Celtic conception of bond and duty. In 'Culhwch and Olwen', for example, Arthur declares that Culhwch will obtain his boon 'as far as wind dries, as far as rain wets, as far as sun runs, as far as sea stretches, as far as earth extends.' The passage shortly continues:

> Quoth Arthur: 'My heart grows tender towards thee: I know thou art sprung from my blood. Declare who thou art.'
> 'I will: Culhwch son of Cilydd son of Cyleddon Wledig, by Goleuddydd daughter of Anlawdd Wledig, my mother.'
> Quoth Arthur: 'True it is. Thou art then my first cousin. Name what thou wilt, and thou shalt have it, whatever thy mouth and tongue shall name.'
> 'God's truth thereon to me, and the truth of thy kingdom?'
> 'Thou shalt have it gladly.'

In fact, Arthur is reprimanded by his retinue for making such a generous offer unreservedly, but he defends himself very righteously, making clear that the blood relationship demands no less a commitment. Culhwch, in turn, invokes his boon of Arthur with deepest ceremonial, asking it in the name of Arthur's warriors and a vast list, several pages long – almost like a genealogy – of heroes, gods, personifications and mythical figures. Some, like Cei (Kay) or Bedwyr (Bedivere) are familiar; others, like Hwyrddyddwg, Drwgddyddwg and Llwyrddyddog ('Late-bearer', 'Ill-bearer' and 'Full-bearer'), seem to be not so much people as attributes, often listed in threes, a typically Celtic practice.

Ferocity and competitiveness were as much part of daily life as they were of organized warfare. Tale after tale begins with a band of heroes seated at a feast, eating huge quantities of meat and drinking gallons of ale and wine, which invariably leads to a drunken insult or challenge, followed by fighting and reparations.

Leisure and wealth

The early Celts sublimated much of their aggression in games and sports. A game much like modern hurley is described in the early texts, along with a team game known in Ireland as 'baire' in which the goal was a hole dug in the ground. Sculpted figures from the Romano-British period are seen holding what appear to be hurley or hockey sticks. The hurling of the silver ball, practised from time immemorial, is an ancient, sometimes violent, game still played annually at St Columb in Cornwall; the accompanying ritual and ceremony, and the enthusiastic involvement of virtually the entire community, are typically Celtic.

Board games were also popular, often played for very high stakes, and frequently associated with religious augury, as if the game were a paradigm of life or the greater cosmic reality. 'Fichell', said to mean 'wooden wisdom' in early Irish, seems to be the same game as 'gwyddbwyll' in Welsh (the name perhaps meaning guard-head), a game similar to chess, in which two sets of men, or armies, were pegged into position on a wooden board and moved to trap or defeat the enemy.[10] 'Brandub' (Black Crow) was another popular board game, and the inclusion of the god's name Bran suggests that it, too, may have had divinatory or other religious significance. In the *Tain Bo Cuailgne*, the playing-board itself is actually given a name, 'Cendchaem' (Smooth head), reminiscent of the mystical practice of naming individual weapons to celebrate their supernatural powers and qualities. The name given seems to describe, or invite, a particular quality: Arthur's famous sword Excalibur, for example, is supposedly derived from an original Celtic name, 'Kalespolgh', the meaning being the rather prosaic Hard Handle. In 'The Dream of Rhonabwy',[11] we find Arthur and Owein playing 'gwyddbwyll' with gold pieces on a board of solid silver, in itself suggesting an extraordinary importance for the game. Each series of moves is accompanied by a series of strange events, until Owein, becoming alarmed, wishes to abandon the game, but Arthur insists that it be played through to the finish, implying an important supernatural doom associated with the game itself.

As well as enjoying substantial leisure, it seems clear that the Celtic tribal aristocracy, at least, also enjoyed substantial individual wealth. The most valuable commodity in the ancient world, apart from fine metals, was common salt. (Most readers will already be aware that the modern English word salary derives from the Latin salarium, the Roman soldier's salt-money.) A tribe which had access to, or control over, quantities of salt was generally wealthy, since salt was essential for preserving meat through the long winter months when very little other food was available. A tribe denied salt would be a tribe denied vital sustenance. Hallstatt, which gives its name to the earliest recognizable phase of Celtic culture, was the site of an ancient salt-mine in the region of the Salzkammergut, close to modern Salzburg (the meaning of both names is obvious).

Wine, imported from the Mediterranean in clay *amphorae*, or jars, was another important indicator of wealth. The general tribal populace drank a kind of ale, known in Gaulish as 'corma' (actually the same word as the modern Welsh 'cwrw', Cornish 'korev'), or barley-beer. Mead (still a very popular beverage in Cornwall) was fermented from honey. The name of the Irish goddess Mebh, related to the word for mead, means 'she who intoxicates' or 'drunk woman'. Drinking to excess seems to have been acceptable behaviour.

Eating to excess, however, was unacceptable. Strabo tells us that the Celts 'try not to become stout and fat-bellied, and any young man who exceeds the standard length of a girdle is fined.' Foods most frequently mentioned by classical authors or in the early vernacular texts include many different kinds of fish, but especially salmon, which, in Celtic mythology, was closely associated with wisdom and divination. Salmon was traditionally baked with honey and herbs. The Roman writer Athenaeus refers to fish baked in salt, vinegar and cummin. Beef and pork were the favourite meats at feasts. There seems to have been a taboo, certainly among some Gaulish tribes, against the eating of any winged creature, associated with the idea that birds represented souls in flight between this world and the other world, or that a god or goddess might frequently shapeshift into the form of a bird. Cattle produced an abundance of dairy products – milk, butter, cheese, curds. Watercress, water-parsnip and seaweed are mentioned as foods in the *Tain*. To this day, seaweed (highly nutritious in its edible forms) is an important constituent of Welsh laver bread. Oat porridge was another staple food, particularly in winter, since dried oats could be stored without difficulty.

The main evidence of Celtic material wealth, at least among the aristocracy, is the vast quantity of elaborately decorated weapons, artefacts and personal jewellery discovered by modern archaeology. These physical items alone, without any other evidence, would be sufficient to convince us of a distinctively Celtic identity and culture. Whole books have been dedicated to Celtic art, and with good reason. The style of decoration and representation developed by the Celts is represented homogeneously over a very long period of time and great geographical distances. More significantly, it demonstrates time and again an extraordinarily sophisticated, developed and elaborated view of the world, quite at odds with the crude, warlike image of the Celts which we might assume from classical sources alone. Paul Jacobsthal, quoted in Anne Ross's book, neatly summarizes the essential differences between classical and Celtic art:

> To the Greeks, a spiral is a spiral and a face is a face and it is always clear where the one ends and the other begins, whereas the Celts 'see' the faces 'into' the spirals or tendrils; ambiguity is a characteristic of Celtic art.[12]

This fluidity in artistic representation suggests a connection with the broader Celtic conception of shapeshifting. Celtic mythography represents a view of the universe in which this world and the other world continually intermingle and flow together. There are instances of gods changing shape at will in several early mythologies, including Roman ones, and most notably in the magician-god figure of Woden or Odin in northern mythology, but nowhere are these changes assumed with such ease and frequency as they are in Celtic mythology, art and literature: Conaire's bird hunt ends when the birds 'put aside their bird cloaks and turn upon him with spears and swords'; Midir wins Etain from her husband King Eochaid, 'and the hosts rose up around the king, for they felt that they had been disgraced, and they saw two swans circling around Tara'; Arthur becomes a chough (related to the divine raven); Merlin becomes an eagle or a salmon (both associated with old age and wisdom); the god Nodons appears as a dog, or shapeshifts into whatever other form he chooses. In Celtic art, these shapeshifts from beast to man to leaf to geometrical line are handled with consummate ease and delicacy. The underlying geometry of the artwork, even of simple knotwork and key patterns, is highly complex and sophisticated, and it seems to be further evidence of mathematical skill as an attribute of the early Celts, associated with Druidic knowledge of mathematics and astronomy.[13]

Taboos and laws

Mention has already been made of the general importance of law in early Celtic tribal society. Many of the prohibitions are of the simple taboo kind, ridiculed by Bertrand Russell. They often survive to modern times as otherwise inexplicable superstitions. For example, the taboo against eating beans (mentioned on page 30 in connection with Pythagoras), was widespread in early cultures. Apart from the indigestion and wind cited by Pliny, it may be that the taboo recognizes the fact that some beans, unless they are cooked in a certain way, contain dangerous, even fatal, toxins. The taboo survives in Asia today in the practice of scattering bean flowers about the house to placate demons; in the old English superstition that one white bean in a row of green plants signifies a death in the coming year; in the old Cornish superstition that beans must only be planted on the third day of May, or bad luck will follow; and in the instructions printed on the packets of reputable kidney bean suppliers that the contents must be boiled vigorously for at least 15 minutes to remove toxins before they are eaten. Another early taboo (also vegetable) was the prohibition against eating leeks. Leeks, very tasty and highly nutritious, were nevertheless reserved for medicinal and prophylactic use only. Warriors would crush leeks and rub the oil over their bodies to promote strength and wound resistance in battle. To this day, the leek (along with the daffodil) is an emblem of Welsh national identity.

Conceptual law, that is law based on moral or philosophical belief as opposed to mere taboo, also featured prominently in Celtic society from earliest times – an unusual characteristic in warrior societies. Often, the concept was pursued in defiance of observation, with laws schematizing and conceptualizing in symmetrical patterns, even if they did not relate exactly to the realities of life. As has already been mentioned, 'fir fer', or 'fair play', was a central concept; so also were the utterance of truth, and appropriateness, often described in the vernacular texts as 'the fitness of things'. Anne Ross gives an example of the power of truthful utterance:

One story tells of a legendary king of Ireland, Lugaid mac Con, who ruled for seven years, from Tara. He took Cormac son of Art into his household as his foster-son. On one occasion, sheep trespassed on his land and ate the Queen's woad. Lugaid said the sheep were then forfeit because they had trespassed. Although Cormac was only a small boy at the time he disagreed with this verdict: he said the shearing of the sheep, not their seizure was a suitable compensation for the shearing of the woad. As the woad would grow again on the plant, so would the wool grow on the sheep. 'That is the true judgment,' said all, 'and it is the son of the true Prince who has given it.' Immediately the side of the house in which the false judgment had been given fell down the slope and became known as "The Crooked Mound of Tara". After that, Lugaid was king in Tara for a year, 'and no grass grew, no leaves, and there was no grain.' After that, he was dethroned by his people for he was a 'false prince'.[14]

The principle of the 'fitness of things' was used to determine appropriate scales for punishments and reparations, and it is virtually certain that the prime arbiters in these determinations were the Druids. In 'Branwen, Daughter of Llyr', the hero Matholwch, whose horses have been maimed and ruined, is offered in compensation a sound horse for every one maimed, with a staff of silver 'as thick as his little finger' and 'a plate of gold as broad as his face', as appropriate and sufficient recompense for the insult and suffering afforded him.[15]

Much of early Celtic law (and lore) is recorded in the early Irish law tracts, some of them dating from as early as the seventh century AD, and clearly based on an oral tradition yet centuries older. Unfortunately, the language of these texts is deliberately arcane, obscure and technical. What is clear is that, as well as ambassadors and priests, the Druids were also makers, givers and arbiters of the law, and that their influence in early Celtic society was powerful and widespread, which brings us to the subject matter of the next chapter, namely the functions performed by the Druids and their retinues.

Notes

1. This is my own translation. The original text is:
   Forþon þaet bið eorla gehwam aeftercweþendra
   lof lifgendra lastworda best,
   þaet he gewyrce aer he on weg scyle
   fremum on folde wið feonda niþ
2. Gaesatae is not a tribal name: it simply means spearmen. They were mercenaries who hired themselves out to different tribal factions.
3. Anne Ross, *Everyday Life of the Pagan Celts*.
4. Robert Graves, *The Greek Myths*.
5. *Tain Bo Cuailnge*.
6. One of the tales of *The Mabinogion*.
7. Alan Garner's excellent novel, *The Owl Service*, is based on this incident.
8. Also in *The Mabinogion*.
9. Anne Ross, above, p. 174.

10. Dr Ken George informs me in recent correspondence that this game, under the Breton name 'Goezboell', is on sale from the Breton Company, Keit Vimp Beo, complete with instructions in 14 languages.
11. In *The Mabinogion*.
12. Anne Ross, above, p. 230.
13. The reader is enthusiastically recommended to George Bain's magnificent *Celtic Art: the Methods of Construction* for further information.
14. Anne Ross, above.
15. In *The Mabinogion*.

· CHAPTER FOUR ·

DRUIDIC FUNCTIONS

THE CONTEMPORARY WELSH GORSEDD acknowledges three classes, or ranks, of membership: Bard, Ovate and Druid, with Druid as the most senior rank. The most senior of the Druids is given the title Archdruid. The Cornish and Breton 'gorseddau' confer the rank of Bard only, with the most senior among them known as Grand Bard. All three institutions are revivals, not survivors of a continuous tradition, and the question of the extent to which the model of the revived Welsh Gorsedd, which is the pattern for the other two, expresses any truth about the structure and function of original Druidism remains moot.

The word 'gorsedd' ('gorsedh' in Cornish) contains two elements. The second, '-sedd', means literally sitting. The first, 'gor-' is an emphatic prefix, which might be translated as great or super. (The Cornish for market is 'marghas', for example, and supermarket is 'gorvarghas'.) So the word 'gorsedd' means something like great sitting, or assembly. It can refer either to a place or to an event.

The Welsh National Eisteddfod, a cultural assembly closely related to the Gorsedd, is sufficiently well known for some of its proceedings, notably the awarding of the Chair for Welsh-language poetry, to be televised in Britain. The three 'gorseddau' (Welsh, Cornish and Breton) also receive brief television reports, and their awards are generally more fully covered in the written Press, but they remain relatively small and obscure institutions.

There is a modern revived Druidism in several variant forms, with a British organization closely associated with Midsummer celebrations at Stonehenge until recent controversy over the safety of the site precluded those ceremonies, and an American organization which is a neo-pagan revival, closely associated with other neo-pagan religions, including Wicca.

All revived forms of Druidism, or institutions based on the original Druidic functions, ceremonies and beliefs, suffer from the same dearth of real information, and are subsequently fertile ground for invention and purely imaginative reconstruction, which makes much of the scholarship about Druidism unreliable. That is not to denigrate those institutions or ceremonies (I myself am a Bard of the Cornish Gorsedh, and immensely proud to be so honoured), but the important reminder needs repeating, namely, that our evidence for the realities of early Druidism is extremely scant, and the presence of some particular element in revived Druidism, or ceremonies based on Druidism, is by no means indicative of that element being part of original Druidism.

The three divisions of rank in the revived 'gorseddau', namely Druid, Ovate and Bard, are supposedly modelled on the subdivisions in the Druidic priesthood of the early tribal Celts attested both by classical writers and the authors of the vernacular texts. In the Irish texts we also find the terms 'filid' and 'ollam', and Hirtius uses the (supposedly Gaulish) term *gutuater* in his account of Caesar's Gallic Wars. All three terms, which will be discussed in more detail shortly, complicate the basic picture to some extent, because it is not exactly clear how the different terms and functions relate to each other. 'Ollam', sometimes interpreted as senior poet, is clearly related to the Bardic role. 'Filid' and *gutuater* seem related to divination.

We have the added difficulty of possessing more information about the differences between, say, Bards and Druids, than we have about the ways in which their religious and secular functions overlapped or combined. For example, the Bards, as the name suggests, were responsible for poetic composition; the Druids, for teaching: yet, presumably, these functions must have overlapped at least to some extent, as, for example, in the composition, learning and recital of the long and complicated royal genealogies which were certainly the responsibility of the Druid and his retinue. An even greater overlap is revealed in the area of divination, or prophecy, a responsibility apparently shared by Druids and Ovates, or Vates as they are also called.

To cloud the picture further, we have several unmistakable references in both classical and vernacular texts to the function of prophetess, yet it is by no means clear to what extent that function duplicated or overlapped with the responsibilities of the Druid and the Ovate. The vernacular texts suggest that women may have been Druids (or Druidesses) as well as men, and there are two obscure and slightly dubious classical references, both from the same Roman author (Vopiscus, described below), to confirm the suggestion. From everything else we know about Celtic society, and in particular about Celtic attitudes towards women, we might easily expect women to appear as Druids as well, although all the references we have indicate that the Druid was always a man. But then, all the written references we have were written by men; moreover by either Romans or medieval Christian monks, both groups deeply immersed in a chauvinistic, patriarchal culture which would be utterly unreceptive to the notion of women acting as priests or wielding real religious power, but which might well accord them the important but lesser role of prophetess, associated with feminine intuition. Romans recognized priestesses, but usually only within clearly defined cults associated with a particular goddess, or with a particular function, as, for example, with the Vestal Virgins. Christian scribes would have the nun as their only role-model for a woman utterly dedicated to religion, and, by the time the early vernacular texts were being written down, they would associate any women involved in religion outside the nunnery with witchcraft and diabolism. Christian misogyny, deeply rooted in the earlier Judaic tradition, would have made the concept of women priests utterly alien. Perhaps that chauvinism has consistently substituted the word prophetess for a real function, in which Celtic women also were Druids. There is some evidence to suggest that the function of shaman, which was widespread in many early cultures, was not necessarily exclusively male. Our only classical source is Vopiscus, who tells one tale of a Druidess prophesying to Diocletian that he will one day be emperor, and another of several Druidesses foretelling the fame of the illustrious descendants of Claudius: in both cases, the priestesses are actually acting as Vates or seers, but the attribution of the title Druidess is quite clear. It seems to me highly likely, in a society in which women could be ruling monarchs, semi-divine representations of deity, chieftains, generals, warriors and hunters, that they could also be priests, if they chose. The Celts worshipped male gods and female goddesses with equal ease, and their ceremonials were very probably led by Druidesses as well as by Druids. There is an important connection between women priests in Druidism and women teachers or priests in Pythagoreanism, which will be discussed more fully in Chapter Seven.

When discussing individual functions within the Druidic retinue, we have to play games with semantics and interpretation to some extent, because of the ways in which the functions overlapped. For example, all the sources make it clear that Bards were not responsible for, or even involved in, any religious rituals. Yet we also know, from a host of different sources, that the Bards were responsible for composing and uttering satires, the effect of which might be to weaken or even kill their intended victim. Utterance of such power must, to some extent at least, appear to our modern sensibility as being of ceremonial or ritual significance. Here is an example from the Irish texts:

> Then Medb sent the Druids and satirists and harsh bards for Fer Diad that they might make against him three satires to stay him and three lampoons, and that they might raise on his face three blisters, shame, blemish and disgrace, so that he might die before the end of nine days if he did not succumb at once, unless he came with the messengers. For the sake of his honour, Fer Diad came with them, for he deemed it better to fall by shafts of valour and prowess and bravery than by shafts of satire and reviling and reproach.[1]

Strabo mentions Druids, Vates and Bards, and describes all three classes as being 'held in special honour.' Caesar, as we observed on page 78, singled out the Druids as being of particularly high rank, equating them in terms of social status with the senior nobles or *equites*. There seems to be a general consensus in the early sources, reflected in the pattern of the revived institutions mentioned earlier, that the Druids were definitely considered senior to all the other Druidic ranks. Caesar also informs us that among the Druids (of Gaul, at least) there is 'one at their head who holds chief authority among them', in other words, an Archdruid.

Leaving aside for the moment the complications of nomenclature and overlap of functions, we can piece together at least some information about the two main subsidiary classes, namely Bard and Ovate.

Bards and Ovates

Bards are described by Strabo as 'singers and poets'; by Diodorus Siculus as poets 'chanting eulogies and satires'; and by Ammianus, quoting Timagenes, as men who 'celebrate the brave deeds of their famous men in epic verse.' Poems celebrating past heroes are also mentioned by Diodorus Siculus and Lucan. Poseidonius, who travelled in Gaul in the first century BC, writes of lettered 'parasites' who accompany warriors to sing their praises, and elsewhere mentions 'their entertainers . . . called Bards . . . poets who deliver eulogies in song', but it is not clear whether these two descriptions are of the same, or different, groups.

We can make some reasonably well-informed inferences about the nature of Bardic poetry in early Celtic tribal society, not least from two distinctively Celtic poetic methods, one Irish, namely 'dinnseanchas', one Welsh, namely 'cynghanedd', which are very well attested and survive, in various forms, to this day.

There is every likelihood that early Celtic poetry was as arcane, complex, fluid and allusive as early Celtic art. It was probably rich in metaphor and verbal puns, full of historical and mythological references, and driven by a strong and persistent musicality: indeed, there is some evidence to suggest that poetry was recited, or performed, to musical accompaniment. Much of its subject matter would have been heroic, historical or genealogical, and its mythological content would have been woven in and out of the factual with consummate ease, just as the geometric spirals and trefoils of Celtic art wander in and out of faces, leaves, or animals. Much of the poetry would have been descriptive, particularly of special geographical areas, most of which were sacred. Some of the poems would be very familiar to their audience, so that subsequent poems would contain many literary references which only that informed audience would understand. A good number of the poems would have been very long, requiring several hours for recital or performance, particularly when associated with ceremonies or rituals. Metres, rhymes, syllabic patterns and rules of construction would generally have been strictly observed, although inventiveness and the creation of new patterns, if sufficiently skilled, would also have been highly regarded. The heightened colour and vigour of a language strengthened by a powerful oral poetic tradition would have been reflected in a generally increased articulateness which, much as it did for early Elizabethan English, would have given even everyday speech a special energy, rhythm, vitality, variety and allusiveness.

The Irish term 'dinnseanchas' (which actually means topography in modern Irish and is also applied to prose descriptions) is used to describe a type of early Celtic poetry in which a noteworthy place, often also a sacred place, is described or recorded. The following is an example from the 'dinnseanchas' on Ard Ruide:

Tri tuili,	(Three flood-tides
bit i ndun Ardda Ruidi,	there are in the dun of Ard Ruide,
tuile ocan, tuile ech,	a tide of young men, a tide of horses,
tuile milchon meic Luigdech	the tide of the greyhounds of Lugaid's son)

The grouping of events or facts into a group of three, or triad, is typically Celtic, and is found in both the Gaelic and Brythonic traditions.

The typical stanza pattern of the poetic 'dinnseanchas' was very strict. Each stanza consisted of four lines, all rhyming, each with exactly seven syllables. A variant form, as in the example above, allowed three syllables for the first line. Rhythms were complex. Both in 'dinnseanchas' and in other forms of early Irish poetry, a highly ornate and complex pattern of rhythmical emphasis was developed, known by the Gaelic term 'dan direach', which is reminiscent of the musical practice, still very much a feature of traditional Irish singing, in which complex, decorated and highly ornate figures are improvised on unstressed syllables, and the singer earns great praise for his or her ingenuity in the performance.

The Welsh 'cynghanedd' was originally an equally strict poetic technique, although centuries of continuous practice have modified and extended its principles considerably. Alliteration, which means the repetition of the same consonantal sound for musical effect (as, for example, in Shakespeare's 'The barge she sat in, like a burnished throne/Burned on the water; the poop was beaten gold . . .'), is very common in many poetic traditions, not least the Anglo-Saxon or early English, where alliteration was considered far more important than rhyme (which was hardly ever used). 'Cynghanedd' is a fiendishly complex and demanding form of alliteration, in that it requires the consonants to be not only similar, but exactly identical, with only the internal vowels changing. Robert Graves gives the following illustration in English:

> Billet spied,
> bolt sped.
> Across field,
> crows fled,
> Aloft, wounded,
> Left one dead.[2]

It is an extremely restricting and difficult poetic technique, requiring tremendous skill and ingenuity for successful practice. Graves describes 'cynghanedd' as 'hoary' and 'ossified' even by the tenth century AD. Ossified or not, the tradition continues into modern times. Hedd Wyn, the famous Welsh shepherd and Bard of the Black Chair, who was killed in World War 1 before he could be declared winner of the Welsh national poetry competition in 1915, was an expert in 'cynghanedd', writing lines like 'Tros fanau hoff Trawsfynydd' – where the vowel transpositions from 'tros fanau' to 'Trawsfynydd' are typical – abundantly in all his work, and showing a complete mastery of ancient poetic tradition. To this day, there are still many capable Welsh (and Irish, Scottish, Cornish and Breton) practitioners of the traditional Bardic skills.

The ancient Bards were reputed to require a training period of at least nine years, during which they would have to memorize some 20,000 verses, before they might be considered qualified as Bards. (Even if only partly true, that observation reminds us that a possibly vast tradition of pre-Homeric poetry may have perished when the Celtic oral tradition was lost. Even allowing for all the intervening cultural changes, who knows what glorious poetic treasures may have disappeared along with the Druids and their retinues?) Diodorus Siculus, describing the Gauls, confirms the Bardic reputation for learning: 'They are boasters and threateners, and given to bombastic self-dramatization, and yet they are quick in mind with good natural ability for learning.'

This is an unusual compliment from a Roman author describing a barbarian people, yet it is echoed by Caesar, who attributes the learning of long poetic tracts – he uses the explicit phrase *magnum numerum versuum*, that is a large number of verses – to the Druids rather than to the Bards, although that may be simply a lazy or mistaken attribution. Caesar goes on to explain the Druidic preference for oral as opposed to written literature by saying that the Druids 'did not wish the rule to become common property', and, more prosaically, that the Druids believed 'the assistance of writing tends to relax the diligence of the student.' Caesar's first observation is corroborated by mention in the Irish texts of a secret language, known as the 'berla na filid', meaning 'tongue of the filid', which was used exclusively by poets and seers. Caesar also informs us that the Celts were certainly capable of writing if they chose. He tells us that Druids used Greek letters, at least for secular purposes 'in their public and private accounts', an observation which is to some extent confirmed by archaeological finds.

The 'filid', mentioned above (the name is Irish) seem to have filled a function part way between Bard and Druid – the exact role is not clear. Originally, the word 'fili' ('filid' is the plural, as 'druid' is the plural of 'drui') meant prophet or seer, but it is frequently used in the vernacular texts to mean 'poet', particularly the writer of destructive satires. The role is also credited with the power of divination, however, and is sometimes associated with the role of Ovate or Vate, rather than Bard.

Another difficult Irish term is 'ollam'. In one sense, its meaning is quite clear: it refers to the third, or highest, class of poet, and therefore equates most nearly with the title of Bard, although the rank appears to be higher. In fact, the Irish texts tell us explicitly that the Ollam was entitled by law to travel with a retinue of 24 men and expect free hospitality for all of them from a host, even a royal host – a level of rank which we would normally associate only with the Druids or higher-ranking nobility.

'Fili' and 'ollam', exclusively Irish terms, may describe roles within the Druidic retinue which were also exclusively Irish – we have no way of knowing for certain.

The second group in the Druidic retinue, the Ovates or Vates (both forms are widely used) are described by Strabo as 'interpreters of sacrifice and natural philosophers.' He says that they differ from Druids in that they do not teach or study 'moral philosophy'. This accords with the general notion that Druids were principally ambassadors, judges and lawmakers, because the moral philosophy which supported the law was their exclusive province. Strabo's description leaves moot the question of the extent and nature of the divinatory sacrifices, and whether Druids were also present or involved, which is strange, since most other classical descriptions make it clear that Druids were present and involved.

Diodorus Siculus also describes a separate group within the Druidic retinue which was responsible for sacrifices and auguries. He uses the term *manteis*, which is Greek. Pliny later constructs a verb in Latin, *manticinare*, from *manteis* and the Latin verb *canere*, meaning to sing, the compound usually translated as meaning 'to play or perform the role of a diviner'. The term seems almost certainly to be related to the name Manto, which was given to a prophetess, daughter of Tiresias, and also to a nymph, mother of Ocnus and founder of the original settlement at Mantua (in other words, a goddess of place) who also had the gift of prophecy.

Another less well-known term is *gutuater*, which is found in Book VIII of Hirtius's account of the Gallic War, and which seems to mean seer or invoker, although the precise social status and ceremonial function are not further specified. It is possible that *gutuater* was a Gaulish word. *Guttur* is the Latin for throat (hence our word guttural) and 'guth' is the Irish for voice. Perhaps the root meaning of voicer or speaker gives a clue to the actual role, which may have involved speaking with the god's or goddess's voice.

We do not know whether Bard and Ovate were permanent ranks within the Druidic retinue, or whether suitable candidates might eventually be promoted to Druid. We do know that the training period for the Druidic priesthood was long and arduous. As has been mentioned, Caesar states explicitly that the training took 19 years. It is also not clear to what extent the functions of Bard and Ovate were duplicated by the Druid. We have plenty of evidence in both classical and vernacular sources of Druids casting satires, composing verses and giving augury, all of which seem to suggest that Druids did, indeed, have earlier training and experience as Bards and Ovates before achieving the rank of Druid.

The three social functions of the Druidic retinue which seem, according to most sources, to have been reserved exclusively for the rank of Druid were: firstly, the conducting of important religious ceremonies, particularly on feast days and significant stations in the calendrical cycle; secondly, the teaching and induction of younger acolytes, perhaps from the ranks of Bard and Ovate, into the Druidic priesthood; thirdly, the giving of arbitration, particularly on matters of law, political analysis and general diplomacy.

Druidic ceremonies

Possibly the most familiar description of Druidic ceremonial – certainly the one which has had the greatest effect on subsequent interpretations in visual art – is the following by Pliny:

> They call the mistletoe by a name meaning the all-healing. Having made preparation for sacrifice and a banquet beneath the trees, they bring thither two white bulls, whose horns are bound then for the first time. Clad in a white robe, the priest ascends the tree and cuts the mistletoe with a golden sickle, and it is received by others in a white cloak. Then they kill the victims, praying that God will render this gift of his propitious to those to whom he had granted it. They believe that the mistletoe, taken in drink, imparts fertility to barren animals, and

that it is an antidote for all poisons. Such are the religious feelings that are entertained towards trifling things by many peoples.

As Piggott points out, at least one part of this description must be inaccurate: mistletoe is a very tough plant, and gold a very soft metal; the knife may have been golden in colour, perhaps made of gilded bronze, but it cannot have been actually made of gold.[3]

Pliny's description is so graphic, and has coloured so many subsequent descriptions of Druids, that it is worth examining in more detail.

Firstly, his attribution of significance to the mistletoe plant in early Celtic society, and his suggested interpretation of the Celtic name for the plant, are both accurate. The mistletoe, or *Viscum album*, is a member of the Loranthaceae family. It is a parasitic plant, found mostly on deciduous trees, especially the apple. The chemical constituents of the plant vary according to the species of the host. According to tradition, Druids favoured mistletoe growing on the oak, although, as Graves points out, all species of British oak are too hard to act as hosts to mistletoe (unlike some Mediterranean oaks) and the equally venerated apple tree is a far more likely candidate for the host.[4] The plant contains 11 proteins and substances called lectins which are currently being investigated for possible anti-cancer effects. Its complete chemistry remains elusive. Its known uses, ancient and modern, include the infusion of the dried leaves and berries to make a tea which is hypotensive (reducing blood pressure), cardio-active (stimulating the heart), diuretic (expelling excess body fluid) and sedative when taken by humans. It has been demonstrated to have an antineoplastic (tumour-reducing) effect on animals.[5] The plant has been venerated in folklore over centuries, long after the passing of the Druids. The custom of kissing under the mistletoe at Christmas seems to confirm Pliny's description of it as an acknowledged aid to fertility, although it was also an earlier custom to hang mistletoe in the porch of a house as a more general and innocent sign of peace and hospitality. In Christian times, mistletoe was carried as a defence against witches, and placed in a baby's cradle to prevent the child from being abducted by fairies, or pixie-led, to use the Cornish expression.

The Brythonic name for mistletoe, in its variant spellings, means high branch – the Cornish is 'ughelvarr', the Breton 'uhelvarr'. The Welsh 'uchelwydd' is almost identical, except that the '-wydd' element means tree rather than branch. Whether the 'high' is literal, that is, signifying that the plant grows a long way above the ground, or metaphorical, that is, signifying that the plant has high rank or status, is unclear: both meanings are possible for the element 'ughel'. The Goidelic word, however, is quite different. In Irish, it is 'uil-ioc', meaning 'all-heal', which accords exactly with Pliny's account. (The English word, incidentally, is from Old English 'mistiltan', meaning missel twig, the 'mistil' being the missel, mistle, mistle-thrush or berry-thrush, all variant names of the same bird.)

Pliny's description of the 'banquet beneath the trees' definitely has the ring of authenticity about it. The Druids certainly conducted ceremonials and feasts in the open air, particularly in the cleared forest grove known by the Greek word *nemeton*.

The sacrifice of the white bulls seems plausible, except that bulls with white hides would have been extremely rare. Perhaps Pliny is trying to make the point that these would have been rare, and therefore valuable animals; the colour may be more symbolic than actual. Perhaps he has imported a detail from a description of some other ceremony in eastern Europe or Asia. Perhaps the bulls were dyed or painted white, in keeping with the braids and ribbons tied around the horns. Or perhaps Pliny made the whole thing up. We have no way of telling.

The white robe for the Druid is now firmly ensconced in reconstructed Druidism. The English Druids who used to meet at Stonehenge and now meet on Tower Hill, the modern Welsh Druids at their Gorsedd and Eisteddfod, all wear white robes, after Pliny's description (except for the Archdruid, who has gold trimmings). Yet the vernacular texts suggest that plain white would have been a very unlikely colour for a Druid – indeed for any Celt – to wear. Far more likely that he would have worn a multicoloured cloak, probably richly patterned, and quite possibly some form of head-dress or mask, perhaps an antlered helmet or totemic animal mask. My own view is that the white robe is a product of Pliny's Roman imagination, in which the whiteness would be associated with the plain white robes of the Roman priesthood, not the Celtic.

The golden sickle, as has been mentioned, is thoroughly implausible. It is, however, quite likely that the mistletoe would have been cut, rather than pulled bodily out of its host's trunk, since leaving part of the plant rooted would obviously give it a chance to survive the pruning and be used again at a future date. But the implement must have been sharper. The cut plant may very well have been thrown down into a cloak, but, again, probably not a white one.

In general, the events seem plausible, but the colours are wrong. White bulls, white robes, white cloaks, and golden sickles – these seem like Roman idealizations.

Whether Pliny's description is accurate in its details or not, his general description of Druids leading religious ceremonies is corroborated by several similar descriptions by other classical authors. Caesar, for example, says that the Druids 'are concerned with the worship of the gods, look after public and private sacrifice, and expound religious matters.'

Pliny is the source of another mystery which has led to a great deal of conjecture and imaginative reconstruction. He claimed to have seen, at first hand, an important Druidic ceremonial object, for which he uses the word *anguinum*. This is the neuter form of the adjective *anguinus*, meaning snaky, from *anguis* meaning snake. Strictly speaking, *anguinum* ought to be translated as a snaky thing, but it is usually translated as serpent's egg. I have laboured the point about the meaning here because there is intense confusion and speculation about what Pliny actually meant by the term.

Pliny's context makes clear that this object was greatly significant to the Druids. He says that it was carried by them because it would 'ensure success in law-courts and a favourable reception by princes' – those would certainly have been important Druidic objectives. He further tells us that the *anguinum* was formed from the spittle and secretions of angry snakes, from which arises the lazy translation, serpent's egg; nowhere does Pliny actually say or imply that the object was an egg, or even egg-shaped. In fact, Pliny gives us a very clear and explicit physical description: 'It was round, and about as large as a smallish apple; the shell was cartilaginous and pocked like the arms of a polypus.'

Piggott, in his attempt to unravel the description, rejects Pliny's literal angry snake secretions as unscientific, not observed biologically; he also dismisses the sea-urchin, suggested by other authorities; finally he settles for:

> the ball of agglomerated empty egg-cases of a whelk (Buccinum), which has a parchment-like texture and a nodulated surface, for since Buccinum is a genus confined to Atlantic and northern waters, its egg-cases, common enough objects on a North Gaulish or British beach, might be quite unfamiliar to a Mediterranean naturalist, and so capable of being endowed for him with magic powers.[6]

This seems ingenious at first glance, but a moment's thought makes it clear that a whelk's empty egg-case would fit the bill only if Pliny had been the victim of some monstrous practical joke. Unfamiliar to Pliny as it may have been, the egg-case would have been a very familiar object to all the peoples living along the Atlantic seaboard, found in their dozens, perhaps in their hundreds, washed up on the beach after stormy weather and hardly likely to have been carried by Druids as a special token or emblem of authority. It would be like a child telling a Martian that the sweets in his pockets were diamonds, and the Martian believing him. Another difficulty is that in Druidic tradition the serpent's egg is bright red, while the Buccinum is white, or a pale yellow at best – in fact, most of those I have seen have been a dirty grey colour, small, damp and squishy, and not in the least bit mysterious, suggestive or emblematic of any kind of power. The Druidic tradition later developed to include painting hens' eggs red in the early part of the year, an ancient practice from pre-Christian times which survives in all the egg games and egg lore associated with Easter (which, in itself, is derived from the name of the pre-existing pagan festival, Eostre or Eastre, a Saxon, rather than Celtic, festival). Pliny is normally a pedestrian writer, so we should expect some real object to match his description, but there does not seem to be a thoroughly convincing one. The majority of snakes lay eggs with soft shells which might be described as 'cartilaginous'. The adder, Britain's only venomous snake, gives birth to live young, however. The only egg-laying snake in Britain is *Natrix natrix*, commonly known as the grass snake, but its eggs are white and very small. Its close European relative, *Natrix viperinus*, is very common in Spain and Portugal, and its affinity for water would associate it with springs, pools and rivers revered by the Druids.

The mystery of the serpent's egg remains unsolved, although the association of Druidism and snakes, and later the winged snakes, in other words dragons, continues undiminished for many centuries after Pliny's description. The horned god Cernunnos, whose cult was widely distributed among the early Celts, is frequently depicted holding one or two serpents, which themselves are mysteriously ram-headed or horned. By Christian times, of course, Cernunnos has become the image of Satan, his antlers transmogrified to Devil's horns, and the hooded, horned or winged serpents have become fire-breathing dragons to be pacified and slain by saints.

Pliny is not entirely trustworthy as a source, and it may be that the mysterious serpent's egg, on which so much interpretative energy has been spent, was just an invention. It should be remembered that Pliny vilified Christians equally vehemently, describing their faith as 'gross superstition' and their courage under Roman torture as 'obstinacy', so that his observation that 'at the present day Britannia is still fascinated by magic, and performs its rites with so much ceremony that it almost seems as though it was she who had imparted the cult to the Persians' has to be seen as written by a very staid and conventional Roman, regular in his dedication of wine and incense to the divine emperor, and for whom all other religious beliefs and practices would have been foolish and unsavoury. In a letter to the Emperor Trajan, he seeks guidance on how to deal with captured Christians, asking *'quid et quatenus aut puniri soleat aut quaeri'* – what method of degree of punishment or enquiry are usual – to which he receives Trajan's succinct instruction that they must capitulate *'supplicando dis nostris'* – by supplication to our gods – or be put to death.

Caesar states quite unequivocally that the Druids were involved in human sacrifice. His assertion is supported by Diodorus Siculus, by Strabo, and, importantly (because he is generally reliable as a historian), by Tacitus, who says specifically of the British Druids: 'They deemed it indeed a duty to cover their altars with the blood of captives and to consult their deities through human entrails.' Such practices are so alien to modern thought that many later writers have denied that human sacrifices ever took place, or, if they did, it was without the active participation of the Druids. This is palpable nonsense, which Piggott eloquently refutes:

> It is hardly realistic to exculpate the Druids from participation, probably active, in both the beliefs and practices involved in human sacrifice (which after all had only been brought to an end in the civilized Roman world in the early first century B.C.) The Druids were the wise men of barbarian Celtic society, and Celtic religion was their religion, with all its crudities. It is sheer romanticism and a capitulation to the myth of the Noble Savage to imagine that they stood by the sacrifices in duty bound, but with disapproval in their faces and elevated thoughts in their minds.[7]

Piggott's point is well made, but, in fairness, it should be pointed out that the context of the above quotation is a long and general attack on any suggestion that the Druidic philosophy or religion had any substance: he is trying to persuade us of the crudity and banality of Druidic thought, a more general argument which I find less persuasive.

The two most striking classical descriptions of Druidic human sacrifice come from Strabo and Caesar. Both describe victims being imprisoned in huge numbers inside a vast wickerwork structure, which Strabo describes using the Greek word *kolosson* and Caesar calls '*immani magnitudine simulacra*', suggesting that the figure was made in the shape of a man. According to the authors, this wickerwork structure was set alight while the victims were still imprisoned within it, so that they were burned alive.

As was mentioned on page 15, however, Strabo also describes ritual exccecution by bow and arrow, which is highly implausible. If Caesar's original description was an invention, a flight of imagination whipped up to reinforce the image of the Celts as a savage, heartless, barbarian people, the fact that the same description appears in Strabo is not necessarily corroborative. Strabo (his name, from the Greek *strabon*, means one who squints) was a Greek, born around 63 BC. He was a geographer (one of the earliest), who spent most of his time in the great library of Alexandria and reputedly had little time for the Roman authorities. However, he was only eight years old when Caesar first invaded Britain, and by the time he came to write his great work, simply called *The Geography*, Caesar's accounts of his adventures (now history by a few decades) would have been widely circulated, and copies would certainly have reached the library at Alexandria. Strabo might well have copied Caesar's description of the wickerwork man simply to add some spice and local colour to his own work. If this is true – and, of course, it is no longer susceptible to proof either way – it would make the description doubly uncertain.

Nevertheless, the evidence does suggest that the Druids practised at least some form of human sacrifice. If, as Caesar suggests, many of the victims were law-breakers and captured prisoners, perhaps the word execution would be more appropriate than sacrifice. Even in Rome, the question was often moot. As just explained by Piggott, the Romans themselves practised human sacrifice until 96 BC, when the Senate prohibited it. However, two soldiers who participated in a rebellion against Caesar were executed for treason and their heads stuck on poles for all to see in the Regia, but their execution was also dedicated to the god Mars. Strictly speaking, one might say that Caesar himself was responsible for at least one human sacrifice. Roman gladiatorial combat and summary execution by crucifixion, neither of which seems civilized to modern Western sensibility, are also both well attested.

Here is another instance of our need to suspend our cultural prejudices if we are to see with a clear eye. Perhaps it helps to remember that in the Bible the author of the Book of Revelation unleashes a frenzy of hatred on Rome and longs for her rivers to turn to blood, her people to be trampled underfoot till their blood 'shall make a sea up to the bridles of their horses'. In the light of our knowledge of the persecutions of Christians under Nero and Domitian, we can understand the anger feeding such violent sentiments, which in every respect are quite contradictory to the spirit of forgiveness and reconciliation preached by Jesus of Nazareth – we have to grant St John his historical context. Similarly, if we suspend our own moral judgement about the Druids and their warrior society, we can see that their historical and cultural circumstances, as well as their precepts and religious beliefs, might well lead them to accept human sacrifice as a normal, reasonable, necessary, perhaps even cleansing and healing institution – as some in our society (myself not included) might see capital punishment. In the Celtic spirit, we observe simultaneously a riotous delight in life and all that comes with it – food, drink, sex, war, glory, art, music, poetry, celebration – and, paradoxically, a complete indifference to life and a willingness to walk into the jaws of death without a moment's hesitation. Against that cultural background, sending a man to his death in sacrifice or execution may not have seemed to the Celts greatly different in moral character from sending him to his death in battle; the only difference would be the gain achieved in denying the enemy, or victim, his share of any battle-glory.

Other than the descriptions by Caesar, Strabo and Pliny, all of which are to some extent unreliable, we have little further description of Druidic functions in the classical texts. We gain more insights from the vernacular texts, but the picture is neither very detailed, nor complete. However, we can guess, or reasonably infer, what other ceremonial duties Druids might have performed. In a society closely tied to the agricultural cycle, it is very likely that Druids performed ceremonies to mark important stations of the year, as well as irregular occurrences, such as eclipses, but that is a line of inference which I shall pursue in more detail in later chapters. We know that Druids rarely fought in battle, but they were frequently present at, or in the vicinity of, battles. As well as the legal and diplomatic tasks which they undertook, it is quite likely that they led battle prayers, cast satires against the enemy and participated in victory ceremonial. The Celts had both marriage and divorce, and an unusual form of concubinage in which a man could legally take a second wife, known in Irish, surprisingly since the relationship was perfectly legal, by the term 'adaltrach', literally adulteress. Presumably marriage ceremonies (and, quite possibly, divorce ceremonies) may have been conducted by Druids. It is inconceivable that the Druids did not play a central and distinctive role in all funeral ceremonies. Particularly for great nobles, burial ceremonies would have been extensive and elaborate, almost certainly with the Druids taking a leading role in the organization. It is equally likely that all the other small stations of the life journey – the taking of a name, initiation into adulthood, tribal initiation, battle initiation, and so on – were also accompanied by appropriate ceremony.

Druids as teachers

The second Druidic function was that of teacher. With no written records, the important task of recording, organizing and handing down a whole culture, an entire racial history, devolved upon the Druid and his retinue. We have already heard Caesar inform us that the Druids were required to learn '*magnum numerum versuum*', that the Bards, in training for nine years, would learn over 20,000 individual verses. Many of these would be genealogical, many would be accounts of battles and heroic deeds, many would be mythological.

Much of this teaching would be esoteric, intended for the Druidic retinue only. As Anne Ross points out, much of the learning would probably have been of the hear-and-repeat kind, with the Druid or senior Bard (or Ollam, in Ireland) intoning what had to be learned and the select acolytes of the Druidic retinue repeating it all together. The Old Irish verb meaning to teach is 'for-cain', literally sing over.[8] The Brythonic verb to teach ('dysgu' in Welsh, 'dyski' in Cornish) also means to learn. Included in this esoteric lore would probably have been all the elements of ceremonial practice, in other words, all elements necessary for training in the priesthood: mathematics and astronomy, including calendrical computation; precepts of law and diplomacy; the geography of sacred places, particularly local ones, and how local gods should be called and propitiated; herbal and medicinal lore; theology.

There would almost certainly have been some public teaching, also, if 'teaching' is the appropriate word: performing might be better. Here the Bards may well have taken a more prominent role than the Druids. Recital of genealogies, songs and perhaps even dramatizations describing great deeds of heroic exploits, poems, mythological tales would have been included.

Druids as politicians

The third Druidic function, and one for which we have considerable evidence, was that of lawgiver, judge, ambassador or diplomat – in other words, a political function. Much of this function has been described already, but it can be summarized briefly here. The Druids interpreted established law, giving judgements on wrongdoers and acting as arbiters in disputes, which were frequent. Their authority was great, even extending over kings, since it was spiritual in essence. They also created new law, by giving judgement where there was no precedent. The guiding principles for such arbitration were 'fir fer', or fair play; the utterance of truth; and the fitness of things, which we might also refer to as proportion, appropriateness, or just plain common sense. They adjudicated disputes, particularly over sensitive issues like divorce or inheritance. They supervised, and perhaps even delivered contracts (probably oral) for relationships and responsibilities entered into by third parties either through clientship or fosterage. They negotiated between tribes in disputes over territory or possessions, particularly important possessions like cattle. They enforced domestic law and taboo, punishing wrongdoing through satire or other utterance and through a range of physical sanctions up to and including execution.

So, we now have some idea of the history and structure of the society within which the Druids operated, and of the functions which they performed. Our next task is to imaginatively reconstruct the pattern of the year as it would have appeared to members of early Celtic tribal society and to describe, from their point of view as far as it is possible empathetically to do so, how the rhythms and cadences of the agricultural cycle would have affected them.

Notes

1. In the *Tain Bo Cuailnge*.
2. Robert Graves, *The White Goddess*.
3. Stuart Piggott, *The Druids*.
4. Robert Graves, above.

5. Malcolm Stuart (ed.), *The Encyclopaedia of Herbs and Herbalism*.
6. & 7. Stuart Piggott, above.
8. Anne Ross, *Everyday Life of the Pagan Celts*.

· CHAPTER FIVE ·

THE AGRICULTURAL CYCLE

PLINY TELLS US that the Celtic year began in July, as did the Athenian. The mythographic attribution of holly and oak, whose gods are twins, to the midsummer months supports the idea that the Celts reckoned the year from high point to high point, that is from midsummer to midsummer. Midwinter to midwinter would also have been feasible and, for some reason, many contemporary writers have assigned special significance to Samhain (the day following Hallowe'en, that is, dusk, on 31 October to dusk on 1 November) as the beginning of the Celtic year – revived neo-pagan Druidism favours this date. For the purpose of this chapter, it makes no difference where we begin the year, but the question will be discussed in greater detail later.

Neolithic man cleared ground for farming in a pattern, or a succession of phases which is often called slash-and-burn. In the first phase, oak or ash forest was roughly cut, the timber burned and the ashes ploughed into the ground as fertilizer. The ground was then cultivated for as long as it would continue to give reasonable crop yields. Eventually, the ground would be worn out and the plot would be abandoned. Weeds associated with cultivation, such as plantain, would invade the plot. Finally, birch and ash would recolonize the area, yielding after some years to hardier and more durable oak.[1]

As early as 3000 BC there were established farming settlements in the British Isles. These were cleared by the long-headed peoples, precursors of the Celts, who had begun their immigrations 500 years earlier. These were the people who built the great stone circles of Avebury and Stonehenge.

By the time the Celts invaded Britain and displaced the earlier settlers – perhaps as early as 900 BC, perhaps rather later – some patterns of land use were long established. Much of the British Isles remained covered in impenetrable forest until well into Elizabethan times, but the Celts would also have found large areas dedicated to farming of one kind or another – established grasslands, pastures and meadows, even long established farm fields, conceivably with a crude system of crop rotation or laying fields fallow in grass or rye. Although the early Celts tended to wander extensively within their tribal areas, moving their flocks and herds with them, the seasonal planting of vital crops, like wheat, barley and oats, would tend to slow down the drift and encourage more settled communities. By the time of the Roman occupation, several tribes were more or less permanently settled, their roundhouses closely grouped, probably with a 'fogou' (see page 75) nearby. For such settlements, a fresh water supply from a stream, river or wells would have been of paramount importance, especially in summer, and an extensive timber supply for fuel would have been equally important, especially in winter. The Cornish place-name Kenidjack is derived from 'keunys', meaning kindling or fuel and the adjective ending '-ek', yielding the meaning 'place rich in fuel or kindling'. The Welsh and Breton cognates are 'cynnud' and 'keuneud' respectively.

Hunting continued all year round and provided an important supplement and variety to the agricultural diet. Fishing, in streams, rivers, lakes and in shallow coastal waters, would have added freshwater fish and seafood, like crabs, clams and mussels, to the diet, as well as dabs, codling, sea bass and other fish easily caught close to shore. There is little evidence to suggest that the early Celts were deep-sea fishermen, although they did undertake regular sea voyages, especially from Roman times onward. Salmon were regularly netted during the annual spawning, and it is possible that the early Celts built ledges and dug pools in stream beds to encourage upriver migration.

Farming duties would almost certainly have been shared extensively among the tribe. While a very small number of kings, chieftains and other nobles may have escaped agricultural labour altogether – as the Druids and their retinues may also have done, although that is less easy to suppose – the vast majority of the men, women and children in the tribe would have been involved in the work of agricultural production for at least part of the year. Especially busy times would be: the hay harvest, since the amount of fodder accumulated would determine how many animals would survive the winter; the different grain harvests, each labour-intensive in itself, but also leading directly to the further tasks of storage and milling; and the winter slaughter, when a great deal of meat would need to be salted quickly.

The earliest agricultural implements were of antler, horn and bone, but the tribal Celts used wooden tools, metal tools, and tools edged or reinforced with metal, including an iron-soled plough. Oxen were used as draught animals, the small Celtic horses being too light for such work. Fields were double-ploughed after the winter frosts had broken up the ground, first north to south, then east to west, so that they tended to be square in shape. (The Anglo-Saxons later used a different system, in which the oxen were turned less frequently, so the fields became long and narrow – in fact, they were a 'furrow long', which is the origin of the word furlong.) Crop fields were not protected by walls or even hedging, but livestock could be contained by light wickets and fences of ash stakes with hazel twigs woven between them, or by barriers of gorse and bramble. As was suggested on pages 62–3, dogs were probably used to help control flocks and herds.

Midsummer

The midsummer turn of the year heralded the first haymaking. In a long, mild autumn, especially if there was plenty of drying wind, there might be two or even three hay harvests before the onset of winter, although the last would probably be of little value as fodder. Winter barley and winter oats might also be harvested soon after midsummer, if they had prospered through a mild spring. This would be the wealth crop: the greater the total harvest, from both winter and spring sowings, the less the danger that the tribe would face starvation in the winter. If either crop failed – usually through the weather being too wet – it would make for lean, hard times. If both plantings failed, it was disastrous: many of the tribe, especially the very young and the very old, would die. At the height of the summer, the lean times ahead had to be planned for – the ancient Cornish proverb expresses it, 'Yn hav, porth kov a wav', In summer, remember winter. Medicinal flowers would be picked and dried. Borage, with its blue, star-shaped flowers and grey-green leaves, was eaten raw to lighten and exhilarate the mind, particularly before battle. Marjoram was crushed, its oil producing a useful painkiller.

Its flowering tops were simmered to make a purple dye for wool. Other dye plants were woad flowers, for blue; madder for brown or red; weld for yellow; and buckthorn berries for vivid green. On the moors, bilberries and cranberries came into fruit around midsummer; both were too tart to be eaten raw in any quantity, but cranberries made a good accompaniment to meat and bilberries made good eating when boiled and reduced to a sticky, sweet syrup. Rowan berries and rose hips received similar treatment.

If barley and oats had been successfully harvested early in the summer, grass would be sown quickly in the empty fields; with good fortune and clement weather it would make a late hay harvest or catch-crop in November, a valuable addition to the winter reserves. More summer flowers would be gathered. Bee-balm was widely planted to produce nectar – some would be harvested and dried for medicinal infusions, the rest of the flowers would be left to encourage the bees in their honey-making. Camomile flowers, invaluable for treating stomach disorders and sleeplessness, were plucked and dried.

Some plants had to be weeded out, rather than collected. The first purple crocuses of late midsummer were poisonous to cattle, and they would certainly taint their milk even if cows survived eating them. Several other noxious plants, injurious both to sheep and cattle, needed clearing from the pastures, and it was part of the shepherd's summer duty to keep a close eye on what his herds were eating.

Autumn

As summer ripened into autumn, everyone would be anticipating the main harvest. Settled weather during this period was critical. A sudden storm, especially of hail, could destroy an entire crop within minutes, and that spelled disaster. Prayers for a bountiful harvest began early and were earnestly maintained. The surest way to judge the ripeness of the crop was by pulling a few ears and rolling the grain between finger and thumb to see how plump and yielding it felt. It was vitally important to allow the crop to ripen as fully as possible, but the longer it stood unharvested, the greater the danger that it might be spoiled or destroyed by rain, wind, flood, or even – after a lightning strike – by fire. Judging the exact, critical moment for the harvest – a day wrong either side could make a difference –

must have been a difficult task, and it is highly likely that the Ovates and the Druids would have been widely and frequently consulted for their opinions.

Once begun, the harvesting occupied the whole tribe. The grain stalks were scythed by hand and gathered in loose stooks. Hand beating and winnowing separated useful grain from chaff. The spent stalks were gathered and stored as straw. The grain was collected, probably in woven baskets, possibly in clay jars and pots. Some grain would have been milled immediately, probably using a simple stone pestle and mortar, while the bulk of the harvest would have been kept in grain. Dry storage, properly ventilated, would have been essential to ensure that the stored grain lasted through the winter without being blighted by rot or mildew. Some writers have suggested that the main purpose of the fogou was to provide a dry, ventilated grain store, but the argument is unconvincing for the simple reason that most fogous are very cool and damp, in summer and winter alike.

At the same time as the main harvest ripened fully, ceps and blewits appeared in the woodlands. These fungi had little nutritional value, but they were tasty, easy to gather and easy to dry and store for the winter. Birthwort came into flower, and its heart-shaped leaves and yellow-green petals were collected to make an analgesic specific for birth-pangs, as its name suggests – it might well have been used on animals in the winter and early spring birthing seasons, as well as on humans. The deer came into rut at harvest time, the barking of the stags echoing through the woodland as they gathered their harems of hinds. On the moorlands, and perhaps occasionally in the cornfields where harvesting was going on, adders gave birth to their young at this season, anywhere from six to twenty at a time.

The weather might well remain mild after the harvest. There might even be a brief autumnal spell as warm as any day in the previous summer, but the intimation of the first frosts would be in the air and there was much to be done. Firstly, the harvested fields would be rough ploughed ready for the winter. If the weather was wet, or cold threatened early, the ground would simply be left untouched. The winter frosts would break the soil apart, and seed would be sown in the spring. On the other hand, if the weather was still warm, an early winter sowing could be achieved before the ground became too cold. The seed would set underground, then overwinter and deliver a very welcome early harvest the following year. The decision was critical. If a winter crop was sown in cold or wet ground, the seed would simply wither and rot underground and be totally wasted. If the following spring sowing also failed, the tribe would almost certainly starve. The general rule was to sow winter seed – winter barley, winter wheat and grey oats – and pray.

Calving from milk cows would continue, with good fortune, until late in the autumn; the later the better, because every cow delivered of a late calf would continue to give plentiful milk through the lean months of winter. Sorting of the rest of the flocks and herds would begin. The hay harvest would determine how many animals could be kept through the winter – usually only breeding animals survived. Goats were easiest to keep, because they could survive on very scanty feed, and gave useful milk and cheese, as well as meat. Sheep were more valuable, but they required better pasturage. Pigs gave excellent meat and soft leather, but they were difficult to raise domestically because of their susceptibility to cold in winter. Most valuable of all were cattle, which demanded large amounts of feedstuff but gave tremendous returns in milk, meat and hide. Horses, particularly breeding mares and young, fit animals also required plenty of winter fodder to stay healthy, but they were essential for warfare and transport. Nevertheless, some horses would probably have been slaughtered for meat, although it may be that cult worship of the horse-goddess Epona made horse-flesh taboo in some regions. Horse-flesh is regularly eaten in modern France, but not in Britain or Ireland.

Autumn brought some late wild harvests. The fat hen plant, whose leaves could be eaten in times of food shortage, also yielded seeds rich in fat, almost as big as beans, which stored well in cold weather. Hazelnuts ripened – they were reputed to give wisdom as well as strength. Split hazel wands and withies made excellent hurdles for livestock when woven between stakes. Hazel wood, which burns with a quick, fierce heat, was probably also used for heating the flat stone hearths on which bread was baked – it has been associated with traditional bread ovens ever since. Sloes ripened on the blackthorn in late autumn. The fruits were too bitter to eat, but blackthorn timber was prized for its strength: it was used to make shepherd's crooks, walking sticks, and the famous Irish shillelagh. As the ash leaves turned yellow and fell, the timber would be cut for a variety of purposes: firm, smooth-grained and supple, ash was used for spears (the Old English word for a spear is 'aesc', meaning ash) and chariot frames, along with a host of non-belligerent uses. Birch timber, on the other hand, was useless for just about anything except firewood, for which it was mostly culled. Holly, just coming into berry, was also a popular firewood because its flame, bright and yellow, gave out great light to send back the darkness.

Winter

Last fruit of all were the mistletoe berries, waxy and white, but with their coming the last of autumn was definitely turning into the first of winter. There might be one very last, desperate hay-cutting of the catch-crop sown in the height of summer, but the fields generally had nothing left to yield. The ground was often wet, and such grass as there was had little or no food value. Sea-cabbage and wild roots could be put out to supplement the grazing for the cattle, but very soon the first of the winter's hay had to be brought out. The cattle would be brought in from outlying pastures to nearby fields or enclosures within the village stockade. Some outlying fields would be left in rye-grass over the winter to provide early outside grazing the following spring. The horses would have to be brought in, too, to be fed on hay, oats and oat straw. Foals born in winter and early spring would be prey to wolves if not closely guarded.

Now was the time for cattle-raids, before the great winter slaughter. Any tribe with insufficient livestock to get it through the lean months would have to consider the possibility of stealing livestock from a neighbouring tribe; for many warriors, these last raids and battles of the autumn would be the last of their lives. Such livestock as the tribe managed to keep intact by the beginning of winter would now be herded and sorted. Only breeding stock would be kept alive. Cattle were easily managed, although prone to disease. Sheep were fairly hardy, but would need careful attention during early spring lambing. Domesticated pigs had to be securely and warmly housed but at least one or two breeding sows would be kept, if possible. They probably slept with the humans.

All other livestock was slaughtered. This, like harvest, was a busy time for the whole tribe. Blood from the slaughter was collected to make blood sausage or black pudding, which had to be eaten quickly before it spoiled. Hides were washed, the fat scraped laboriously from them, then stretched on wooden frames to cure and dry. Carcasses were divided into manageable joints, heavily salted and close packed for storage. Any tribe which had plenty of livestock, but had neglected to maintain a healthy supply of salt, would starve in the midst of a banquet – unsalted meat would spoil within weeks.

The basic diet for the winter would be oat porridge, supplemented by carefully rationed portions of salt meat. There were no more fruits, berries, or fresh vegetables, so to ward off scurvy and skin disease, bittercress and other watercresses were collected from streams. Brooklime, which grew on the stream's banks, served the same purpose: its leaves, while not especially palatable, could be chewed to provide essential vitamin C.

Hunting supplemented the winter diet. At least in Ireland, birds were hunted: Strabo describes a spear designed especially for that purpose, and we meet Cu Chulainn in the Irish texts bringing down 16 swans in flight with a single cast of a stone, although these were shapeshifted souls in flight, as Cu Chulainn was aware, rather than plain food. In parts of Gaul, there seems to have been an actual taboo against eating bird flesh, because birds in flight were so often associated with souls of the dead.

The favourite animal to hunt was the boar, or wild pig. Several of the vernacular texts mention or include boar hunts, and make it clear that the hunt was generally carried out on foot, aided by hunting dogs. In *The Mabinogion*, the Twrch Trwyth is a boar with supernatural attributes, and it is clear that the mythology of the boar hunt was generally widespread and very important in early Celtic culture. The boar is frequently described as emblem or totem of the warrior's finest virtues: ferocity, swiftness, courage, stamina, and so on. Any hero given the epithet 'boar' was highly honoured.

Deer were hunted, too, but their timidity and swiftness made them more difficult targets. One trick was to set blocks of salt in cleared fields close to the forest edge. If the deer were tempted out to the salt lick, they could be chased into open ground where a rider on a swift pony could pursue them, but if they escaped back into the forest, they were difficult to catch, even with dogs.

As autumn moved into winter, salmon began returning to spawn in the river pools, and their arrival made a welcome addition to the winter diet. They were usually baked with honey and herbs, and their flesh, like the fruit of the hazel tree, was associated with wisdom. Young cod, or codling, could be netted in shallow coastal waters or estuaries. Oysters, winkles and other shellfish were collected in coastal areas. Voles and mice were easy to trap, but provided little meat; nevertheless, in a hard winter, even the smallest food source would not be spurned. The Roman occupation brought many new food sources to the native British, notably peas, cherries and rabbits.

Dried peas later became a staple food of the Romano-British diet, particularly in winter.

The first half of the year came to an end with the longest night and shortest day. It was a turning-point, almost certainly marked by propitiation and ritual ceremony. The first green shoots of winter-sown wheat might just be showing above ground, but everywhere the earth would have appeared bare and cold – no leaves, no flowers, wild animals in hibernation, livestock and tribesmen alike holding out through frosts, fog and snow, waiting for the cycle of life to roll forward again.

Lambs would be the first harbingers of new life. Often born while the weather was still bitterly cold, even in snow, the first lambs were also susceptible to predation by foxes and wolves. Male lambs were castrated at two or three weeks of age, ready to fatten as wethers for mutton.

Such manure as was available from the much smaller winter flocks and herds was gathered and spread on the crop fields, ready for the first spring ploughing. Frost and rain would break up the earth and wash the manure's nutrients down into the soil.

Spring

As the first fox and badger cubs were born, the first spring flowers also appeared. They were welcome for their medicinal properties as well as for giving evidence of the coming spring. Coltsfoot provided a very effective remedy for coughs, and primrose flowers, boiled with pig fat, made a protective and healing ointment for cuts and battle wounds.

Soon, other flowers confirmed the onset of spring. Alder trees, cultivated by riverbanks and on marshy ground for their timber, which provided the best charcoal, brought forth their first catkins. Wood anemones flowered, and the first yellow petals on the spiky, dark-green gorse. Gorse would sometimes be used to make a quickly erected thorny barrier to corral livestock. The sacred mistletoe came into flower. Willow catkins appeared – willow twigs were woven to make baskets. Even apple trees might come into blossom, but early blossom meant a light or spoiled crop. The first ground-ivy flowers appeared and were carefully picked: they were added to the barley mash to clear beer in fermentation and to impart a refreshing bitterness.

As soon as all the natural flowerings and blossomings were unmistakable, it was time to plough the fields to a fine tilth and plant spring barley and oats. Rye was planted on poor soil, or to help break new ground. The black oats sown in the spring (grey oats in winter) made excellent porridge and oat-bread. Oat mash and even oat straw were ideal feed for the horses.

The barley crop affected the tribe in a number of different ways. The best of the grain at harvest time was used to make barley beer, or ground into flour for barley bread. Soaked to soften the husks, raw barley mash was excellent fodder for horses and pigs, even for humans at a pinch.

Boiled barley, barley broth or barley water were used as a food substitute and restorative for invalids, or for the very young or very old. Barley straw made good bedding, good flooring for houses and good litter for livestock. So, while wheat and oats, and, to a lesser extent, rye were also essential crops, it was the barley sowing and the barley harvest which affected the early Celtic tribe in the greatest variety of ways.

The first animals to be sent out to graze on the nutritious new grass were the dairy cows in milk with their calves, and ewes with lambs. New-born beef calves would be fed by their mothers all summer and be ready for fattening and slaughter by the beginning of the next winter.

Once the ploughing and spring sowing were complete, the rest of the flocks and herds were sent out to graze. The spring pastures were often still cold, with wet ground underfoot. Livestock weakened by overwintering would be especially susceptible to disease at this time of year.

At the turning-point of Beltane, when the spring sun began to presage summer warmth, the flocks and herds were driven between two fires to protect them against disease and to encourage fertility. Once that ceremonial was complete, they could be driven to summer pasture on higher ground. On a diet of lush and nutritious new grass, livestock would fatten quickly.

In late spring, bees swarmed and settled new hives. Bee-keeping was an important part of the tribe's general husbandry. Honey was the only sweetener available, apart from natural fruit, such as berries, and it was used extensively in cooking and as a food in itself. It was also fermented to produce mead, a sweet and intoxicating liquor. At swarming, the bee-keepers would encourage the bees to divide into as many new hives as possible.

Summer

Various blossoms and flowers appeared in early summer. If the apple blossom was late, it signified an abundant crop. The first beech catkins appeared. Beech was a durable timber, but difficult to work with hand tools. Its most important use was to provide abundant supplies of nuts in the autumn: domesticated hogs were driven through beech forest to feed on the fallen mast. The first blackberry or bramble flowers appeared. All through the summer, blackberries provided sweet fruit, although there was a taboo against them in Wales (see page 199). The leaves, when boiled, made a good poultice, and the boiled roots provided an orange-yellow dye. Catkins flowered on the oak, and the first holly flowers appeared. The woods would be filled, almost overnight, with the heady smell of ramsons, or bear's garlic – the oil, like leek oil, was rubbed on the skin before battle to protect against wounds, both figuratively as a charm and literally as an antiseptic. Wild strawberries flowered and came to fruit in the woods, as did wild cloudberries on the moors.

A host of other flowers and herbs was gathered as summer came into the full: betony, effective in reducing fever; bugle, to make poultices for ulcers; mallow root, to soothe burns and wounds; henbane, whose leaves, flowers and seeds were all deadly poison if eaten raw, but which could be processed to yield an effective painkiller, especially prized as a remedy for toothache.

Sheep-shearing took place at high summer. The wool was washed, carded, dyed and spun ready for weaving, which would last all through the winter. The quality of wool garments was so high that, during the Roman occupation, Celtic woollen cloaks were popular imports to Rome. In the tribal lands of Gaul and Britain, the weaving would conform to established plaid patterns, and the tartan of a warrior's cloak or robe would identify his tribe or clan.

Trees were in full leaf, birds in full song. Barley, wheat, oats and rye were all growing strongly. New-born fawns and boar farrow sported in the forests, fattening up for the autumn hunts. If all had gone well, this high point of midsummer, the end and beginning of the year, was a time of great prosperity. Celebratory midsummer fires were lit. In the other world, Tir na Nog or the Land of the Ever Young, it was always midsummer.

Agriculture and astronomy

The transitions of this agricultural cycle followed a well-marked pattern, and the deep understanding of the pattern exemplified by the Druids' calendrical and astronomical lore would have been, at the least, impressive to the ordinary Celtic tribesman. We cannot prove the extent to which early Celtic agricultural practice was affected by religious thought and ceremony, but the evidence strongly suggests a very firm connection. Mark Graubard (discussing Babylonian and Egyptian agriculture) dismisses the idea that early farmers welcomed calendrical information:

> There does not seem to be adequate evidence for the oft-encountered assertion that ancient astronomy originated in the farmer's need for knowledge of the precise time for ploughing or sowing. Even today farmers do not really watch the calendar to tell them the time for initiating these activities, but rather go by the season generally, that is, by warmth and thaws, time of sunrise, length of day, the succession of blooming plants, or the appearance of migrating birds which are as accurate chronometers as any which nature could devise . . ... In Egypt where agricultural needs were supposed, we are told, to have obliged man to look heavenward for a calendar, the very floods of the Nile were an excellent time indicator by themselves. What could the Egyptian farmer have required celestial reminders for, anyway? If the helical rising of Sirius came together with the floods, could not the latter have reminded him of all he needed to think about, just as efficiently as the former?[2]

It is true that the ancient connection between agriculture and astronomy has been assumed without a great deal of investigation, but that is because, contrary to Graubard's assertion, there *is* an obvious and natural connection between the stars, the time of the year and appropriate agricultural activity. In ancient societies, where the tolerances for error were far more critical, and the consequences of failure far more immediate and dire for all concerned, these interdependencies would have been much greater than they are in our own time. In the geographical context of early Celtic tribal society, Graubard's point that regular phenomena, like the flooding of the Nile, would have been sufficient indicators in themselves falls at the obvious first hurdle, namely the infamous *irregularity* of climate in the temperate maritime zones of western Europe and Britain: the Nile might flood on more or less the same day every year, but British apple blossom could set in February or in May, and be preceded by sunshine and followed by frost and snow. In a climate where small but critical differences could occur with great variety, calendrical observation and prognostication of good weather and propitious times for sowing and harvesting would have been of tremendous importance. Our general impression of the Celts as a deeply religious and superstitious people, much given to consulting Ovates and Druids on a host of social, moral, legal and political as well as religious questions, strongly reinforces the notion that the Druids were also actively and closely involved in the necessary magic of the successful agricultural cycle.

That thought leads us directly to the next chapter, which attempts to reconstruct the likely ceremonials and religious practices, some of them partially described or implied in the classical and vernacular texts, which might have marked the stations of the year and the agricultural cycle.

Notes

1. John G. Evans, *The Environment of Early Man in the British Isles.*
2. Mark Graubard, *Astrology and Alchemy: Two Fossil Sciences.*

CHAPTER SIX

THE ANNUAL CEREMONIES

THE FOUR GREAT CELTIC FESTIVALS, attested and described in the vernacular texts, recognized in centuries of folk tradition, and even celebrated to this day in various ways, are Imbolc, Beltane, Lughnasa and Samhain. They have been assigned to dates in the modern calendar, as follows: Imbolc, 1 February; Beltane, 1 May; Lughnasa, 1 August; and Samhain, 1 November, thus dividing the year into four parts of approximately three months each. Strictly speaking, a Celtic day is a night followed by a day, so Imbolc would be better described as the period from dusk on 31 January to dusk on 1 February, the other dates being modified in similar fashion. But, in any case, the modern assignation of the dates is, in fact, only an approximation necessitated by a solar calendar. Actually, 6 February, 6 May, 6 August and 6 November would be more accurate, since those dates fall more or less halfway between the equinoxes and solstices. In addition, the actual celebrations may not have taken place only on the dates now assigned: Lughnasa, for example, was a long festival, taking perhaps up to 30 days for all its rituals and events to be completed. The division of the rest of the year, and the significance of the midwinter solstice, vernal equinox, midsummer solstice and autumnal equinox, will be discussed more fully in subsequent chapters. The purpose of this chapter is to examine what we know about the attested festivals, and to see whether we can infer or form a plausible reconstruction of what ceremonial might have accompanied them.

We know that all religious festivals were important to the Celts, not just to the Druids and the religious élite, but to the ordinary tribesmen too. Caesar tells us:

When a private person or a tribe disobeys their ruling they ban them from attending sacrifices. This is their harshest penalty. Men placed under this ban are treated as impious wretches; all avoid them, fleeing their company and conversation, lest their contact bring misfortune upon them; they are denied legal rights and can hold no official dignity.

It is possible that this is an invention by Caesar, or an idealization, prompted perhaps by wishful thinking about how a more devout and religious Roman citizenry ought to behave; but there is no real reason to suspect Caesar's motives here, and the description accords well with his earlier descriptions of the Celts as exceptionally religious-minded.

It seems equally probable that all major festivals would also have involved ritual sacrifice of some kind. Animal sacrifice would, of course, provide meat for the associated feast. As was suggested on pages 100–1, it seems very likely that human sacrifice was also practised on a regular basis, but precisely which festivals or occasions would warrant human sacrifice is not clear. It seems unlikely that every single religious ceremony, of which there might be very many in any given year, would of necessity be accompanied by human sacrifice. There is no evidence in the vernacular texts, which would be more reliable than the classical authors on this topic, to tell us whether human sacrifice was seen as more significant or propitious than animal sacrifice, or what criteria would determine when human sacrifice was appropriate. Human sacrifice as such does not appear in the vernacular texts, but only in classical references, confirming for some commentators their hypothesis that human sacrifice was falsely and maliciously attributed to Druidism by Greek and Roman authors. Assuming, however, that some kind of human sacrifice did, in fact, take place, we can guess – but it is only a guess – that human life was generally valued more highly than animal life, and occasions leading to human sacrifice would be generally more important or significant than occasions leading to animal sacrifice. Although the Celts hunted heads (see page 71), there is no suggestion of the eating of human flesh anywhere in either the classical or vernacular sources, and it seems safe to assume that human sacrifice did not imply or lead to any form of cannibalism.

There is plenty of evidence, mostly from Irish sources, to suggest that the annual festivals were also feasts. Lavish eating and drinking, sports, games, entertainments and special markets and fairs are all associated with religious festivals. There are several square or rectangular enclosures found in early Celtic sites which contain apparent evidence of ritual sacrifice, and even some classical references to square enclosures set aside for feasting, which suggests that some kind of site, or building, may have been constructed specifically for celebration and sacrifice on feast days: it would be meeting place, feasting hall and temple all in one – the long enclosure known as the Banqueting Hall on the Hill of Tara, one of early Ireland's most sacred places, is cited as an example. As a reminder, it was noted earlier that Tacitus is careful to use the adjective *castum*, meaning chaste, when describing the outdoor worship site of the *nemeton*, or sacred grove, which suggests that such outdoor sites were not used for sacrifice, although that interpretation obviously relies rather heavily on a single word.

The survival of the four major festivals (in the vernacular literature, in the transmogrified Christian festivals inlaid over them, and in neo-pagan revivals) is a good indicator of how important they must have been in the Celtic calendar, but they were not the only festivals held during the year. Professor Alexander Thom, whose pioneering work on Stonehenge and other early stone circles and alignments awoke new excitement in the field, suggested that prehistoric people divided the year into 16 equal periods.[1] That may be an oversophisticated analysis but the pattern of eight annual stations, on which it is based, is virtually undeniable in the early Celtic schema of religious festivals. Aubrey Burl, who later collaborated with Thom, selected eight of the 16 stations which Thom called 'Megalithic Months', and setting them out in the table reproduced below, showed the remarkable correspondence between the annual dates of solar alignments, prehistoric and Celtic festivals and the later Christian festivals associated with them.[2]

The significance of these eight stations will be discussed much more fully in Chapter Eight but, for the moment, it is sufficient to make the simple observation that Druidic religious ceremony seems to have been closely related to calendrical observation, which would have required some knowledge of mathematics and astronomy, and that important Druidic festivals seem to have been closely associated with precise astronomical alignments.

We can guess at some of the ceremonies associated with the solstices and equinoxes from the centuries-old folk traditions which are still observed at those times of the year. The Cornish and Breton traditions of lighting bonfires on the tops of hills, carns and ridges on

Midsummer's eve are now dedicated to the Christian St John, but they are clearly pagan in origin. Similarly, the Crying of the Neck, the ceremony of cutting and preserving the last stook of corn in the field, now overlaid with centuries of Christian interpretation, and conducted to this day by the Grand Bard of Cornwall every year, has its counterpart in many pagan and folk traditions of the last stalks of corn symbolically harbouring the fertility of the next year's crop (the ancient craft of corn-dolly making is based on this tradition). The cutting, hauling and burning of the Yuletide log was undoubtedly a pagan ceremony long before it was associated with the Christian festival of Christmas.

The four major Celtic festivals have very well-documented associations and, from those, it is possible to infer or guess at some of the ceremonial practices which may have accompanied them.

Solar alignments and festival dates*

| | | Azimuths (55°) | | Festivals | |
Date	Declination	Sunrise	Sunset	Prehistoric	Christian
8 May	+16.6°	60°	300°	Beltane	Whitsun?
21 June	+23.9°	45°	315°	Midsummer solstice	St John's feast
9 August	+16.7°	60°	300°	Lughnasa	Lammas
23 September	+0.4°	90°	270°	Autumn equinox	Harvest festival
6 November	−16.3°	119°	214°	Samhain	All Souls All Saints Martinmas
21 December	−23.9°	135°	225°	Midwinter solstice	Christmas
5 February	−16.2°	119°	241°	Imbolc	St Brigid's Candlemas
23 March	+0.4°	90°	270°	Vernal equinox	Easter?

(Adapted from Aubrey Burl, *Prehistoric Astronomy and Ritual*.)

*The selected latitude of 55°N represents an approximate midpoint of Britain. Each of the major Celtic festival dates is also a few days later than the dates assigned by modern convention.

As stated on page 106, my view – the evidence for which I shall give in later chapters – is that the early Celts reckoned the year from midsummer to midsummer. This would be a time of high feasting, with meats, fishes, fruits, berries, vegetables, honey, barley beer and mead all available in abundant supply. High summer, with its long days of comfort and plenty, was associated with the everlasting joy of the other world. The Goidelic name for paradise was Tir na Nog, the Land of Youth, sometimes also translated as Land of the Ever Young. The Brythonic equivalent was Avallon, a summer apple orchard in full fruit. Marriages were often solemnized at midsummer: June is still considered the traditional wedding month. We shall investigate the solstices and equinoxes in greater detail later, but for the moment we concentrate on the four named festivals.

Lughnasa

The first major festival after the beginning of the year would be Lughnasa, which was probably also the longest festival of the year. Traditionally in Ireland, the festival began in mid-July and lasted until mid-August. The eponymous god of the festival is Lugh, a divinity who appears in several guises in both the Goidelic and Brythonic traditions. Lugh is his Goidelic, or Irish, name. It seems to be related to the Latin *lux*, meaning light, although Graves also suggests Latin *lucus*, meaning grove, and even *lug*, the Sumerian for son.[3] A Dionysus- or Hercules-type deity, he is sometimes called Lugh the Long Handed. In Wales, he was Lleu, or Lleu Llaw Gyffes, meaning the Lion with the Steady Hand. The 'Lleu' element is not a variant spelling of 'Lugh': it is an epithet, meaning lion, derived from the Latin *leo*. The Gaulish name was Romanized to Lugus. Lyons, in France, was originally Lugudunum, or the fortification of Lugus, in Roman Gaul, and a festival held there on 1 August was later redesignated the Feast of Augustus. The towns of Laon, Leyden and Carlisle (originally Caer Lugubalion) also take their names from the god. The modern name Hugh is directly descended from the Goidelic form.

The '-nasa' element of the festival's name is from Celtic 'nasadh', meaning commemoration, which suggests, as Graves points out, that the festival was essentially a mourning festival, celebrating the death of the god-king associated with oak.[4] The Anglo-Saxons used the term Lughmass for the festival period which, because it took place between the hay harvest and the corn harvest, later became confused with the term 'hlafmass', meaning literally loaf mass, from which combination the modern Christian name, Lammas, is derived. In medieval times, Lammas was a mourning feast, and the tradition of symbolic funeral processions at this time of year continued in the Lancashire Wakes Week, and the Wakes processions across ancient moorland trackways, the most famous being the Lyke Wakes Walk across the Yorkshire moors, in which groups of (usually) young men carried an empty coffin 40 miles (64 kilometres) within 24 hours across the ancient track, which is still occasionally undertaken to this day.[5]

In both Brythonic and Goidelic traditions, Lugh or Lleu is closely associated with the oak, the most venerated of trees, and with the eagle, a symbol of supreme godhead to the Celts, as it was to the Romans, who ascribed it as a totem animal to Jupiter. It is highly likely that the Roman soldiers who brought the cult of the sun-god Mithras to Britain found in Lleu Llaw Gyffes a familiar and sympathetic representation of their vision of the supreme male deity.

In Ireland, the festival was also associated with powerful goddesses, and there were two important assemblies which took place during the festival, Oenach Tailten, meaning the assembly of Tailte, which was held at Teltown in County Meath, and Oenach Carmain, meaning the assembly of Carman. Tailte was Lugh's foster-mother, the significance of which relationship was discussed in Chapter Three, page 79. The assembly seems also to have commemorated Lugh's two wives, Nas and Bui. The goddess of the second assembly, Carman, was a mother-goddess and sorceress, whose sons were expelled from Ireland, and whose assembly commemorated her grief. The dedication of these assemblies to high goddesses, their association with motherhood and marriage, and their association with a goddess of sorcery, suggest strongly that they signified an important meeting time for Celtic women, especially for priestesses and Druidesses, and that ceremonials associated with the rites of passage of womanhood, with childbirth, with fecundity associated with the time of harvest, with marriage, with women's roles in burial funerary, and with other mysteries appropriate to and associated with women, may have been conducted during Lughnasa. In medieval times, the Lughnasa games and festivities attracted huge crowds in Ireland, and there was a special kind of trial marriage, called a Tailtean (or Teltown) marriage which could only take place at the festival, which lasted 'a year and a day' (the formula means

365 days, as will be explained in due course) and which could only be dissolved if both parties returned to the Lughnasa games at the end of the year and ritually walked apart, one to the north, the other to the south.

The legend of Lleu Llaw Gyffes is told in the 'Story of Math', which is the fourth story, or 'branch', in *The Mabinogion*. It is essentially Celtic in virtually every respect, although one important character, Gwydion, belongs to another tradition – the name is a Celticization of the Nordic god's name Odin, or Woden, the magician-god. Summarized as briefly as possible, the story runs as follows.

Lleu is born the son of Arianrhod (the mother-goddess, whose name means Silver Wheel), who imposes three taboos, or fates (what the Irish called 'geis'), on him at the time of his birth: only his mother may name him, only his mother may arm him, and he may never marry a human woman. The magician Gwydion thwarts the first two fates by trickery. With the magician Math, he also attempts to thwart the third 'geis' by constructing a woman out of flowers, called Blodeuwedd, and breathing magical life into her. However, Blodeu-wedd takes another lover, called Gronw, and the pair plot Lleu's death. Lleu has been protected by a further 'geis' which says that he can only be slain if he is standing with one foot on a goat's back and the other on the edge of a vat of water. Blodeuwedd contrives to persuade Lleu to take up this position, and Gronw runs a spear through him. At the moment of impact, however, Lleu shapeshifts into an eagle and flies to a magic oak tree. Here, Gwydion finds him and transforms him back into a man. Gronw is killed, and Blodeuwedd is transformed into an owl.

This complex, allusive tale is spun around a central relationship which is the ancient archetype of a central platform of Druidic belief: the renewal of the power of the god through the goddess, and the renewal of the power of the goddess through her son(s) the god (twin-gods). As will be discussed in more detail later, the trees associated with the midsummer months are oak and holly, whose respective mystical letters are the twin letters of D and T, representing the twin gods of midsummer, the god of the old year and the god of the new. The earthly representation of the twin gods is the twin kings, the old king and the new king. In Ireland, the relationship between the High King and the kingdom was often described in terms of a sexual relationship, either son and mother, or husband and bride.

So, the essence of the Lughnasa festival was a 'nasadh', or commemoration of the passing of the old king, or god, or year, idealized by the sun-god Lugh, accompanied perhaps by funerary rites and processions, and a celebration of the arrival of the new king, or new god, or year, or rebirth of the sun-god, accompanied perhaps by games and feasting, and by spectacles of magic.

If this mythographic depiction of Lughnasa is essentially correct, we can infer, or at least make a reasoned guess, at what ceremonies might have accompanied the festival.

Firstly, some of the ceremonies may have been literally funereal. Real victims of sacrifice, or animal substitutes, or effigies and symbolic representations of the dead, may have been carried in procession and led to burial. Votive offerings, which were frequently cast into pools or down into deep burial shafts, may have been especially welcome or potent during Lughnasa. It may have been a time for paying special homage to the dead, particularly warriors and heroes in the mould of Lugh or Lleu, and there may have been special performance of eulogies or genealogical poems praising ancient gods or heroes and their descendants.

Solemnizations of kingship (the word coronation implies crowns, which the Celts did not use) may have been celebrated at midsummer and confirmed one month later, at Lughnasa. In the ancient pattern, the king would literally die at the end of the year (midsummer), freely allowing himself to be put to death so that the new king could take his place. In ancient Greece, where the same pattern obtained – it is quite possible that the Celts acquired the practice from the Greeks – the death was literal.

Later, the king's one year of rule was extended to 100 months and, later still, a symbolic death was substituted for the real one. Lughnasa would be the time for the king to make a reaffirmation of his divine 'marriage' to the well-being of the kingdom. The Arthurian stories place Arthur's symbolic drawing of the sword from the stone in the depths of winter, but the coronation of Arthur takes place in high summer.

Real marriages may have been celebrated more frequently at midsummer and Lughnasa. We have ample evidence of the Tailtean marriage ceremonies, and it may well be that the long festival of Lughnasa, lasting a whole month in the height of summer, was seen more generally as a good time to marry. Between the two harvests, and with food abundantly available, it was the least demanding and most relaxed time of the year.

Samhain

After the autumnal equinox, the next major Celtic festival was Samhain, occasionally also spelled Samain. The name is recorded on the Coligny Calendar, a Gaulish bronze tablet dating from the first century AD, as 'Samonios'. The word 'Samhain' is Irish: it means November, as well as describing the ancient festival. In Irish, the broad mh is absorbed by the preceding a into a diphthong represented phonetically as /au/. In other words, the proper pronunciation is much closer to sowan than the frequently heard, but incorrect, Sam Hayne. The Irish for Hallowe'en is 'Oiche Shamhna' (ee-uh shown-uh), the Eve of Samhain.

The evening part of the festival is now widely celebrated, more so in America than in Europe, as Hallowe'en. This creates a particular difficulty for our present purpose, in that the traditions of Hallowe'en are essentially Christian in origin, and we need to untangle the Christian elements from the associated, but not necessarily identical, earlier Celtic ones. To confuse matters still further, a Roman festival dedicated to Pomona, a goddess of fruit (she still has tinned pears and peaches named after her, by companies probably not fully aware of the significance of her name) fell at about the same date, and was grafted on to the Celtic celebrations when Roman troops conquered Britain – the Hallowe'en tradition of bobbing for apples comes from the Roman games played during Pomona's festival.

The 'e'en' of Halloween is the 'even', meaning evening, of All Hallows, the Christian festival which celebrates the dead, or, more accurately, the Hallows, that is, the saints and redeemed sinners (hallow means holy) restored to Heaven now and at the Day of Judgement by Jesus Christ. The festival of All Hallows, also called All Saints and Hallowmass, was traditionally celebrated on 1 November. It was a catch-all festival, one of its theological tasks being the appropriate celebration of all those souls worthy of sanctification who, because of human rather than divine fallibility, had not been named and numbered among the saints. This was an important duty of reconciliation, and the day was marked by a solemn Eucharist, or Communion.

All Saints was immediately followed by an associated festival, All Souls, on 2 November. This second festival, in which *all* the dead, redeemed or not, were celebrated, was established, according to tradition, by Saint Odil or Odilo, Abbot of Cluny, a town in eastern France, in the ninth century AD. According to the legend, a pilgrim returning from the Holy Land was shipwrecked on a rocky island, where he found a gaping chasm leading down to Purgatory. Tormented by the desperate wailing of tortured, unredeemed souls which came from the chasm, the pilgrim could find no rest until, after being rescued by a passing ship, he found Abbot Odil and begged him to intercede on behalf of all the souls still suffering in Purgatory. Odil made the necessary petitions, and All Souls' Day was established in the Church Calendar. In due course, the festival became very popular among ordinary folk. The custom sprang up of baking 'soul cakes', which were set out, usually accompanied by a glass of wine, for the dead to enjoy. Candles were lit and the home made tidy. Many people visited cemeteries and prayed bareheaded, kneeling on or close by the gravestones. Later, during the Reformation, these folk traditions had become so confused with the earlier pagan elements of Samhain, and with witchcraft and popular superstition, that Christian authorities grew alarmed, and All Souls was removed from the Church Calendar. The feast was restored only as late as 1928, when it was presumably felt that superstition or the pagan influence no longer offered any significant danger to Christian orthodoxy.

Many of the modern cultural appurtenances of Hallowe'en – the witches, ghouls and goblins – were originally associated with All Souls on 2 November. From the original custom of leaving fires lit in the home and setting out little gifts of food, drink and tobacco, intended to appease the visiting souls of dead relations, grew the idea that this was a night when all the dead roamed the world. In time, the friendly dead were remembered less, and the evil spirits and practitioners of witchcraft and magic who conjured up the dead, or associated with them, became more closely linked with the festival. Trick-or-treat, the ritual of children demanding presents of sweets, is a corruption of the long-established practice of alms gathering on the eve of All Souls. Originally, it was soul-cakes which were sought, rather than sweets. In Aberdeenshire in Scotland, the soul cake was usually called the Dirge Loaf; in Wales, particularly in Dyfed, the term Dole Cake was used; and in Yorkshire it was called the Saumas or Soul Mass Cake. One traditional song which accompanies the soul-cake seeking ran as follows:

> *Soul! Soul! for a soul-cake!*
> *I pray you, good missis, a soul-cake!*
> *An apple, a pear, a plum or a cherry,*

Or any good thing to make us all merry.
One for Peter, two for Paul,
Three for Them who made us all.
Up with the kettle and down with the pan.
Give us good alms, and we'll be gone.[6]

All these later developments from All Souls have coloured descriptions of the ancient Celtic festival of Samhain, so that it is difficult to be certain which elements are unequivocally Celtic and original. It seems that Samhain was associated with the dead, and that the popular conception was that at the time of the festival the dead were especially likely to appear or move through the world. The reader should be reminded, however, of two important and fundamental early Celtic beliefs already described. Firstly, this world and the other world were closely interconnected at all times, and gods, demigods, heroes, shapeshifters and the spirits of the dead came and went at all seasons of the year. Secondly, the dead brought no special terrors with them but were only as intimidating or as threatening as they might be if they were living. This last notion is especially difficult for the modern Western mind to grasp. No matter how rationally sceptical we pretend to be, images of Hell and Purgatory, founded on a Christian doctrine of original sin and necessary redemption, are deeply ingrained in the Western psyche, so that the dead, or their ghosts, terrify and appall us in a manner, and for reasons, which would have puzzled the early tribal Celts had they encountered these attitudes.

The decoration of the humble pumpkin, now strongly associated with Hallowe'en, may, in fact, be derived from an original Samhain practice. Because pumpkins, gourds and squashes are harder to find in Britain than they are in America, and because Americans carve and display pumpkin lanterns at Hallowe'en with far greater enthusiasm than the British, it is often assumed that pumpkin carving is a fairly recent American addition to the Hallowe'en tradition, perhaps derived from the popularity of pumpkins and pumpkin pie at Thanksgiving in late November. In fact, mangel-wurzels (a kind of turnip) were hollowed out and made into tallow lanterns at Hallow Tide as early as Elizabethan times in Britain. At Hinton St George in Somerset, these lanterns were called 'punkies', and their lighting was accompanied with songs, dances and the lighting of bonfires. It is quite likely that the original Samhain festival also included the lighting of bonfires, and the carving of special lanterns, to symbolize the life-giving energy of fire, in particular the fire of the Sun, and to celebrate and encourage solar regeneration. The ancient god called Sol by the Romans, the original and unadulterated representation of the Sun, was called Samas by the Babylonians, and that name may be related to the Celtic Samonios found on the Coligny Calendar.

Samhain is an important feast in the Old Irish tales, and it seems that its significance there is the source of the now widespread notion that it marked the beginning of the Celtic New Year. It was at Samhain that the annual mating took place between the Dagda (the name simply means Good God), the tribal father-god of all Ireland, and the Morrigan (Great Queen), a war-goddess, seer and sorceress, whose totem animal was the raven, like the god Bendigeidfran in the Brythonic tradition. Samhain was the occasion of the triple killing of the Irish king (by wounding, burning and drowning), an annual ceremonial of the transfer of the divine right to rule. The assemblies at holy Tara of the five Irish provinces took place at Samhain, accompanied by horse races, fairs and markets. Cu Chulainn becomes romantically entangled with women from the other world, in other words manifestations of the mother-goddess, at Samhain.

Two of the Irish tales deal with an episode or adventure which recurs annually at Samhain, and so they may give us an even better insight into the themes and philosophical beliefs associated with the festival – these are stories which are specific to the station of the year.

The first is the tale of Oenghus and Caer. Oenghus is an interesting figure. He is the Goidelic equivalent of the Brythonic Maponus or Mabon, which simply means son. (Mabon and Madron, Son and Mother, were mentioned earlier in connection with St Madron's Baptistry and the associated holy well in Cornwall, see page 57.) Oenghus is also given the epithet 'mac Oc', literally son of Youth. He is the archetypal divine youth, and, in the Irish tradition, he is strongly associated with romantic and sexual love. He appears in three important legends: the story of Midhir's wooing of Etain; the story of Diarmaid's love for Grainne; and in his own story, *The Dream of Oenghus*. In his dream, he is given a vision of a beautiful young girl, with whom he falls in love. Her name is Caer Ibormeith (meaning Yew Berry – the yew tree, then as now, was associated with death) and she is a shapeshifter, who takes the form of a swan. Caer's father, Ethel Anbual of Sidh Uamain – in other words, the king of a 'sidh', which is loosely translated as fairy mound, but it means more generally a hill or mound, sometimes burial chamber, which is the dwelling place of spirits – refuses to allow Caer to be wooed by

Oenghus. The god's only recourse is to shapeshift himself also into a swan at the festival of Samhain, the one time of the year when Caer is not confined to human form. Successfully transformed and united, Oenghus and Caer fly three times round a lake, sending Caer's companions into a dream-sleep lasting three nights and three days. They then fly to Brugh na Boinne, Oenghus's palace (his mother was Boann, the eponymous goddess of the River Boyne). The metamorphosis of the lovers into swans is almost identical to that of Midhir and Etain, in their similar legend. Cu Chulainn is also associated with a flock of swans at Samhain. We recognize the swans as spirit-beings because they wear delicate chains of gold and silver. In a legend obviously bowdlerized by Christian doctrine, the children of the god Lir (sometimes Llyr or Lear) are cursed by a Druidic spell to live as swans until the coming of St Padraig to Ireland releases them. (The curse is, of course, a blessing, but the monk who transcribed the tale could hardly be expected to endorse that interpretation.)

The second Irish legend closely associated with Samhain is that of the annual destruction of Tara, the magical hill, or 'sidh', which is the ancestral seat of the gods and High Kings of all Ireland. According to the legend, every year at Samhain a goblin, called Aillen, cannot be prevented from destroying the halls of Tara, which he sets on fire. The goblin's name is interesting: it seems to be related to the abstract noun 'aille', which means beauty, and the related subsidiary concrete noun 'ailleanach', which is translated in the *Gearrfhocloir Gaeilge-Bearla*, or *Irish-English Dictionary*, as 'dressed-up useless person' – a neater translation might be fop. This is an unusual title for a malicious goblin intent on the annual destruction of the most holy seat of Ireland. There may be implied in the name some reference to personal vanity and overweening pride in appearances, which was a very distinctive characteristic of the early Celts, frequently mentioned by classical writers. Aillen achieved his objective by playing the harp with supernatural skill, so lulling all the hearers into charmed sleep before setting fire to the palace. The hero Finn overcomes Aillen's magic by holding the sharp point of an enchanted spear against his own forehead – the pain allows him to resist the enchantment. The spear was made by Len, swordmaker to the gods, and symbolizes the warrior's attributes of courage and indifference to pain.

So, apart from the visitations of the dead and other themes traditionally associated with Samhain (and, later, with All Souls and

Hallowe'en), there are three distinct mythological themes also closely associated with the festival: it is a time of ritual mating and pair-bonding; it is a time when the mythological symbolism of the swan is especially important; it is a time when order is restored by valour conquering enchantment.

It may be that all these themes are connected. The swan is found in Urnfield and Hallstatt representations harnessed to wagons, possibly funerary. A similar depiction is a wheeled cauldron, drawn by a swan, found at Orastie and dating probably from the seventh century BC. The Celts would have observed closely many of the swan's natural characteristics: an unusually strong and courageous bird, willing to face much larger and more dangerous adversaries in defence of its young, the swan is also one of the most elegant and graceful creatures living, its white plumage more dazzling than that of any other bird; it is faithfully monogamous and mates for life; it has a neck shaped like the sacred serpent, and hisses like a snake when threatened; it passes at will over land, over water and through the sky; its flight is accompanied by a distinctive and evocative beat of rushing air. (The swan is also a big, fleshy bird and makes good eating, but – on the strength of nothing more informed than intuition – I suspect that its flesh was taboo because its symbolic importance was so great.) Perhaps the festival of Samhain celebrated, through legends of shapeshifting into swans, not just the return of the dead, in whatever form they chose to appear, but the very crux of the religious question: the transformation of life from one state to another, the passage-making between time and timelessness, the interrelation of life and death, the necessary magic by which souls escaped the ties of earthly life, and – like swans released from their gold and silver chains – flew to the joys of eternity. In other words, the doctrine of metempsychosis, or karma, closely related to the idea of a universal order which requires ritual pair-bonding of the god with the goddess, ritual restoration of the sacred palace through courage and pain, may have been at the heart of Samhain, as well as the celebration of the actual dead.

What rituals and ceremonies might have expressed these themes is a matter of pure speculation. Samhain may have involved symbolic or ritual copulation, as in many forms of witchcraft and revived Wicca, to celebrate the ritual mating or pair-bonding of the god and goddess. There may have been swan dances, or ritual re-enactments of other shapeshiftings and transmogrifications. There may also have been trials of courage, trials by strength, ritual pain inflictions, or sacrifices, to celebrate the heroic valour needed to restore the well-being of the kingdom, to rebuild the figurative palace of Tara.

Midwinter festivals

Midwinter, or the winter solstice, marked the end of the first half of the year. The Coligny Calendar, which was mentioned on page 130, and will be described in more detail on page 141, tells us that the Druids divided each lunar month into two halves, one half (of the waxing moon) propitious, the other (of the waning moon) unpropitious. They may have thought of the year as being divided into two distinct halves in similar fashion. The vast majority of stone-circle and other standing-stone alignments (created not by the Celts but by the long-headed people who preceded them) are based on midsummer, rather than midwinter, solar alignments, but the precise date of midwinter would have been easily calculated by the Druids.

Rather like Samhain, which has the Roman festival of Pomona and the Christian festival of All Souls grafted on to it, the Celtic festival of the winter solstice subsequently became confused with a Roman festival, the Saturnalia, and the important Christian festival of Christmas. The winter solstice marked the date of the southernmost rising and setting of the sun – the word solstice means sun standing still. By our modern calendar, that day, the day of the longest night, is (usually) 21 December.

The Roman festival dedicated to Saturn, the Saturnalia, began on 19 December. It celebrated the overthrow of the old father-god, Saturn, by the new, Jupiter or Deus Pater (God the Father, although in our context he is actually God the Son). These gods have direct counterparts in Greek mythology (Cronos and Zeus) and in Celtic mythology (Bran and Bel or Belin). The basic symbolism is very ancient: the goddess (Madron, mother of all creation, the Moon) is married to the god (Mabon, her son, the Sun), but the renewal and continuation of the marriage (creation, the kingdom, life and the harvest) depends on the ageing god (or king) being replaced by the young god (his twin, also Mabon, the new Sun, the new king). The Saturnalia was known to the Romans as *Dies Natalis Invicti Solis*, the Day of Birth of the Unconquered Sun. As a result of this ancient connotation, the Saturnalia also became associated with the turn of the year, and a new god was designed to accommodate the transition

on the immediately following Kalends, or first month-day; he was
Janus, the two-headed god who looked back over the past and looked
forward to the future, whose name is now incorporated in our month
of January. The Saturnalia was a fire festival, with homes being
decorated with evergreens, candles, and specially constructed coloured
lanterns. Officially the whole month before the Kalends of Janus was
dedicated to Saturn, the original father-god and still patron of
harvests, but the formal festivities lasted only for seven days. There
were thanksgiving ceremonies at shrines and temples, public feasting,
and private feasts to which family and friends would be invited.
Courts, markets, government offices and schools all closed for the
holiday, and slaves were given special dispensation to perform light
and urgent tasks only, and they were even invited to dine with the
family. Personal gifts were exchanged, wrapped in coloured cloth.
Popular foods at the festival were figs, dates, plums, pears and
apples, fresh pomegranates and melons from Africa, quince preserved
in honey, sweet bread, cakes and pastries pressed in the shape of
stars, nut breads, cheese pies, shelled pistachios, filberts, pine nuts
and walnuts, accompanied by cider and mulled wine.

Any reader familiar with the Christian festivities at Christmas will
immediately recognize in the above description many similarities
between the Roman and Christian celebrations. In fact, Christ's
birth-date was deliberately and artificially set, during the third
century AD, to coincide with, absorb and supersede the pagan festival
dedicated to Saturn. It is not even certain that Christ was born in the
winter: many legends speak of his being born in the spring. The
controversy caused by the switch from the old Julian calendar to the
Gregorian calendar persists in the popular folk story that Christ was
actually born on 6 January, and that at midnight on the eve of that
day animals kneel in homage to the Christ Child in mangers and
stables. Many of the original customs of the Saturnalia have survived
into the Christmas celebrations with remarkable persistence. The
theme of the Advent and the Virgin Birth is, of course, not Celtic or
Roman, although there are virgin births in other religions and
mythologies. Specifically Christian is the story of the three Magi, or
Wise Men, the supposedly Persian astrologers who predicted and
attended Christ's birth. As has been mentioned (see pages 21–2),
several writers on Druidism have attempted to reconcile Christianity
and Druidism by calling these figures Druids, or associating them with
the Celts, although there is no direct evidence for the connection.
Earlier mention (see page 46) was made of the medieval legend which

says that the Druid Bachrach, of Leinster, foretold Christ's coming after a dream vision.

The midwinter tradition of the Yule Candle and the Yule Log is almost certainly Celtic in origin. Early Welsh texts, especially the *Romance of Amergin*, which will be discussed in detail later, give us detailed evidence of the Druidic preoccupation with trees and their mythological and religious significance. The Yule Log was directly associated with fire as the purifying emanation of the sun-god. To bring the Yule Log indoors was symbolically to bring the blessing of the sun-god into the house, and the collecting, hauling and kindling of the wood was conducted with great ceremony. The word Yule, however, is derived from Middle English 'yole', the earlier Anglo-Saxon spelling being 'geol'; its meaning is unclear, but it is possibly related to 'geolo' (yellow) or even to 'geoleca' (yolk). The word appears in a variety of spellings, in Old Norse and other members of the Teutonic family, but it appears to have no Celtic counterpart: the Goidelic for Christmas is 'Noillach' (Scots Gaelic) or 'Nollaig' (Irish), clearly related to the Brythonic 'Nadelik' (Cornish) or 'Nadolig' (Welsh), all derived from Latin *Natalicia*.

The Yule Candle was a very large ornamental candle, usually blue, green or red in colour, which was lit at the beginning of the Christmas season and associated with a number of superstitions. It could only be extinguished using a pair of tongs – blowing out the flame invited bad luck. Only the head of the household could light or extinguish the flame. The unconsumed remnant of the candle was preserved as a protection, to be lit during thunderstorms to prevent the house being struck by lightning. Its tallow was rubbed on the sole of the plough before spring ploughing, to bless and promote the seed.[7] The lit candle was displayed in a window, to promote goodwill, a custom which is still widely observed in Connecticut and elsewhere in New England. All these associations derive from the ancient Celtic veneration for the candle as a symbol of light in the darkness of winter. The Romans used oil in purpose-built lamps, but the Celts made candles, with wicks or reed in tallow made from beef lard and pig fat.

The Yule Log had a number of similar associated superstitions. It had to burn steadily without being extinguished, or bad luck would follow. It could be cut down on one's own land, or accepted as a gift from a neighbour, or be stolen from the forest, but it could not be bought or sold: the exchange of money for a Yule Log would destroy its magic properties. Wine, cider or ale – and sometimes corn – was sprinkled over the log before it was lit. Part of the unconsumed log was kept safely to one side and used to ignite the new log in the following year. It was decorated with evergreens and dragged to the house by oxen if it was too heavy to be manhandled. In Cornwall, the figure of a man was chalked on the log, to be consumed by the fire.

It is likely that the midwinter celebrations conducted by the Druids included ceremonial lights and candles, and we know from several texts that bonfires were lit at the winter solstice, as well as at midsummer. The Cornish man chalked on the Yule Log may represent an earlier real sacrifice by fire. The two plants still associated with the Yule, namely holly and ivy, were also associated with the Saturnalia (Saturn's club was of holly wood, and his sacred bird, the gold-crested wren, nested in ivy), and both had sacred and calendrical significance in Druidism, as will be discussed later.

Imbolc

The first festival of the second half of the year was Imbolc, also called Oimelg, and now allocated to 1 February. It was dedicated to the goddess Brigit, who was later transmogrified into the Christian St Brigid or Bridget. The feast took place at the time of the first lambing, and was closely associated with the ewes' coming into milk. In practical terms, it would have marked a vital turning-point in the winter, since the first sheep's milk and cheese would have been of enormous importance with no other fresh foodstuff available and stored meat and grains perhaps beginning to run low. Brigit was an archetype of the great mother-goddess and was the protectress of women in labour and childbirth. Birthwort, the plant analgesic collected and dried in summer, may have been administered by priestesses in her name. This element of worship of the mother-goddess and her son survives in the Christian tradition of Candlemas, which is held on 2 February and commemorates the Purification of Our Lady, that is the Virgin Mary, and the Presentation of Christ to the Temple. The name Candlemas may also be related to the Roman festival of Lupercalia, formerly held on 15 February, which was a festival of lights. It was traditional on Candlemas to offer special prayers to St Brigid and to the Virgin Mary and to honour motherhood. Some of these celebrations were branded 'popish' by Protestants, and the rituals of Candlemas subsequently engendered some controversy within the Christian Church.

We may well suppose that Imbolc was a Druidic festival dedicated to the mysteries of motherhood, and it is quite possible that its ceremonial was conducted principally by Druidesses and priestesses, rather than by male members of the order. The lamb, as a symbol of all things new-born and innocent (including Christ, the Lamb of God) is a figure of great antiquity. A real new-born lamb, representing the mythic creature and symbol, may have been paraded or temporarily venerated. There may have been special ceremonies associated with the first drinking of the milk, incorporating other pastoral associations.

By the time of the vernal equinox, even in unusually cold or wet springs, the regeneration of the world would be obvious and indisputable, with new growth everywhere observable. The vernal ceremonies would probably have celebrated this regrowth, perhaps with ritual directly related to buds, blossoms and new leaves. If the ritual was conducted in the *nemeton*, or sacred grove, evidence of the ceremonial's objective would be immediately to hand.

Beltane

The last great festival celebrated before the year turned full circle back to midsummer was Beltane, now allocated to 1 May. There are so many folk customs and traditions associated with May Day that picking out the Celtic thread alone is a little difficult. However, for Beltane we are fortunate in having good evidence not only for the nature of the ritual practised, but also for the religious belief behind the ceremony.

The name Beltane consists of two elements. The first is the god's name Bel (also known as Beli, Belin or Belinus, and perhaps associated with the Phoenician or Canaanite word 'Ba'al, meaning master, found in the Old Testament). The variant Belenos is found widely distributed in early inscriptions in Gaul and northern Italy. Beli Mawr (Great Beli) appears in *The Mabinogion* as a King of Britain, and founder of the Welsh royal line. There is an older name, also Bel, which is that of the Babylonian Earth-god, which in turn is related to the Sumerian Belili, who was a goddess of trees, the moon, love and the other world – in other words, a manifestation of the great goddess, mother and creatrix of all things. This very ancient name element, 'Bel-', is found in the Latin *bellus*, meaning beautiful, and all the words subsequently derived from it; in the Goidelic 'bile', meaning sacred tree; in the medieval Latin *billa* and *billus*, meaning branch and trunk, and in other words of distant origin.[8] The second element is 'tan' (Cornish, or Brythonic) or 'tine' (Irish, or Goidelic), meaning fire: fire is associated both with the god, since he is a sun-god, and with the ceremonial ritual itself.

The principal attested Druidic ceremony which took place at Beltane was the driving of livestock between two fires for purification. As was mentioned in Chapter One (page 20), the early Celts, like the ancient Persians, associated fire with ritual purification and healing. Livestock emerging from the rigours of winter would, indeed, tend to be sickly and prone to disease, particularly if the ground underfoot was still very cold or wet. The animals were herded and driven between two fires, which was probably much harder than it sounds. Cattle can be prodded in just about any direction, although they can be very stubborn when frightened. Sheep will follow a leader, but need considerable urging and prompting, usually assisted by dogs, to be persuaded to go where they are supposed to. Horses are naturally terrified of fire and will run away at the sight of it, even into apparently greater danger. So, the actual gathering and driving of the flocks and herds must have been quite an enterprise, probably requiring the cooperation of the whole tribal community. Once the ceremonial was completed, the grazing animals were taken out to new pastures, often on higher ground, where they would thrive on the nutritious new grasses.

Bel was the young-god counterpart of the old-god Bran, as Jupiter was the counterpart of Saturn, or Zeus was the counterpart of Cronos. His festival, appropriately, would be at the centre of the second half of the year, when the new god had supplanted the old and all things were growing towards the high point of midsummer. In general, the first half of the year may well have been associated with Bran, the second half with Bel or Belinus. The months either side of midsummer (modern June and July) are associated with oak and holly, represented mythologically in the sacred tree alphabet (which will be discussed later) by the twin letters D and T, signifying the old god and the new, the old king and the new, the brother and his twin, Mabon and Mabon, sons and husbands of Madron. The Beltane ceremonies would therefore have been of special importance, as great as for Lughnasa, which would be the great festival in Bran's half of the year (Lugh and Bran were gods of the same type).

The dancing around a Maypole, which has survived despite some vigorous opposition from Christians at various times, may be Celtic in origin, and may have been practised as part of the Druidic festivities in early Celtic times. However, as Paul Devereux pointed out to me, the idea of a central tree or pole at the axis of the cosmos is very ancient and widely found in other cultures. The Maypole is plainly a phallic representation, and the dancing around it, along with other celebrations of the juices flowing through the world and its people in spring, drove later Christian commentators into fits of apoplexy. Here is Philip Stubbes's view, expressed in *The Anatomie of Abuses*:

> All the young men and maids, old men and wives, run gadding over night to the woods, groves and hills, where they spend all the night in pleasant pastimes. In the morning they return bringing with them birch and branches of trees, to deck their assemblies. There is a great Lord over their pastimes, namely Satan, Prince of Hell. The chiefest jewel they bring is their Maypole. They have twentie or fortie oxen, every one having a sweet nosegay of flowers on the tip of his horns, and these oxen drag the Maypole (this stinking idol, rather) which is covered with flowers and herbs, bound round with string from top to bottom and painted with variable colours.[9]

If we ignore the references to 'Satan, Prince of Hell' and 'this stinking idol', this might well be a description of the Druidic festivities as they took place at Beltane in early Celtic society. Other folklore customs associated with May Day, which might or might not have been associated with the original Beltane, include: May birching, in which different tree branches were set before people's doors, each tree representing a characteristic – pear for beauty, gorse for sluttishness, and so on; washing in the first dew collected on May Day, which was reputed to have healing, as well as beautifying, qualities; May dolls, associated both with the Virgin Mary, to whom the month of May is dedicated, and with the Roman goddess Flora; May garlands, in cross or hoop shapes, sometimes associated with silver ornaments; May hobby horses, the most famous being those of Minehead and Padstow, which are of great antiquity.

We have left unanswered one obvious and important question. The cutting of the sacred mistletoe is the most famous Druidic rite. When did it take place? Traditionally, in the popular imagination, it is associated with midwinter, because mistletoe berries are associated with holly berries and the general evergreen proliferation around Christmas. The plant, which is evergreen, sets flower rather erratically: it may be as early as March, it may be as late as May.

Almost invariably, however, the fruit, or berries, appear by mid-October, which would mean that the mistletoe-cutting ceremony might have taken place at Samhain, rather than at midwinter. Samhain, if it does indeed celebrate the mystery of pair-bonding and the ritual mating of king and queen, or god and goddess, would be appropriate for the connotations of fertility and sexual love which have come to be attributed to the mistletoe. There is no certain evidence either way. Perhaps Pliny's white bulls were covered with a fine dusting of fresh snow. We shall return to this question in Chapters Nine and Ten.

Notes

1. Alexander Thom, *Megalithic Sites in Britain*.
2. Aubrey Burl, *Prehistoric Astronomy and Ritual*.
3. & 4. Robert Graves, *The White Goddess*.
5. The reader is recommended to the excellent article by Paul Devereux in No. 117 of 'The Ley Hunter', issued mid-1992, which deals with the subject of paths dedicated to the dead, or associated with symbolic funerary procession. Copies are obtainable from PO Box 92, Penzance, Cornwall TR18 2XL, United Kingdom.
6. & 7. Christina Hole, *A Dictionary of British Folk Customs*.
8. Robert Graves, above.
9. Quoted in Victor J. Green, *Festivals and Saints' Days*, p.72.

CHAPTER SEVEN

DRUIDIC MATHEMATICS AND ASTRONOMY

MENTION WAS MADE in the last chapter of the Coligny Calendar, the first-century bronze tablet which gives us our only archaeological evidence of Druidic computation of days and months. Found at Coligny, near Bourg-en-Bresse in France, the bronze tablet, originally measuring 5 feet by 3½ feet (1.5 by 1 metres), but now greatly fragmented, is engraved with a calendar of 62 lunar months and two additional, or intercalary, months. The language is Gaulish, but the lettering is Roman. Each month is divided into two halves, the propitious half (of the waxing moon) indicated by the word 'MAT' (which means good; the Breton word is 'mad') and the unpropitious half (of the waning moon) by the letters 'ANM', which obviously stand for bad despite the fact that the presumed missing full word 'ANMAT' is not actually found in any surviving Brythonic language, although the negative prefix 'an-' is very common. Many of the inscriptions are obvious abbreviations. The calendar is reckoned in nights followed by days, which we know from Caesar's observation and from other sources to have been the Celtic method of reckoning.

However, even the apparently indisputable evidence of the Coligny Calendar leads to controversy and uncertainty, as is so often the case with the Druids. Robert Graves dismisses the Coligny Calendar as not truly Druidic; he states clearly that, in his view, the tablet represents a stage in the Romanization of Gaul, when the Celts tried to please their Roman masters by adopting foreign calendrical systems. Crucial to his argument is the fact that the calendar is based on lunations, that is, periods of twenty-nine and a half days, rather

A fragment of the Coligny Calendar. The text is Celtic, the lettering and numbers Roman. The holes on the left were probably used for pegs to mark feast days.

than on the 'lunar months', of twenty-eight days to which he subsequently devotes much attention.[1]

To set the background, and to further explain the problem of the Coligny Calendar, here are some very basic facts about the year. A year is 365.24219879 days, or 365 days 5 hours 48 minutes and 45.975 seconds, in duration, a day being 24 hours. The sidereal year, which means the year measured as if we were on the surface of the Sun watching the Earth in orbit against the background of the other stars, is about 20 minutes longer. We shall examine this difference in more detail in Chapter Ten. Our modern Gregorian calendar is very slightly out of step with the physical reality of the year, since it is based on the slightly different year length of 365.2425 days. As a result, our calendar gains an extra day once in every 3,320 years – a problem our descendants will have to deal with in due course.

This precision of number may seem drearily modern and scientific, but civilizations considered primitive by our standards were capable of similar precision. Mayan astronomers successfully calculated the length of the year as 365.242 days, which is certainly accurate enough for many purposes. The Druids probably calculated the Golden Year to an accuracy of two days in 18.61 years, despite having no clocks (see Chapter Ten).

Days are measured by the movements of the Earth and the Sun. The calendar of modern Western civilization is a solar calendar. The awkward additional hours, roughly a quarter of a day, which are left over at the end of the year are accommodated by the system of making every fourth year a leap year of 366 days. This system was first proposed by the Greek mathematician Eudoxus, a pupil of Plato's, who lived from 408 to 355 BC, and so it is remarkably ancient, as well as being reasonably effective, despite its simplicity. It is not entirely effective, however, and the great shift from the Julian to the Gregorian calendar brought with it the loss of 11 days, necessary to reconcile the gains accumulated over centuries. The change was proposed by Pope Gregory in 1582 and introduced into Italy and other Catholic countries, but the new calendar was not introduced into Britain until 1752, when the loss of the 11 days precipitated riots because people thought that they had been deprived of part of their lives by 'popish' machinations.

The solar calendar, complex as it is, is child's play by comparison with the lunar calendar, in other words the system of reckoning the year by the apparent waxing and waning of the moon. Nevertheless, many religions are still based on the lunar calendar, which explains why the feasts and festivals of many religions and nations, particularly the Eastern ones, appear on different dates from year to year in the solar, or Western, calendar. The best-known movable feast in the Christian calendar is Easter, based as it is on the variable date of the full moon preceding it. A full lunation, that is, the complete cycle from one moon phase to its repetition, is 29 days 12 hours 44 minutes 3 seconds, although that is only a mean value. As with the Sun, the period required for the Moon to complete one revolution measured against the stars (or sidereal revolution) is different from the observed period between identical phases (called the synodic period). While the synodic period is just over twenty-nine and a half days, the sidereal revolution is only 27 days, 7 hours 43 minutes 11.5 seconds.

There are four separate but related apparent celestial movements, as seen from Earth, which would have been obvious to ancient man:

the rotation of the stars; the movements of the brighter planets, Jupiter, Saturn, Venus, Mercury and Mars; the movements of the sun; the movements of the moon. Stars and the 'wandering stars', or planets, caused immense difficulty to the ancients, as we shall see shortly. The apparent movements of the sun and of the moon seemed far more obvious and easy to accommodate in a mathematical model. Even so, there were complications which could only apparently be understood by close observation over periods of time.

The complication with the sun was that the positions of its rising and setting varied with the seasons. In winter, when the days were short, it would rise and set further towards the south. In summer, when the days were long, it would rise further to the north, climb higher and stay longer in its journey across the sky, and set further to the north. An additional complication was that the precise positions of these midsummer and midwinter risings and settings depended on how far north the observer was. At 60° of latitude, up in the highlands of Scotland, the midwinter sun remained in the sky for about two and a half hours longer than it did at 50° of latitude, down by Stonehenge. Any considerable journey northwards or southwards – say from Britain to Rome, or Rome to Britain – would have made these differences all the more noticeable.

The complication with the moon was more subtle, and it required very careful observation. Any observer seeing the rising of the full moon at a given point of the year – say, for example, the first full moon at midsummer – might fix its rising point by aligning it with a hill, a tree, rocks, or any other natural feature. However, precisely the same rising on precisely the same date one year hence would not be in precisely the same place – the rising position would have moved just slightly. If our hypothetical ancient observer had been very patient, and continued these observations year after year, he would eventually notice, after almost 19 years of observation, that the moon had returned to its original rising position and was beginning a new cycle. At latitude 55°, in the middle of Britain, the midsummer full moon would have risen at about 148°. Nine years later, it would rise at only 124°. After a further nine years, it would be approaching the return to the 148° position. Most of us in the modern Western world have never seen a single moonrise, let alone made the countless observations which ancient man had to make before attempting to reach an understanding of these celestial movements. When 40 would have been a ripe old age, precise astronomical observations and recordings over a period of eighteen and a half years seem all the more remarkable. It seems highly likely that the 19-year period of training and study which Caesar tells us was necessary to be received into the Druidic priesthood was symbolically, perhaps actually, related to the 18.61 year great lunar cycle, or Golden Year. This topic will be discussed more fully in Chapter Ten.

Now we can perhaps appreciate a little more clearly the difficulty with the Coligny Calendar. Whichever way the months are calculated, they do not come to a recognizable unit of time in total. If the 62 months listed are full lunations of approximately twenty-nine and a half days, as they appear to be, the total time period represented is 1,829 days, or 5.007529 years, which does not seem to make much sense as a recognizable time unit. Even if the two intercalary months are added, we are still left with an awkward number. If the months are reckoned as lunar months of 28 days, the total comes to something under five years. The essence of the objection made by Graves is that the strict period of lunation is extremely difficult to reconcile with the solar calendar: 12 months of full lunation give us the simple approximate multiplication $12 \times 29.5 = 354$, which leaves a very awkward period (actually about ten and three-quarter days) to be accommodated to reach the full solar year.

However, if we assume a lunar month of 28 days (Graves associates it with the menstrual cycle), and calculate 13 months to the year, we now have this multiplication: $13 \times 28 = 364$, which only leaves us the odd day and a quarter to accommodate. Graves makes the convincing point that the very ancient phrase 'a year and a day', found in many of the Celtic law tracts, as well as in countless myths, legends and fairy stories, accords very neatly with this calendrical method.

All this to some extent anticipates the arguments of later chapters. We need first to look back over the available evidence to see if we can observe, deduce, infer and possibly reconstruct some kind of model, however limited, of how the Druids calculated the stations of the year. We know that they must have maintained a calendar to meet the schedule of attested festivals, and there is abundant esoteric and poetic evidence about that calendar which we shall examine in subsequent chapters, but for the moment we are concerned with simple mathematics and astronomy. The point was made in Chapter One that there are many apparent similarities between Druidism and Pythagoreanism (see pages 27–31), which is where we must begin, after briefly looking at the mathematics of peoples who were ancient even to Pythagoras.

Chaldeans and Babylonians:
the first astronomers

The first organized astronomers of any significance were the Chaldeans and the Babylonians.[2] Although their observations may have begun around 3000 BC, a recognizable cosmogony does not emerge until about 800 BC (at about the same time as the first Celts may have been invading Britain and displacing the builders of Stonehenge). The Babylonian calendar was lunar, based on the full lunation cycle of 29.5 days. A year consisted of twelve months (i.e., 354 days), and the 'missing' ten and three-quarter days at the end of each year were reconciled by the addition of a thirteenth month every three years. It was a very imprecise calendar, and its use for predicting events, and for interpreting and offering augury, was complicated by ill-informed observations of the five bright planets and some of the brighter stars, which were associated with good and evil consequences. It was the Babylonians who first attached significance to the constellations which lay along the apparent pathway of the sun through the sky, which we now call the ecliptic. They divided the ecliptic into three regions, each assigned to a divinity. This division was later increased to 12, and because 11 of the 12 regions, or constellations, were associated with animals, the division was later called the *zoidiakos* by the Greeks, related to *zoion*, meaning animal, and *kukos* (circle), from which is derived our term zodiac. Three of the signs of the modern zodiac represent human figures: Gemini, Virgo and Aquarius. These are Graeco-Roman figures, who may have displaced animals in the earlier Babylonian zodiac. In the time of Hipparchus, the appropriate constellations corresponded with their signs. However, stellar precession has now shifted each constellation, so that the sign Aries is now occupied by the constellation Pisces, and so on.

The Babylonians deemed the moon the most significant of the observable heavenly bodies. It was considered the manifestation of a masculine god, named Zu-en or Sin, to whom the great city of Ur was dedicated. On the basis of an approximate computation of a full lunation, the day of each full moon was predicted. If the full moon arrived early (because the computation was wrong, despite the astronomers' best efforts) it was considered especially ominous – crop failures or plagues might follow.

The planets Venus and Jupiter (which the Babylonians thought of as stars) were accorded special status. Jupiter's great brightness at perigee heralded periods of prosperity. Venus, recognized as a morning star and an evening star, was associated with the goddess Ishtar, a type of earth goddess who brought fertility to crops and natural vegetation. The astronomers recognized the other naked-eye planets, Mercury, Mars and Saturn, also calling them stars.

During the decade 639 to 630 BC, the Babylonian Empire fell to the Persians. Around 626 BC, the Persians took stock of what they had conquered (much as William did with the *Domesday Book* in Britain after the Norman Conquest of 1066). Among the stocktaking was a reckoning of what the Babylonians had discovered about the cosmos, as recorded in the great library of Assurbanipal. For that early date, their list of achievements is impressive: the Babylonians had traced the path of the ecliptic and related it to the seasons of the year; they had drawn up a partial list of the constellations whose rising corresponded to the months of the year; they had determined the revolutions of the five observable planets, Mercury, Venus, Mars, Jupiter and Saturn, in relation to the sun; they knew that eclipses were regular, and tried to devise a system for predicting them; they recognized that a full lunation lasted about twenty-nine and a half days.

Some time during the sixth century BC, new and different astronomical notions from Chaldea and Babylon infiltrated the long-established and deeply conservative Egyptian priesthood. Temples dedicated to Thoth and Set were decorated with depictions of the zodiac, and the ancient records of the flooding of the Nile were recalibrated.

Astronomy and astrology in Greece and Rome

The Greeks absorbed astronomy with ferocious intellectual enthusiasm, and developed it along far more recognizably scientific lines. Pythagoras, in particular, began a series of speculations which profoundly influenced the whole of subsequent Western thought, through his successors, most notably Plato. For broadly political reasons, Greek astronomy developed along different lines from the Babylonian. Divination and augury had been the chief concerns of the Babylonian priesthood, and the astronomers' first duty was to the emperor. The Greeks were also concerned with fate, but in a less monolithic fashion: they were more concerned with the individual, and with the general intellectual and philosophical adventure epitomized by the study of pure number and geometry. The greatest of the early Greek astronomers were Eudoxus, Theophrastus the disciple of Aristotle, and Hipparchus; all of them were indebted to the genius of Pythagoras, whose influence we shall examine more closely in a moment.

The Greek passion for numbers and astrology found its way in time to Rome, where it became a semi-religion. Augustus and Tiberius were both keen proponents of astrology and maintained retinues of soothsayers and numerologists, some of them Greek or Persian, to assist them in their divine imperial duties. The Greek for 'to learn' was *manthanein*, from which came the noun *mathema*, or learning. This new sect of soothsayers and numerologists called themselves *mathematekoi* (in Greek) or *mathematici* (Romanized), meaning men of learning, and this is, of course, the origin of our term mathematics. The *mathematici* were feared as well as respected. The general Pythagorean notions of number being at the core of all things, of harmony and reciprocity between celestial and earthly motions and events, of the magic symbolism of pure number as a representation of the eternal, all became bowdlerized and popularized in the Roman imagination into a highly superstitious semi-religion of augury and divination by number. Fortunes were read, fates prognosticated (as they are to this day) by numerologists. Astrology, numerology, reading fates in entrails, interpreting the movements of clouds or flight of birds, and so on, all popularized by imperial enthusiasm, rapidly replaced the more objective Greek view.

At the same time, however, the nobler Pythagorean ideals and concepts also gained wide acceptance among Roman intellectuals, and, because Rome was at peace and involved with widespread trade across the known world at that time, these profound new ideas were widely disseminated. In the long run, the Pythagorean idea of an unobservable yet eternal truth lying behind observable reality – especially as it was subsequently developed by Plato – was the foundation for Rome's gradual abandonment of its simple, ancient pantheon of gods and goddesses and its equally gradual movement towards the concept of a single, universal deity, until, finally, Christianity came to Rome and completed the transition.

Redefining the divinity as male

A great mythographic shift, of considerable importance to our present study, took place during this time. The Chaldeans seem to have been the first to record that the movements of certain stars were not only very erratic, including apparent backwards rotation and dramatic changes in luminosity, but they were also very closely linked with the sun. The Greeks were the first to call these unusual stars *planetes*, meaning wanderers, from the verb *planasthai*, to wander. The mythographic shift came about because these astronomical observations coincided with early Hellenic warrior cults associated with the earlier Mycenaean invasions, with a cultural shift towards the hegemony of men over women, and a far greater emphasis on military conquest and territorial expansion. The sun became more important than the moon, and became indisputably masculine. In earlier cosmogonies, the sun could be female or male, and there are several early goddesses who are clearly sun-goddesses. However, as soon as astronomical observations tied the planets to the motions of the sun, the figurative orbits of lesser gods and goddesses began to be tied to the image of the sun-god, or father-god. It hardly needs pointing out that the subsequent conceptualization of the divinity as being essentially male has had the profoundest effect on Western culture. The sun had always been masculine: the sexual imagery of shafts of sunlight penetrating and fertilizing the receptive earth is so basic that it would have been recognized even in Neolithic cultures. But the sun had also been capable of being feminine. Now it was not. The sun was male. The earth was female. The moon was female. These fundamental conceptualizations were cemented in place by astronomy, and in particular by observation and interpretation of the movements of the planets, begun by the Babylonians, developed by the Greeks, and carried forward into the Roman pantheon.

We know that the Celts in their societal organization had far more open views about the equal nature of sexuality than did the Romans (or, subsequently, Christians). If the Celts and Druids worshipped gods and goddesses equally, and moreover held to the most ancient matrix (exactly the right word) of the universal mother-goddess continually giving birth to her son(s) and husband(s), the universal father-god(s), does that mean or imply that they did not recognize the motions of the planets, or that they failed to understand their significance? The answer is almost certainly no.

It was the Romans (once again the villains of this story, so it seems) who worked and developed the father-god centered cosmogony into a rigid paternalism. The divinity of *Deus Pater*, or God the Father, or Jupiter, was associated with the divinity of the emperor, with the divinity of the Roman Empire itself. New Agers sometimes use the vague term 'the Old Religion' to indicate a maternalistic, or at least non-paternalistic, conception of the universe, and, while the term is vague and much abused, it does reflect a real, historical truth. The oldest human communities – pastoral, hunter-gatherers emerging from the Neolithic, through the Bronze Age, towards settled farming – held the fecundity of the earth, the mother and provider of all sustenance, at the centre of the different philosophical or religious conceptions they had. Despite the paucity of evidence, and our heavy reliance on archaeology, there is little argument that ancient societies worshipped the great divinity as a woman, called her mother, thought of themselves as her children. As civilizations – and, in particular, military empires – rose and fell, from Babylonians to Assyrians to Persians to Egyptians to Greeks to Romans, the father-god, warrior and chastiser, grew in importance and eventually superseded the mother-goddess. When the planets were subjugated and tied to the sun, the father-god reigned supreme. The chauvinism and misogyny in Judaism, Christianity and Islam are rooted in this very ancient and fundamental shift in cosmic power.

The Druids would certainly have observed the motions of the planets, and would have recognized that their movements were restricted to the ecliptic and directly related to the movements of the sun. However, the Celts were not empire-builders: their territorial ambitions were fierce at times, but always limited in scope because of their underlying belief that places are sacred, and limited in scale because the fundamental, unchanging Celtic social unit was the tribe, which was of necessity limited in size. Their aristocracy was limited to petty kingships, and small royal territories, by the systems of clientship and fosterage; it was only after the Romans arrived that Celtic leaders even thought about declaring themselves kings or queens of all Britain. There was a long tradition of matrilinear inheritance. Women were used to wielding political and religious power. For all these reasons, the great shift from worship of the mother-goddess to exclusive worship of the father-god seems to have bypassed the early tribal Celts. They certainly worshipped male gods, Bran and Belin (the counterparts of Saturn and Jupiter) especially. These cults would have been greatly reinforced by the arrival of Roman soldiers devoted to the great sun-god Mithras. However, the Celts also worshipped all the female goddesses with equal enthusiasm, and the Celtic cosmic reality mirrored the earthly reality, in which both sexes are necessary for the continuance of life.

Pythagoras's influence on the Celts

If, as seems likely, there was a vital intellectual commerce between Greeks and Celts (perhaps via the Galatians in Asia Minor), and particularly between Pythagorean priests and Druids, then number mysticism would certainly have been one of the commodities in the trade. As mentioned in Chapter One (page 26), both Greeks and Celts seemed obsessively preoccupied with the number 3, and there are some other number correspondences which we shall examine shortly. The essential point is that the rich and complex cycle of mythological attribution in the Druidic calendar (described in Chapters Eight, Nine and Ten) seems to have had as its foundation a system of calendrical computation either taken from the Greeks or developed through contact with Pythagorean number mysticism.

The mathematical models behind the astronomy effecting these great mythographic shifts were complex, even by modern standards, although none of them was capable of accurately describing just our own solar system, let alone the wider cosmos. Pythagoras believed the earth to be spherical, a fact we take for granted with such ease now, that it is easy for us to forget that the notion of the flat earth persisted for centuries long after Pythagoras. To Pythagoras is attributed the invention of trigonometry, which is not only useful in the measurement of right-angled triangles, but also essential in accurate calculation of celestial movements. For centuries either side of Galileo Galilei's great debate about the Ptolemaic and Copernican models of the solar system, the rumour persisted that Pythagoras had described the planets, including the earth, all circling in orbit around the sun. In fact, the rumour was mistaken, because the Pythagorean model of the solar system was slightly more complicated, requiring a balancing mass, or 'counter-earth', and placing the sun among the orbiting bodies, as we shall see in a moment.

Pythagoras was of Tyrrhenian stock. The Tyrrhenians, originally called Tursha, were a tribe of the northern Aegean who spread westwards into northern Italy and Etruria, where they eventually became known by their more familiar name of Etruscans. Pythagoras was born on the Greek island of Samos, but he is believed to have travelled widely. His theory of metempsychosis, or karma, is Indian, or possibly Egyptian, in origin – it is certainly not Pelasgian or Greek – which has led to the supposition that Pythagoras must have travelled to India or Egypt at some time. As mentioned on page 28, he is also believed to have travelled to Britain. Later in life, between 540 and 530 BC, he settled at Crotona, in southern Italy, a powerful Greek settlement and trading port in the region known in modern times as Calabria. He established a school of some 300 disciples, including the famous Olympic athlete, Milo.

Pythagoras was worshipped as a semi-deity, the reincarnation of Apollo, in part because he had undergone a severe ritual initiation at the sacred Orphic temple on Crete. The significance of Orphism – the cult associated with Orpheus – was that it postulated, in a way very similar to the concept of karma, the pre-existence and indestructibility of souls; if the human being in whom the soul temporarily resided led a sufficiently worthy life, it would return to dwell among the gods with whom it was originally created, but if the human being failed to achieve a worthy and enlightened death, the soul would be forced into a further reincarnation.

Pythagoras is also supposed to have undergone initiation by the Daktyls, specifically into the mystical connotations of number and the relations between sacred numbers and sacred letters. The Daktyls (the name means fingers) were the five Phrygian or Cretan deities, sometimes named as Herakles, Paeonius, Epimedes, Jasius and Idas, whom the mother-goddess Rhea created to be handservants (literally) to her lover Cronos, the first father-god. A mystic finger-alphabet was also used by the Druids.

Pythagorean moral philosophy has profoundly influenced all Western thought. By the laws of karma, man was not driven inexorably by fates over which he had no control: he had a choice between good and evil, a responsibility for determining his own fate, and the consequences of his choice would be reflected in subsequent reincarnations. If, as seems likely, this notion was – by whatever means – introduced at an early stage in the development of Celtic society, it would help to explain the Celts' deep respect for moral law and the religious precepts in which the law was enshrined, for the fitness of things, for fair play, for the solemnity of oaths and true utterance, for adherence to contracts and alliances. It would also help to explain why Druidism and Christianity seemed so compatible from their earliest meeting: in both religions, a man's deeds could earn him eternal life. The Druids had no concept of original sin, or redemption from it through divine grace, but the general moral precepts of Christianity would have seemed very familiar to them. Russell ties the thread by saying of Pythagoras:

> I do not know of any other man who has been as influential as he was in the sphere of thought; I say this because what appears as Platonism is, when analysed, found to be in essence Pythagoreanism. The whole conception of an eternal world, revealed to the intellect but not to the sense, is derived from him. But for him, Christians would not have thought of Christ as the Word.[3]

At the core of the Pythagorean philosophy of human knowledge was the significance of number. The idea is often quoted simply as 'all things are number', but, in fact, the original Pythagorean proverb was 'all things are assimilated to number', which represents a slightly more complex idea. Numbers were actually venerated, as mystic representations of eternal and divine truth. The numbers 3, 5, 6, 7, 8, 9 and 10 (the number of perfection) were specially venerated. The *tetraktys*, a simple figure of ten dots arranged in a pyramid (see below), was worshipped as an ikon of the entire universe.

The top dot represents unity, position, eternity. The two dots below represent distance, separation, distinction, opposition, movement. The three dots represent all surfaces, maps, plans, arrangements, extensions in two-dimensions, all geometric figures. The four dots represent three-dimensional space, the entirety of the universe. The mystic dimension of time is represented on each side of the pyramid by the combination of the four dots on the side with the one dot at the centre, the number 5 also representing colour, volume, everything susceptible to the five senses. The number of life, 6, is found in the hexagon of six dots formed by the central pair of dots on each side, and the number 7, the number of intelligence, health, light and

The *Tetraktys*.

inspiration, associated with the goddess Athene, is found by adding the central dot to this hexagon. The total of all the dots is 10, the number of perfection.

In these same simple numbers (i.e., 1, 2, 3, 4 and 10) was discovered a quality which has had the widest significance for Western culture and philosophy. Pythagoras observed that if a string or cord is stopped in the ratio of 2 to 1, it will produce a note, when plucked, exactly one octave above the original note. The ratio 3 to 2 produces the note we call a perfect fifth in modern terminology. The ratio 4 to 3 produces a perfect fourth. The significance of the discovery is that the relationship is not created by man, or by the action of performing the experiment, but it is mathematically *inherent* in the universe. Pythagoras called the octave of notes the *harmonia*, but the term very quickly came to signify a much wider general relationship:

> In the Pythagorean application of the theory of concord in music, *harmonia*, which originally signified the octave or a musical scale, comes to mean a system of relations and eventually the plan, scheme, or system which things compose . . .. In these meanings, *harmonia* is applied by the Pythagoreans to sciences as varied as medicine and cosmology. Medicine, on Pythagorean grounds, must have as its end the proper restoration of the complex harmony of the body, a harmony disturbed by illness. The soul is considered to be a harmony or attunement of the body . . .. There is also a *harmonia* of the cosmos.[4]

The cosmic harmony, in so far as it could be discovered and enjoyed by mankind, depended on the imposition of *peras*, meaning limit, on the *apeiron*, or unlimited, to produce *peperas-menon*, or limitation. All the notes possible, sounded together without limit, produce nothing but noise, the Pythagorean exemplar of evil. Imposing limits, recognizing the natural order and structure inherent in the universe, sounding only certain notes, produces harmony, which Pythagoreans would call divine, or the exemplar of good:

> Owing to Pythagoras's discovery, music provided for his followers the best instance of this principle at work. Its suitability was enhanced by the *beauty* of music, to which Pythagoras like most Greeks was sensitive, for the word *kosmos* carried to a Greek the suggestion of beauty as well as order. It was thus further evidence for the equation of limit with goodness that its imposition on the field of sound

brought beauty out of disharmony . . .. Limit is represented by the numerical system of ratios between concordant notes which reduces the whole to order. It is marked out according to an intelligible plan. The plan is not imposed on it by man, but has been there all the time waiting his discovery.[5]

There is no definitive proof of any connection, but there seems an obvious connection between the notion of an eternal, underlying cosmic harmony, a *peperas-menon*, towards which all human activity should attempt to direct itself, and the Celtic concepts of the fitness of things and fair play, based on the notion of a permanent and inviolable standard of appropriate moral conduct. In the ancient world, such relatively sophisticated moral philosophies were rare. Whatever there may be about early Celtic society which is indisputably crude and barbaric – and there is plenty – it is also undeniable that within the law maintained and administered by the Druidic priest-hood appears a high religious awareness very like the underlying principles of cosmic harmony expressed by Pythagoras and his followers.

The Pythagoreans, who used compound fractions with ease (unlike the Egyptians, whose system was hopelessly cumbersome), were, however, dismayed when they found some numbers which defied expression; they seemed also to defy the whole concept of an infinite and ordered truth in the cosmos waiting to reveal itself. For example, as soon as they looked at right-angled isosceles triangles, it became clear that if the equal sides were of any length measurable in integers, the length of the hypotenuse was a number which could not be written as a fraction (i.e., it was irrational, incapable of expression as a fractional ratio).[6] This was a devastating setback, and it led directly to the separation of arithmetic and geometry, since the study of geometry could advance significantly by its own logic, as long as the arithmetical difficulties of number theory were kept out of the way. Since the Druids kept no written records, we have no way of telling whether they understood irrational numbers, although there is a consistent balanced asymmetry in Celtic art which suggests that they may have known one of the most famous of all irrational numbers: namely 1.61803 . . . (as with all irrationals, the decimal continues to infinity) which is the number of the Golden Ratio or Divine Proportion, much beloved of Renaissance artists. Many of the figures in Celtic art, notably the spirals and interlocking knotwork, seem based on the Divine Proportion, quite apart from the overwhelming sense of delight in geometric patterns generally observable. A spiral found frequently in nature, and in Celtic art, is easily traced within rectangles drawn in the Divine Proportion (see below).

Similarly, we find in the scales of a fir cone, the florets of a sunflower, the parastichies (spiral rows) of a pineapple, a series of patterns all of which are directly related to the Divine Proportion.[7] In other words, there is an unmistakable relationship between the ineffable mystery of life in all its diverse forms and the ineffable mystery of number in its pure and unchanging form. God (or the Goddess) is a mathematician. Celtic art seems to show an understanding of that concept.

For the Pythagoreans, the number 3 was the first number, because, unlike 1 and 2, it possessed a beginning, a middle and end. It was also the first number which was greater when multiplied by itself than when added to itself, since $3 + 3 = 6$ but $3 \times 3 = 9$. It was the first male number: all odd numbers were male, all even numbers female. The Fates, the Furies and the Graces all came in threes, and the sacred Muses were three times three, or nine, although these were all female figures: it seems that the masculinity of this number was very specific and limited.

Three was a divine number to the Celts. When Culhwch reels off the great list of Arthurian heroes in whose names he invokes his

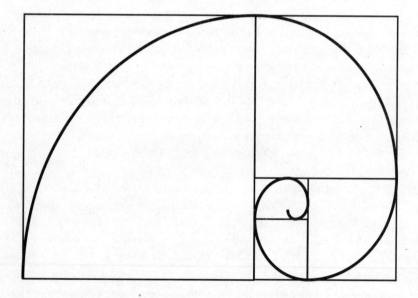

A spiral drawn from the Golden Ratio, or Divine Proportion.

boon, many of these names come in groups of three, some of them clearly divine attributes, rather than real or even mythological figures. It may be that the grouping in threes simply made the names easier to remember – an old Bardic trick, perhaps – but there seems to be more to the practice than that. Here is the opening of Culhwch's long list; not all the names form trios, but the pattern is obvious:

> He invoked his boon in the name of Cei and Bedwyr, and Greidawl Gallddofydd, and Gwythyr son of Greidawl, and Greid son of Eri, and Cynddylig the Guide, and Tathal Frank-deceit and Maelwys son of Baeddan, and Cnychwr son of Nes, and Cubert son of Daere, and Fercos son of Roch, and Lluber Beuthach, and Corfil Berfach, and Gwyn son of Esni, and Gwyn son of Nwyfre, and Gwyn son of Nudd, and Edern son of Nudd, and Cadwy son of Gereint and Fflewdwr Fflam Wledig, and Rhuawn Bebyr son of Dorath, and Bradwen son of Moren Mynawg, and Moren Mynawg himself, and Dalldaf son of Cimin Cof, and the son of Alun Dyfed, and the son of Saidi, and the son of Gwryon, and Uchdryd Host-sustainer, and Cynwas Cwryfagyl, and Gwrhyr Fat-kine, and Isberyr Cat-claw, and Gallgoid the Hewer, and Duach, and Brathach, and Nerthach, sons of Gwawrddur Bow-back (from the uplands of hell these men were sprung), and Cilydd Hundred-holds, and Canhastyr Hundred-hands, and Cord Hundred-claws . . . [The list goes on for a further six or seven pages.][8]

The term 'triad' is used to describe the Welsh poetic practice of linking descriptions or statements of ideas in groups of three, a practice which is also common in Irish poetry and prose. Many of the laws expounded in the early Irish law tracts are grouped in threes, or given a threefold application, sometimes even in defiance of common sense.

In Celtic mythology, the greatest significance of the number 3 is that it represents the three aspects of the principal deity, the great Triple Goddess: as virgin princess, she fuels men's desires; as mother queen, she bears their sons and perpetuates the cycle of life; as crone, hag or witch, she lays them out in death. In all the complex diversity of the Druidic myths, this pattern is endlessly repeated, with the goddess in many guises but always recognizable.

The Pythagoreans associated the number 5 with marriage, since it was the sum of the first even, female number, 2, with the first odd, male number, 3 (this in despite of the belief that 2 was not a number). Five units represented the length of the hypotenuse in the smallest right-angled triangle (i.e., a triangle with side lengths of 3, 4 and 5 units, the only right-angled triangle which has the lengths of its sides in arithmetical progression).

The number 6 also symbolized marriage for the Pythagoreans, as the product of female 2 and male 3. It was associated with childbirth and with health. The Jewish *Mogen David*, or Star of David, is a six-pointed star formed by two intermeshing triangles, and is also associated with marriage and divinity, as well as many other connotations and kabbalistic interpretations of the number 6. The Jews, like many peoples who used the letters of their alphabet to designate numbers as well, developed a complex numerology, which they call the *Gematria*, and which shares some similarities with Pythagorean numerology. The Beth-Luis-Nion alphabet used by the Druids also used letters to signify numbers.

Partly because of the *tetraktys*, the Pythagoreans considered 10 the perfect number. We in the West are now so familiar with 10 as the base of our counting system, that we forget what enormous difficulties early peoples had in reckoning large numbers. The Romans, vastly more sophisticated than most, could handle addition or subtraction well enough: they would write 257 + 369 as –

$$\begin{array}{l} \text{CCL VII} \\ \underline{\text{CCCLXVIIII}} \\ \text{DCXXVI} \end{array}$$

which is fairly straighforward, but simple multiplication or division caused immense complications. Ten is an ideal base for these operations, since the value of a digit simply increases tenfold with every step to the left: 2, 20, 200, 2,000, 20,000, etc. Unfortunately, 10 is a very poor base for measuring fractions of a quantity, since the only fractions expressible by integers are ½ and ⅕. For that reason, merchants continued to use a variety of fractions – 8ths, 12ths, 20ths, and so on – for measuring and dividing, until in 1791 the French introduced the Metric System, in which units of length, weight, volume, etc., were also measured in multiples of 10. The Pythagoreans were so devoted to the properties of 10 that it affected their astronomical theory, as we shall see in a moment.

The largest integer of significance in Pythagoreanism is 216, which also has the unusual attribute of being the smallest cube that is the sum of three cubes, which themselves are the cubes of the significant progression 3, 4, 5:

$$3^3 + 4^3 + 5^3 = 6^3$$
$$27 + 64 + 125 = 216$$

216 is often called Plato's number because it occurs in a famous but obscure passage in his *Republic*, which begins as follows:

> But the number of a human creature is the first number in which root and square increases, having received three distances and four limits, of elements that make both like and unlike and wax and wane, render all things conversable and rational with one another.[9]

The language of this passage, which has received a great deal of attention from mathematicians and mystics alike, is not deliberately obscure. As Wells points out:

> It illustrates perfectly both the intimate relationship that Plato, as a Pythagorean, perceived between numbers and the real world, and the difficulty that he had in using the then available language to express himself.[10]

The integers 8 and 13 were also significant to the Pythagoreans, and these numbers are especially important to our present subject since they represent the festival stations of the year and the number of months in the year respectively; in fact, the first numbers in a famous series directly related to the Divine Proportion, namely 1, 2, 3, 5, 8 and 13, are all highly significant in Druidism.[11] Further explanation follows in subsequent chapters, but for the moment we note that 1 is the number of the eternal; 2 is the number of the twin gods, father and son; 3 is the number of the great goddess; 5 is the number of her unspeakable name, in five vowels; 8 is the number of the principal Celtic religious festivals; and 13 is the number of the months of the year.

The early Celts left us no written records, which was very unaccommodating of them – a few sentences of text might have been sufficient to give us some idea of their actual mathematical and astronomical knowledge. However, they did leave us – in their arms, their cauldrons, their shields, their torques and other jewellery – a vast amount of utterly distinctive, unmistakably Celtic, rich, complex, mathematically sophisticated art, and in their mythology – especially the arcane and allegorical material in early Brythonic sources which conceals the alphabet mysteries – at least the suggestion that their understanding of number was profound.

The basic tenets of Pythagoreanism are so deeply embedded in Western thought that it is not difficult to see (or create) connections with other cultures. Through Plato, Galileo Galilei, Copernicus and Leibniz there flows a continuous stream of ideas which is essentially Pythagorean. Even Sir Isaac Newton, founder of our present conception of the mathematical and physical realities of the universe (Einstein notwithstanding), might be called a Pythagorean – he was certainly sufficiently stimulated by the work of the Pythagorean mystic, Jakob Boehme, to undertake experiments in alchemy.

However, in two respects Pythagoreanism and Druidism seem to be uniquely and distinctively linked. The first is the connection of silence. Pythagorean disciples were bound to secrecy, and they were required to learn their lore by heart. No written accounts were allowed. Several ancient religions were secret and preserved their mysteries by select initiation and so forth, but the specific ban on written records and the requirement to learn great tracts of lore by heart seem to be mutual and exclusive to Pythagoreanism and Druidism. Secondly, and, I believe, even more convincingly, Pythagorean disciples adhered to a principle of social organization quite unusual and remarkable in the ancient world – they treated women as equals. Women taught mathematics (which means they taught divinity) and were accorded absolutely equal status with men. There is only one other ancient society in which any similar equality of opportunity and status for women is observable – and that is early Celtic tribal society. We shall never be certain whether Abaris, the British Druid, went to Greece (or Italy or Egypt) to meet Pythagoras, or whether Pythagoras came to Britain to meet Abaris, or whether Abaris even existed in real life, but at least some reciprocity of ideas between Pythagorean priests and Druids seems very likely.

Lastly, we turn more specifically to Pythagorean astronomy and the Pythagorean model of the solar system.

The Pythagorean solar system

As we noted earlier, the Pythagorean observations of the universe were remarkably sophisticated for their time. They were aware of the planetary motions, and correctly associated them with the sun. Although its association with eclipses was perhaps not recognized until the third century BC, the Pythagoreans were aware of the eighteen and a half year cycle which reconciled the movements of the

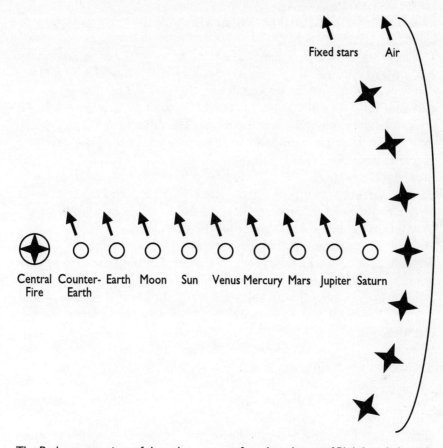

The Pythagorean view of the solar system, after the scheme of Philolaus (adapted from Mark Graubard, *Astrology and Alchemy: Two Fossil Sciences*).

sun with the movements of the moon. They knew the path of the sun across the sky, or ecliptic, and marked the days when it cut the plane of the celestial equator, thus establishing the equinoxes and solstices as stations of the year. Even before Pythagoras, Greek philosophers had speculated that the moon shone with light reflected from the sun, and Leucippus stated that the moon's markings were caused by the shadows of hills and valleys cast on its surface. Pythagoras seems to have recognized that the earth is a sphere, rather than a flattened dish. Eudoxus (408–355 BC), a much admired pupil of Plato, calculated the Golden Year as being 18.61 years. It was the same Eudoxus, as mentioned earlier, who proposed the system of measuring the year as 365 days and making every fourth year 366 days long, or a leap year, the system which we still use in our modern calendar.

There were many ingenious attempts at explaining planetary motions, none of them entirely successful. The Pythagoreans certainly recognized the retrograde motions of the planets, but their explanations depended on increasingly complicated models of interlocking spheres and unusual orbits. They did, however, recognize that the earth is in motion, and not fixed at the centre of the universe. They placed at the centre of the solar system a body which they called the central fire (page 161). This was a hypothetical construct only because Greece was on the wrong side of the planet to observe it – a visitor to the side of the earth beyond India would be able to see it, they felt. All the bodies observed in the sky, including the earth, sun and moon, rotated around this central fire. Unfortunately, even including the central fire, the observable bodies only came to nine in number, which was one short of the divine ten, so a tenth body, called 'counter-earth', was assumed. Like the central fire, it would have to be inside the earth's orbit, which would explain why we cannot see it.

Ingenious as this model was, it still had obvious deficiencies. We have no way of telling to what extent the Druids also accepted it, if at all. They had arrived in Britain and subsumed the culture of the people who, some centuries earlier, had built Stonehenge, Avebury, and the other great stone circles and alignments whose astronomical significance has only recently been studied in any depth. It seems likely that the Druids would have understood the alignments, certainly the very obvious ones at midsummer, midwinter and the equinoxes, and they would have continued to use the stone constructions at the very least for observation. Whether these observations were accompanied by human sacrifice on Stonehenge's 'altar' stone, or any of the other ritual practices associated with Druids in the popular imagination, remains moot.

Nevertheless, the combination of mathematical knowledge and astronomical knowledge (however deficient by modern standards) was certainly good enough to create and use a serviceable calendar, and that is the topic of our final three chapters, beginning with a return to the major festivals which marked the eight major stations of the revolving year.

Notes

1. Robert Graves, *The White Goddess*.
2. The distinction between astronomer and astrologer is not very important for the purposes of this chapter. Nowadays, we use the terms to distinguish a person who observes celestial phenomena scientifically and objectively (the astronomer) and a person who interprets celestial phenomena for mystic or divinatory purposes (the astrologer). Astronomers hold low opinions of astrologers, generally speaking. Ancient astronomers were also, by and large, astrologers.
3. Bertrand Russell, *History of Western Philosophy*.
4. Milton C. Nahm, *Selections from Early Greek Philosophy*.
5. W.K.C. Guthrie, *The Greek Philosophers from Thales to Aristotle*.
6. The demonstration, found in Book X of Euclid, and quoted by Russell, runs as follows. Suppose each of the equal sides of a right-angled isosceles triangle to be 1 in long.

   Let the fraction representing the length of the hypotenuse be expressed as m/n. By Pythagoras's Theorem, $m^2/n^2 = 2$. If m and n have a common factor, divide it out, then either m or n must be odd. But $m^2 = 2n^2$, meaning that m must be even, which means that n must be odd. However, suppose $m = 2p$. Then $4p^2 = 2n^2$, therefore $n^2 = 2p^2$, therefore n must be even, *contra hyp*. Therefore, there is no fraction m/n, for which m and n are both integers, which will measure the hypotenuse. Russell assumes that this proof was known to Plato.
7. David Wells, *The Penguin Dictionary of Curious and Interesting Numbers*.
8. 'Culhwch and Olwen', in *The Mabinogion*.
9. Plato, *The Republic*, viii, 546 B–D, quoted in David Wells, above, source listed as J. Adams, *The Republic of Plato*, 1929.
10. David Wells, above.
11. The series is called the Fibonacci series, after Leonardo da Pisa, also known as Fibonacci, who published his *Liber Abaci* (The Book of the Abacus) in AD 1202. Among other things, it explained Arabic numerals, and Fibonacci is often considered the originator of modern number notation. The series is continued by adding the last two numbers together, as: 1, 2, 3, 5, 8, 13, 21, 34, 55, 89, 144, and so on. The ratio of each term to its predecessor approximates to the Divine Proportion, and the further the series is progressed, the closer is the approximation, e.g. $21 \div 13 = 1.615384615$; $34 \div 21 = 1.619047619$; $55 \div 34 = 1.617647059$, etc.

CHAPTER EIGHT

THE EIGHT STATIONS OF THE YEAR

IN CHAPTER SIX, I noted that some of the Celtic festivals seem to be closely associated with later Christian festivals: Lughnasa with Lammas and the Harvest Festival; Samhain with All Saints' Day, All Souls' Day and Martinmas; the midwinter solstice (Yule) with Christmas and Epiphany; Imbolc with St Brigid's Day and Candlemas; Beltane possibly with Whitsun. These are represented diagramatically in the illustration below.

We now return to these eight stations of the year to examine them in more detail, and, in particular, to see if there is a viable mythographic pattern to the suggested dedications. Pattern-finding is always dangerous. Like the Welsh triads which defy common sense, the apparent matrices of thematic connection can become so appealing in themselves that real information is ignored or distorted to complete the appealingly symmetric pattern. I must confess that a good deal of this chapter will be speculative; I wish it were possible to offer more absolute and incontrovertible proof of the suggestions I am about to make, but I have to be honest and admit that it is not. Nevertheless, it seems to me that some of the mythographic patterns in the Celtic year are very striking, and that there seems to be at least the possibility of an overall pattern which makes mythographic sense. To some extent, the pattern is built on the attributions made in Chapter Six, which were themselves speculative, so we are now building a house of sand on a foundation of sand: the reader will have to judge how well it stands up.

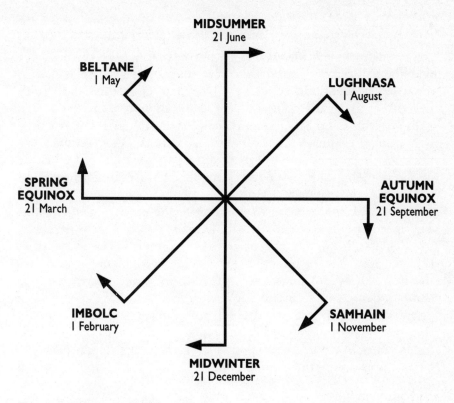

MIDSUMMER
21 June

BELTANE
1 May

LUGHNASA
1 August

SPRING EQUINOX
21 March

AUTUMN EQUINOX
21 September

IMBOLC
1 February

SAMHAIN
1 November

MIDWINTER
21 December

The eight stations of the year.

Calendar dates

First, a note about dates. The calendar dates given in the illustration above are all from the modern, solar calendar. Revived neo-pagan groups hold celebrations on them. Virtually every textbook on the Celts, even some highly respectable academic texts, lists the festival dates as they are given above, with no further explanation or comment. However, the Celts did not wear watches or carry Filofaxes and appointment diaries, nor was there a picture calendar hanging on the wall of the thatched hut. It is highly likely that the week as a time unit only came into the Celtic way of thinking after the Roman occupation. So, the ordinary Celt – without watch or calendar – would have had two basic time units: the day (night followed by day) and the month (full lunation). He or she would know what time of the year it was, by the weather and common

165

sense. The person could recognize the full moon, and count the number of full moons since the year began, and keep track of the count easily enough in his or her head. It therefore seems probable that the great popular festivals were movable feasts, their precise dates set by lunations rather than by whatever method the Druids were using to calculate the full year. In other words, the calendrical knowledge necessary to maintain an accurate annual calendar would be arcane, a mystery reserved for the Druids and their retinues, the priest-mathematicians. The great festivals, however, were in the public domain, and they would probably have been celebrated on days which the ordinary person might easily recognize. The obvious choice would be the nearest full moon to the precise calendar date. The central point here is that, although a solar calendar is necessary to calculate precise dates accurately, the Moon is far easier to 'read' than the Sun – for the uninitiated tribesman, recognizing precise days by distinctions in phases of the Moon would have been a comparatively simple matter. A long festival like Lughnasa would perhaps begin with the new moon before the appropriate full moon, continue right through the full and on into the wane to the next new moon (which would certainly make mythographic sense in the commemoration of the passing of Bran, the old father-god or the old king).

If that is true, our precise solar calendar dates are only approximations. While we have 1 November written on our calendars for Samhain, the Celt might have had in his or her head that Samhain would be held on the fourth full moon after midsummer; that would be easy enough to remember, and easy enough to recognize when it came along. If, because of the vagaries of lunations against the solar calendar, Samhain was going to fall on the third full moon, or the fifth, in the coming year, that information might well be disseminated by the Druids in advance at the large midsummer gatherings. In this way, the difficult and complex computation of the calendar, including the reconciliation of solar and lunar motions, did not have to be understood by the general populace: they only had to keep track of their days and their lunations. It may be that the persistence of the full moon as a marking point in so many of our surviving superstitions about when certain plants should be planted, or what times are propitious for other activities, is derived from this very simple and ancient method for keeping track of the days. It might also explain why the week – which Romans and later Teutonic invaders certainly used – took such a long time to become established in Celtic culture: an artificial unit of seven days would have been of little interest and of little use to our hypothetical Celt, who had the dates of all the important festivals in his or her head, as 'fourth full moon', 'seventh full moon', and so on (there was a maximum of 12 to deal with) and could use days, or obvious parts of the lunation ('I'll lend you my plough until first quarter') for any transactions in between. It was only when the mythological attributes of the days of the week (Sun, Moon, Tiw, Woden, Thor, Frig and Saturn, or their counterparts) became important that the week itself meant anything in Celtic culture.

If we take 1992–93 as an exemplary year, and set each festival date at the nearest full moon, we derive this simple calendar:

Festival	Full Moon	Equivalent solar date
Midsummer	First	14 June 1992
Lughnasa	Third	13 August 1992
Autumn equinox	Fourth	11 September 1992
Samhain	Sixth	10 November 1992
Midwinter	Eighth	8 January 1993
Imbolc	Ninth	6 February 1993
Spring equinox	Tenth	8 March 1993
Beltane	Twelfth	5 May 1993

It is immediately obvious that the solar dates wander quite a distance either side of the precise dates traditionally associated with the festivals. If that seems perplexing and unlikely, consider that the only real alternative would have been for the general populace to have understood the Druidic solar calendar ('Today is the 15th of Reed Month' – further explanation follows in the next chapter), as well as the Druids themselves, which seems unlikely. For comparison, we have the models of the Jewish and Islamic calendars, both based on alternating 29- and 30-day months, which are too complex for the average citizen – most believers simply accept the calendrical computations handed down to them.

There is evidence for several attributions to each of the festivals, some from the classical and vernacular sources, some from an understanding of the Celtic agricultural cycle and natural seasonal phenomena, some from speculation about the origins of apparently associated Christian festivals and religious and secular folklore. (See the illustration on page 168.)

The midsummer transition makes good mythographic sense. The old king is succeeded by the young king when the young king is old

167

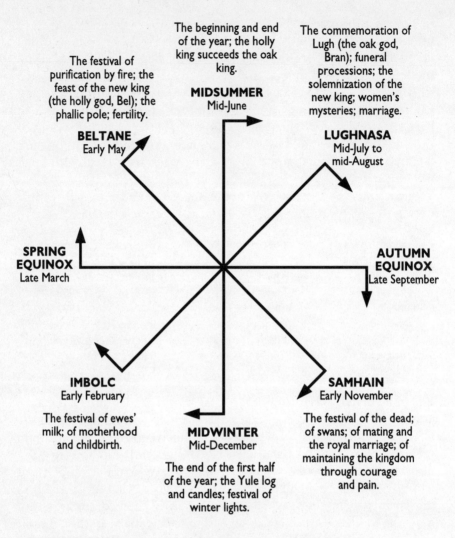

The festival of purification by fire; the feast of the new king (the holly god, Bel); the phallic pole; fertility.

BELTANE
Early May

The beginning and end of the year; the holly king succeeds the oak king.

MIDSUMMER
Mid-June

The commemoration of Lugh (the oak god, Bran); funeral processions; the solemnization of the new king; women's mysteries; marriage.

LUGHNASA
Mid-July to mid-August

SPRING EQUINOX
Late March

AUTUMN EQUINOX
Late September

IMBOLC
Early February

The festival of ewes' milk; of motherhood and childbirth.

MIDWINTER
Mid-December

The end of the first half of the year; the Yule log and candles; festival of winter lights.

SAMHAIN
Early November

The festival of the dead; of swans; of mating and the royal marriage; of maintaining the kingdom through courage and pain.

A mythographic representation of the eight stations of the year.

enough; he becomes the old king in his turn. It seems likely that the human transition represented is the transition from boyhood to manhood. Perhaps midsummer celebrations included male puberty rites and initiation rites as a warrior. At the other end of the year, by which I mean at midwinter, we have an almost equally obvious transition, from Caer the virgin bride to Brigit the mother; in other words, the even greater mystery of the transition from girlhood to womanhood. The onset of menarche, and therefore of fertility, was by its very nature a female mystery.

But a proper understanding of these transitions – if, indeed, they make any real mythographic sense at all – depends on an accurate understanding of the mythographic significance of the four great festivals, so we need to look back over them, gathering together what we already know. Since we are interested primarily in transitions, we shall start with Beltane and see what we can safely carry forward towards Lughnasa.

Beltane

Starting with the obvious: Beltane is dedicated to Bel (Belin, Belinus, Belenos), a sun-god, the counterpart of Zeus and Jupiter. His festival is associated with fire because the word fire ('tan' in Brythonic, 'tine' in Goidelic), is part of its name, and because a well-attested rite at the festival was the driving of livestock between two fires as a purification rite, almost certainly intended to be prophylactic against disease. We noted in Chapter 6 (page 137) the widespread inscription of the name Belenos in Gaul and northern Italy. Of the many folk customs still current around May Day, and therefore perhaps related to Beltane, we noted the decorating of and dancing around the Maypole, fairly unmistakably a celebration of the phallus, and therefore of the young male.

But here is our first anomaly, the first piece which refuses to fit in the jigsaw: it is on Beltane Eve that Gwyn ap Nudd, Lord of Annwn, rides out with the Wild Hunt, related to *Walpurgisnacht*, which takes place on 30 April, the night when witches fly up spiral mountains. The old British legend is that the distinctive whirring of the wild geese flying north on their summer migration is the sound of the flight of damned souls towards the frozen wastelands of the northern Hell. Gwyn (the name simply means the white one) is an Underworld god, the equivalent of Bran. He is also called Herne the Hunter, or Gabriel, and his dogs, white with red eyes and red-tipped ears, are the Hounds of Hell, the Yell Hounds or Gabriel Hounds. In Scotland he is called Arthur, which may be nothing to do with the warrior-king of the sixth century, but a name based on the epithet 'ar ddu' (the black one). Our problem is that he is definitely a Bran-type god, the counterpart of Cronos or Saturn, and not a Bel-type god, although his Wild Hunt is associated with Beltane, and more importantly, with the northward migration of the geese, which can only take place before midsummer. Gwyn was also an oak god, not a holly god; at his death (gods are allowed to die in the Celtic pantheon) he was buried in a boat-shaped coffin made of oak, in honour of his father Llyr, Lludd or Nudd. His name is commemorated in the many British place-names which begin with Win: for example, Winchester, Wincanton, Winford, Wingate, Winscombe, Winston.

However, all is not lost, despite appearances. The prominent constellation on the ecliptic at Beltane is Taurus, the Bull. Above the ecliptic, the dominant springtime constellation is Perseus. Now we have no way of knowing whether the ancient zodiacal associations and attributions, or the classical depictions of the major constell-ations, had anything like the same significance for the early Celts. Perhaps the constellation we call Ursa Major, or the Great Bear, or the Big Dipper, or the Plough, was known to them as the Fat Squirrel or the Big Floppy Hat. But the zodiacal attributions, at least, are very ancient – as was mentioned in the last chapter, they were Babylonian in origin – so it may well be that the attributions were also carried forward with the astronomical lore of the zodiac itself. Perseus is the ideal counterpart for Bel; originally Pterseus, he is the epitome of the young warrior-god, rescuer of maidens (Andromeda) and slayer of dragons (the snake-headed Medusa). Taurus the Bull would be a fitting attribution, although we find Gwyn (a Bran-type, not a Bel-type) also described in the early Welsh text, *The Black Book of Carmarthen*, as 'a bull of conflict, quick to disperse an embattled host'. Gemini, the Twins, takes its name from the legend of Castor and Pollux, but it is also mythographically appropriate following Taurus and anticipating the transition of the twin-gods, oak king and holly king. The real clue to the apparent mystery of Gwyn the father-god appearing in his son's rightful place at Beltane lies in the person of his mother. The goddess most closely associated with Beltane is Arianrhod, whose name means Silver Wheel. Triad 14, part of a collection of early Welsh poems,[1] tells us that she is the mother of the twin heroes Gwengwyngwyn and Gwanat – this is the Madron and Mabon matrix discussed earlier. But Gwengwyngwyn simply means 'the white one-the white one-the white one': this is Gwyn trebly honoured. Arianrhod of the silver (or white) wheel, is also Blodeuwedd of the white spring flowers, who shapeshifts to become an autumnal (i.e. white) owl, and Cerridwen the white sow of approaching winter and death. In autumn, her son Gwyn, or Herne, or Gabriel, or Arthur, leads the *autumnal* Wild Hunt, chasing the souls of the dead into the maw of midwinter. In other words, when Arianrhod took her place at the spring feast of Beltane, she brought her autumn son Gwyn along with her.

Geoffrey of Monmouth, whose *Historia Britonum* (History of the Britons) was published in AD 1139, tells us that in the fourth century BC there was a great battle for the throne of Britain between two brothers, named Belinus and Brennius. Belinus won, and Brennius was forced to retreat north of the River Humber. What Geoffrey did was to present myth as history (not just in this instance: the device is typical of the whole book). The two contestants are, of course, Bel and Bran; they are brothers, but they are also son and father. Their battle is not for kingship of Britain (which, as I suggested earlier, was not a real political aim of the early Celts until the Romans made it one), but for the kingship of the year, or at least for their rightful half of the year. And of course Bel won – he wins every midsummer.

Lughnasa

The defeated king, or god, is commemorated at Lughnasa, the next of the four major festivals, which takes place after midsummer. The zodiacal constellation could hardly be more precisely appropriate: it is Leo, the Lion. Lugh, the god of the 'nasadh', or commemoration, is also Lleu LLaw Gyffes, or the Lion with the Steady Hand. The prominent constellation above the ecliptic is Ursa Major, who is a she-bear, not a he-bear. Perhaps the attribution (which comes from Roman mythology) was quite different from the Celtic one, or perhaps the she-bear represents a goddess associated with the god; the most likely contender would be the Morrigan, the Great Queen, who shared Bran's totem animal, the raven, but who might also appear as a bear, in the same way that Brigit can appear as wolf, vulture or snake. A further animal anomaly is that Lugh is frequently represented by the eagle yet in Roman mythology it is Bel's counterpart, Jupiter, who owns the eagle, not Lugh's counterpart, Saturn. Perhaps the eagle – as in more recent history – is a symbol of the kingship itself, and therefore passes between the two kings, or gods, or brothers, or son and father, as each succeeds the other. Lleu's legend, in which he grapples with his rival Gronw Lord of Penllyn for the love of Blodeuwydd (a reincarnation of his mother Arianrhod) has an exact parallel in the legend of Gwyn grappling with his rival Gwythyr ap Greidawl for the love of Creiddylad: it is in essence the same tale with different names. The peculiar 'geis' (see page 125) of the manner of his death – one foot on the back of a

171

goat, the other on the rim of a vat of water – represents the lustral bath taken by sacred kings at coronation. As Graves points out, it has counterparts in Greek myth: Minos dying at the hands of the priestess of Cocalus and her lover Daedalus, or Agamemnon at the hands of Clytemnestra and her lover Aegisthus.[2]

The commemoration of Bran, the father, is also in a sense a continuation of the reverence for Bel, the son, because Bel, by crossing through the midsummer threshold into manhood, has become Bran, his own brother and father. (If any extremely pedestrian or literal-minded reader has somehow managed to stick it out this far in my argument, the question 'How can somebody be brother and father to the same man?' is met by the answer that these are not real relationships: they are archetypal, or mythographic relationships, the fundamental matrix being the pattern of the eternal and unchanging goddess giving birth to a son who, in his time, will become a lover, and, therefore, a father. The mother, Madron, gives birth to the son, Mabon, who becomes the lover, or husband, Mabon, who fathers the child, Mabon; or Bran fathers Bel who fathers Bran who fathers Bel, year in year out, through all eternity.

Samhain

However, to the goddess and her son-brother-father-husband is born not only an archetypal son to maintain the cycle, but also an archetypal daughter. We have met her already: she is Caer Ibormeith, Caer of the Yew Berry, the virgin princess who elopes with Oenghus, the pair of them shapeshifted into swans flying over Sidh Uamain. Her festival is Samhain.

The zodiacal constellation at Samhain was – what else would one expect? – Virgo, the virgin. However, in 400 BC the sun was in the constellation of Scorpius at Samhain. At night, there was no clear or prominent constellation high above the ecliptic at the time of the festival. Draco and Boötes were both high in the sky, but neither is mythographically appropriate, unless we see Draco, the Dragon, as a serpent associated with the goddess; but, in any case, both constellations are faint and unimpressive.

The mythologically appropriate constellation, Cygnus, or the Swan, is high in the sky throughout the northern summer, although not directly above Virgo. The name, more properly written as Cycnus, was given to four different characters in Greek mythology, all of them male. The one who gave his name to the constellation was Cycnus, the friend of Phaethon; but another Cycnus, son of Ares and Pelopia, became a swan after he was slain by Herakles, the Greek counterpart of the Celtic Bel. In Celtic mythology, the swan is more frequently associated with goddesses or other female figures than with male gods. We know that the swan is closely associated with Caer at Samhain, and in a moment we shall see how it is also associated with Brigit at Imbolc. The pattern of the constellation is very simple, and the attribution of a long-necked bird in flight could easily transfer from one culture to another.

It is in the figure of a swan that Zeus violates Leda, wife of Tyndareus. Leda sleeps with her lawful husband that same night, and from the two couplings, two sets of twins are born: Pollux and Helen, children of Zeus; and Castor and Clytemnestra, children of Tyndareus. In fact, Zeus undergoes a series of transformations to satisfy his lusts: a cloud for Io, a shower of gold for Danaë, a bull for Europa, and so on.

These changes are reminiscent of the Celtic tales of shapeshifting, the most famous of which has the goddess chasing the god, rather than the other way round: this is the legend of Taliesin. The boy Gwion (a Mabon figure) is set to guard the goddess Cerridwen's magic cauldron. When three burning drops of its contents splash on to his finger, he licks them up and he is instantly granted knowledge of all things past, present and future. Cerridwen pursues him through a series of changes. First, Gwion becomes a hare, and Cerridwen becomes a greyhound. Next he becomes a fish, and she shapeshifts into an otter. He flies into the air as a bird, and she becomes a hunting hawk. Finally, Gwion becomes a single grain of wheat on the threshing floor. Cerridwen becomes a black hen and pecks him up. Nine months later, she gives birth to a son, who is eventually given the name Taliesin and becomes the greatest of seers and poets.

The Caer of Samhain appears in many guises in Celtic literature and mythology – she is, after all, the great goddess in her most appealing aspect. Her Greek and Roman counterparts are Aphrodite and Venus. She is Blodeuwedd, Rhiannon, Gwenhwyfer or Guinevere, Morgana, Vivienne and Nimuë, among others. In the Goidelic tale which we have already discussed, the goddess is the virgin Caer, wooed by Oenghus. The corresponding Brythonic tale, which constitutes the first part, or 'branch', of *The Mabinogion*, features Rhiannon as the virgin goddess, and its sexual symbolism is far more explicit. It also includes familiar motifs, like the tryst of the single blow. Like most of the Celtic myths, it seems long and rambling; even when reduced to simple plot summary, it remains fairly tortuous. The reader already familiar with the tale is asked to excuse the full summary following, which is given to illustrate the point that within these myths is contained a symbolic representation of Celtic moral and religious lore. For simplicity's sake, I have separated the story synopsis and my commentary.

Rhiannon's tale in *The Mabinogion*

Pwyll (A) is prince and lord over the seven cantrefs (B) of Dyfed (C). His favourite hunting place is Glyn Cuch (D). While hunting, he meets a huntsman on a grey steed, wearing a horn around his neck (E). The huntsman's hounds are a brilliant shining white and their ears are red (F). The huntsman's hounds kill the stag which Pwyll had been pursuing, and Pwyll is aggrieved. The huntsman offers to make amends. He announces his name and title: he is Arawn Pen Annwn (G). Arawn is being oppressed by a rival, Hafgan (H). He asks Pwyll to take his place a year hence at a battle tryst with Hafgan, at the river ford (I). He warns Pwyll that he must give Hafgan one blow only, even though he will beg for another (J). In return for his service, Pwyll is granted to live in Arawn's kingdom for the year before the tryst. Arawn works magic which transforms their appearances, so that Pwyll may pass as Arawn in Annwn, and Arawn may pass as Pwyll in Dyfed (K).

When Pwyll arrives in Annwn, he is given rich silk robes to wear, with gold brocade. Servants and chamberlains attend his every desire (L). The queen, exceptionally beautiful, greets him as Arawn. Pwyll sleeps in the same bed with her that night, and every night for the remainder of the year, but always with his back to her. During the day, their conversation is sweet and affectionate; the queen cannot understand why Pwyll (whom she takes to be Arawn) will not make love to her at night (M). At the end of the year, Pwyll meets Hafgan at the river ford, and delivers a single, mortal blow. As Arawn predicted, Hafgan begs Pwyll to dispatch him and end his pain, but Pwyll refuses. Hafgan tells his retinue, 'My trusty gentles, bear me hence. My death has been completed. I am in a state to maintain you no longer' (N). Pwyll completes his conquest of Hafgan's territories, and now the two kingdoms are within his power (O).

He returns to Glyn Cuch to meet Arawn again. Each returns to his own shape and semblance. When Arawn returns to Annwn, he sleeps with his queen and makes love joyfully to her. She tells him how pleased she is, after the long year with no lovemaking. Arawn thus learns how steadfast and unswerving Pwyll has been in not succumbing to the temptation to violate his wife. Pwyll, in turn, discovers that Dyfed has been remarkably well governed in his absence (an absence of which only he and Arawn are aware, of course). The kingdom is prosperous and fruitful. A bond of friendship between Pwyll and Arawn now exists, and exchanges of greyhounds, hawks, horses and other treasures take place (P). Pwyll, whose title was Pendefig Dyfed, takes the name Pwyll Pen Annwn (Q).

Later, at a high place called Gorsedd Arberth (R), Pwyll sees a wonder. A mysterious maiden, the most beautiful any man has ever seen, rides by on a pale white horse. She wears a robe of shining gold brocaded silk (S). Although her horse is only walking, none of the human riders can catch up with her, even at full gallop. After several attempts to catch her, Pwyll eventually calls out, 'Maiden, for his sake whom thou lovest best, stay for me.' The lady answers, 'I will, gladly, and it had been better for the horse hadst thou asked this long since' (T). The lady announces her name as Rhiannon (U), daughter of King Hefeydd (B). Pwyll declares his love for her, but she tells him that she is betrothed against her will to another. She makes a tryst for Pwyll to attend a feast a year hence at the court of Hefeydd.

At the appointed time, Pwyll attends and is greeted warmly by Hefeydd. Towards the end of the feast, a red-haired young man, dressed in gold brocaded silk, enters and craves a boon of Pwyll. Pwyll replies, 'Whatever boon thou ask of me, so far as I can get it, it shall be thine' (W). The stranger is Gwawl son of Clud (X), the suitor whom Rhiannon has been avoiding. She tells Pwyll, 'Never was there a man made feebler use of his wits than thou hast' (Y). Honour demands that Pwyll keep his word to Gwawl. Rhiannon tells Pwyll to fulfil his promise and grant her to Gwawl. She will make a tryst to allow him to take her virginity a year hence. In the meantime, she gives Pwyll a small magic bag, which she tells him to keep safe (Z). She tells him to bring 100 men with him to the feast a year hence, and to place them in hiding in the orchard (AA). Pwyll himself is to wear rags (AB).

A year later, Gwawl arrives at the court of Hefeydd and is feasted. The feast is interrupted by Pwyll arriving, dressed in rags and with rag boots on his feet (AC). He asks a simple boon: he wishes to fill his small bag with food. Gwawl, unsuspecting, grants the request. However, no matter how much food is put into the bag, it never fills. Finally, in exasperation, Gwawl asks, 'Friend, will thy bag ever be full?' Pwyll, coached earlier by Rhiannon, replies, 'It will not, for all that may ever be put into it, unless a true possessor of land and territory and dominions (AD) shall arise and tread down with both his feet the food inside the bag, and say: 'Sufficient has been put herein''. Gwawl falls for the ruse, and as soon as he has stepped into the bag and uttered the words, Pwyll ties the bag with leather thongs. He blows his horn (AE) and his hundred men emerge from their hiding-place in the orchard. They begin beating the bag, from which comes the name of the game Badger in a Bag (AF). Gwawl complains that being beaten to death in a bag is not a fitting way for a warrior to die. Hefeydd agrees, and orders Gwawl released from the bag. At Rhiannon's prompting, Pwyll extracts Gwawl's parole that he will not seek vengeance or retribution for his humiliation. Pwyll takes Rhiannon's virginity. Hefeydd wishes to send his daughter to Pwyll in a year's time, but Pwyll takes her immediately (AG). They return to Dyfed to rule as king and queen.

However, after three years, the kingdom is troubled because Pwyll and Rhiannon have not yet had any children (AH). The elders beg Pwyll to take another wife, but he refuses. Within another year, Rhiannon gives birth to a son, born at Arberth (AI). She and six women tend the baby, but one night all of them fall asleep and, in the morning, the baby has disappeared. The six women, waking before Rhiannon, kill some pups newly born to a stag-hound bitch (AJ) and smear the blood on Rhiannon's face and hands, scattering the small bones around. The whole court is convinced that Rhiannon has killed and eaten her own child. Her punishment is to do a penance which requires her to stand for seven years by a horse-mounting block near the gate of the court and offer to carry any guest or stranger on her back (AK).

In the meantime, a good man, by name Teyrnon Twryf Liant, lord of Gwent Is-Coed (AL), has a mare, the most beautiful in the world, who delivers a foal every year on the night of Beltane Eve (AM). Every year, however, the colt mysteriously disappears soon after birth. This year, Teyrnon keeps vigil. Shortly after the colt is born, he sees a great claw coming in through the stable window. He hacks off the arm bearing the claw and rushes outside, but the monster has disappeared into the darkness. Returning to the stable, he finds, instead of the colt, a golden-haired baby boy (AN). He gives the boy to his wife to look after (AO) and they call him Gwri Golt Adwyn, or Gwalchmei Gwyn (AP). Teyrnon recognizes that Gwri looks remarkably like Pwyll. Hearing of Rhiannon's penance, he takes the boy to Pwyll's court, where he is warmly received. Rhiannon offers to carry Teyrnon and his retinue on her back, but Teyrnon refuses, and Rhiannon is absolved from her penance. Joyfully, the royal couple recognize Gwri as their true son. Rhiannon gives him the new name Pryderi (AQ).

(A) 'Pwyll' means sense or discretion.

(B) The word 'cantref' means, literally, a hundred: it is a measure of land area.

(C) Dyfed is one of the ancient Welsh tribal kingdoms. Its name survives in modern Wales to denote an administrative district.

(D) 'Glyn Cuch' means, literally, the red valley. Metaphorically, it signifies the vagina.

(E) The horn around Arawn's neck tells us immediately that he is Gwyn the White, or Herne the Hunter, or Arddu the Dark One, or Gabriel, leader of the Wild Hunt.

(F) The white, red-eared hounds are the Hounds of Hell, or Gabriel Hounds.

(G) He gives his name and title. 'Arawn' has no meaning, but it is similar to 'arawd', which means speech. 'Pen' means head, literally and metaphorically; it is often translated as king. 'Annwn' means the Underworld, abyss or hell; Dr George derives it from 'an down', meaning the deep, but a speculative derivation might be the negative prefix 'an-' and 'duw' (god), conveying the sense 'godless place': a meaning which would suggest that it was a late term, influenced by the Christian monks who wrote down the tales. The Irish used 'Tir na Nog' (Land of Youth), but the only Brythonic term frequently used before the Christian influence is 'Avallon', which is derived from 'avallen', meaning apple tree.

(H) 'Hafgan' means Summer Song. Of course, he and Arawn do not get along: Hafgan is the god of the sun and light, Arawn is the god of winter and the Underworld.

(I) The battle tryst takes place at a river ford because 'crossing the river', for the Celts as well as for the Greeks (and us), was a metaphor for dying.

(J) This is the motif of the tryst of the single blow. It appears very frequently in Celtic and Arthurian legends, most notably in the story of Gawain and the Green Knight, where Gawain strikes off the mysterious knight's head with one blow, but the knight picks up his head and walks away, vowing to claim his return blow in 'a year and a day'.

(K) When the dead appear among the living, they may do so in the guise of someone actually alive, and no one (apart from a Druid perhaps) would be able to tell. It is noteworthy that Pwyll's year in hell is seen as a gift, as a recompense for the wrong done to him, not as a punishment. The other world is a place in which one would *want* to spend a year, or longer.

(L) The silk robes with gold brocade are worn by every other-world figure in the story, including Rhiannon. Pwyll may wear them because he is dead, albeit temporarily. Servants attend him not just because they think that he is Arawn, but because the other world is a place of ease and luxury for all who manage to attain it.

(M) Gawain undergoes exactly the same trial. He succumbs to temptation in a minor way, however, and receives some small wounds as a result, when he later completes his tryst with the Green Knight, who (of course) turns out to be the husband of the lady concerned. The Pythagorean notion of *peras*, or limit, mentioned in the last chapter, seems to apply here. This is not simply an adherence to the Christian commandment against adultery: it is a far broader notion, in which due respect for the 'fitness of things', the sacred bond of honour, is important. The Celts were generally faithful in marriage (although marriages were easily dissolved), avoided overeating, and had a number of taboos, but they did not go in for self-denial in the way of Christian or Hindu ascetics. The motif of a lover shapeshifted into the semblance of a husband reappears significantly in the Arthurian legend, which begins with Merlin shapeshifting Uther Pendragon into the semblance of the Duke of Gorlois so that he may sleep with Ygraine, who accommodates him (thinking him to be her husband), and later gives birth to Arthur. In that tale, also, the child mysteriously disappears: Merlin had laid claim to the baby as part of his bargain with Uther.

(N) The summer king, defeated (as he believes) by the winter king, Arawn, yields up his power. His half of the year is complete and he no longer has any right to maintain the kingdom.

(O) The two kingdoms are the two halves of the year. At any given time, one king or the other, Hafgan or Arawn, Bel or Bran, the holly king or the oak king, has control of the year.

(P) The gifts of treasure are, of course, sacrifices made throughout the year.

(Q) Pwyll was 'Pendefig' ('pennsevik' in Cornish, meaning chieftain or noble, often translated as prince) of Dyfed. Now that he has been dead in the Underworld, and he has returned to this world not only unharmed but also with the assured patronage of the winter god, he can take the title of 'Pen Annwn' (Head or King of the Abyss). In other words, he now has Arawn's title.

(R) 'Gorsedd' means, literally, 'Great Sitting': it can describe a sacred site, as here, or a gathering, usually of priests or nobles. 'Arberth' means 'the bush', significance unclear.

(S) Rhiannon wears the brocaded silk of the other world.

(T) Rhiannon upbraids Pwyll for spending so long on action before thinking to try words. Her point is central to Druidic thought: correct and appropriate utterance has great magical power. Pwyll would have saved himself a lot of time and trouble if he had said the right thing at the right time. This point is made again after the feast at the court of Hefeydd.

(U) Rhiannon's name is related to 'rhiain', which means virgin, exactly as one would expect.

(V) Hefeydd appears to be a compound name, derived from 'haf' (summer) and the substantive terminal '-ydd', mentioned in Chapter One (page 32), which we find at the end of 'derwydd' (Druid, from 'derw', meaning oak, plus '-ydd'). It is difficult to translate exactly – 'Summer-ness' comes close. Rhiannon as the virgin daughter of summer makes perfect mythographic sense, as does Bel as the virgin son of winter.

179

(W) The mistake Pwyll makes is to utter the formulaic response to a request for a boon without stopping to consider the consequences. What he says is perfectly normal, part of the important Celtic law that a host must honour his guest by giving whatever his guest asks for – to do any less would not be honourable. But he utters the formula without thinking, which leads to potential disaster. This is a further example of the Celtic belief in the power of correct utterance.

(X) 'Gwawl' means light (the noun, not the adjective). 'Clud' means luggage or baggage, so the suitor is 'Light, son of Baggage', but that name 'Clud' seems peculiar enough to be unlikely: it may be a scribe's error in the manuscript. The main names, however, seem to match reasonably: 'Sense' (Pwyll) and 'Light' (Gwawl) are contending for possession of the virgin.

(Y) Rhiannon tells Pwyll in no uncertain terms what an idiot he is for speaking without thinking.

(Z) The small magic bag, into which the whole universe can be placed and from which the whole universe can emerge is, of course, the womb. An alternative symbol for the same concept is the magic cauldron, which feeds the universe and can never be emptied. The transition from Samhain, through midwinter, to Imbolc, or from Rhiannon the virgin to Brigit the mother, is the mystery of the menarche, through which the womb derives its power and all life is renewed.

(AA) Pwyll's men hide in the orchard because the orchard is Avallon; in other words, they are in the other world.

(AB) Pwyll wears rags as a token of self-abasement and humility before the virgin goddess.

(AC) He may not wear leather shoes because the bull is sacred to the god which he has not yet become.

(AD) This reference to the 'true possessor of lands' sounds almost as if it comes from a law tract; it is clearly related to a concept of regal legitimacy which is fundamentally spiritual, and that is in accord with what we already know about the nature of Celtic kingship.

(AE) The horn summons Pwyll's men from the orchard, or

Underworld, just as Gwyn's horn summons the dead from their graves to join the Wild Hunt. According to the legend, a horn will rouse Arthur and his men from the mountain under which they are sleeping, at the time of Britain's greatest need.

(AF) It is not clear whether the reference to the badger is scatological, with the badger's bristles in the bag as a euphemism for female pubic hair, or topical, to some real game or amusement involving real badgers. Badgers were semi-venerated by the Celts; nocturnal, secretive, boar-like in many ways, they commanded respect, and it seems unlikely that they would have been stuffed in a sack and beaten for amusement; they were not hunted, either for meat or for sport. Their distinctive colouring about the head was widely copied, particularly by male warriors: Cu Chulainn and other warrior-heroes are described as having hair dyed like the bristles of a boar or badger. 'Brogh', meaning badger, is one of the few Celtic words to have been borrowed into English, in the form of the epithet brock.

(AG) Now that Pwyll has taken Rhiannon's virginity, her father no longer has any rights over her.

(AH) The mythological virgin queen remains a virgin until she bears children, regardless of the technicality of her virginity.

(AI) The divine son is born at Arberth because it is the appropriate place: it is where Pwyll and Rhiannon first met and it is a 'gorsedd', or seat of high wonders.

(AJ) The blood and bones for the deception have to come from a bitch's puppies for the practical purpose of achieving the deception, but also for the mythological purpose of associating animal birth with human birth.

(AK) The strange and cruel punishment is mythologically very apt. Rhiannon now takes on the attributes of Epona, the horse-goddess. It places her in a humiliating position in human terms, but in mythological terms it allows the mystery of the foaling of Teyrnon's mare and of Gwri's birth to take place.

(AL) Teyrnon's name is related to 'teyrn', meaning kingdom. 'Twryf' seems to be a variant of 'twrf', meaning noise, significance unclear.

(AM) The virgin's festival is at Samhain, or early November, and the birth of the son, the new god and king, is at Beltane, or early May. That makes an incubation period of six months, which may be mythologically correct even if biologically unusual.

(AN) The boy is Rhiannon's son, but he appears at the place and time where the colt should have appeared because his mother has become Epona, the mare-goddess.

(AO) Teyrnon and his wife looking after the boy, even though he is not their own son, is a paradigm of the common practice of fosterage, discussed in Chapter Three (page 79).

(AP) Gwri is related to 'gwr', meaning man or husband. 'Gwri Golt Adwyn' means 'Gwri of the Shining Hair' – very fair hair was greatly admired, and limewashing to whiten the hair was common practice, for men as well as women. 'Gwalchmei Gwyn' means 'White May-hawk'. Both names eventually merged into the ancient Brythonic name Gawan, later spelled Gawen or Gawain. Gawan is the name of my own son. (It is a pure accident – or one of the goddess's jokes – that my arbitrarily chosen method of annotation should have generated 'AP', the Brythonic for son, precisely when I am discussing my own son's name.)

(AQ) Once Rhiannon is allowed to recognize her son, she gives him the name 'Pryderi', which means thought, care, anxiety or concern. The generally accepted interpretation of the name is that it represents all the worry Rhiannon had to endure before her son was returned to her, but it may also refer more widely to all the cares and vicissitudes of life which mortals have to endure before they are welcomed to the eternal joys of the apple orchard.

What is immediately noticeable and remarkable about this story, certainly by comparison with any legend from classical mythology, is how dominant and significant a role is played by the female protagonist, Rhiannon. While she is constrained to accept certain vicissitudes because honour and the 'fitness of things' demand it (even though it was Pwyll's stupidity which caused the difficulty), and to undergo a humiliating penance for a crime which she did not in fact commit, it is her machinations and devices, and above all her divine power to work the horse magic of Gwri's extraordinary reappearance, which bring the tale to a satisfactory conclusion. The power in this story lies with Rhiannon, the goddess.

Going line by line through the Rhiannon story was rather laborious, but I hope the effort will have helped convince the reader that there is a discernible mythographic pattern behind the great Celtic festivals and the legends of the deities with whom they are associated.

Midwinter

Now we cross the threshold of midwinter, and the mystery of menstruation, to go from the virgin-goddess to the mother-goddess, Brigit. She, too, appears in many guises and under different names. Brigit is Irish; her Brythonic counterpart is Arianrhod, although there was also a strong cult in the north of mainland Britain devoted to her in the name Brigantia. Her classical counterparts are Hera and Juno. In the time of the early tribal Celts, the sun rose in the constellation of Aquarius at Imbolc. The constellation should represent a ewe giving milk to a lamb, or a mother breast-feeding her baby; instead, we find Aquarius, a man carrying water, another anomaly, which may suggest that the constellation was given a different attribution by the Celts which is now lost to us. The mythographically more appropriate constellation of Cygnus, as was mentioned when discussing Caer or Rhiannon, was high in the sky and close to the Sun, but during the day, and it was therefore invisible.

Brigit is frequently depicted as the three goddesses, or aspects of the single goddess – virgin, mother and crone – in one. Her name means 'the shining one' ('breo' in Irish is a firebrand or torch, and 'breoch' means glowing), and she is associated with the colour white. She is, in fact, the White Goddess made famous by Robert Graves's book of the same name. She is sometimes called Alba (the white one), from which was derived the name Albion, an archaic alternative name for England. In the Celtic languages, the name Alba now refers to Scotland.

Her primary role was goddess of fertility, but she was also the divinity of healing, of craftwork, and of poetry (and let us be reminded that, to the Celts, poetry was not a minority occcupation for an intellectual élite, but rather a magical and powerful occupation closely associated with the religious notion of correct utterance). All cows, and their milk, were dedicated to Brigit, as well as ewes, and she naturally came to be associated with brewing beer, too: a partly Christianized (i.e., bowdlerized) medieval tale has her presiding over a brewing at Easter, in which she produces enough beer for 17 churches (i.e., parishes) from a single measure of malt.

Her name was elided to Bride in Ireland, and modern Irish now has a noun, 'brid', which is a literary term meaning (inappropriately) maiden or virgin. The English 'bride' is found in Old English ('bryd') but not in other Teutonic languages, which seems to confirm that this is another rare example of a word which the early English borrowed from the Celts. She had (still has) many holy wells and springs dedicated to her, which accounts for the many surviving variants of Brideswell in place names, in Britain as well as in Ireland. Her name is also supposedly contained in the Hebrides; Uist, Barra, Harris and Lewis were formerly connected in a single island known as 'Eileana Bride', meaning Bride's Island.[3]

Her association with fire and craft naturally makes her also the patroness of the smithy and metalwork, a craft of great magical importance to the Celts, since their weapons were given whatever strength they had at the time of their making. Weapons were given individual names, like dogs and horses. The most powerful of the smith's creations was a weapon of a very particular kind – the mirror, usually made of beaten and polished copper. Almost certainly then as now, the mirror was used for looking, or 'scrying', into inner or unrevealed truth, including events still to take place. The Celtic mirrors found by archaeologists are beautifully worked pieces, suggesting that they had great value. Brigit is sometimes depicted holding a mirror; unlike Venus (or Rhiannon or Caer), however, it is not herself she is looking at but rather the truth she is scrying.

Brigit is associated with the swan, like Caer, and is sometimes depicted carrying a white rod, which may be similar to the white hazel rods carried by Druids as symbols of their authority. The white rod symbolizes both the serpent and the swan, the bird with a serpent neck and a serpent hiss. Brigit's other totem animals are the cow, for obvious reasons, and the wolf, whose perhaps less obvious attributes are its faithful and devoted attachment to a single partner and its patient protectiveness as a parent.

Like the Virgin Mary in Christianity, Brigit's attributes as virgin are sometimes given greater prominence than her attributes as mother, although the theological reasons are quite different. In Roman Catholic Ireland, Brigit was soon transmogrified into a Christian saint, St Brigid or Bridget, who was widely venerated from very early times. She is supposed to have founded the nunnery at

Kildare, which seems to take its name from 'cill', meaning church, and 'darog' meaning oak.

Bride or Bridie dolls were small figures made of straw and decorated with flowers which were traditionally brought to the door by women, who would call out 'Let Bride come in!' The doll was set down in a cradle inside the house with a white wand of birch, broom or willow beside it to represent Bride's consort. The custom, Scottish in origin, has been renewed recently around Glastonbury in Somerset.[4]

From the mother, Brigit or Arianrhod, we move on to the son, Bel, and to the last of the four cross-quarter festivals, Beltane. We gave Bel a fair amount of attention in Chapter Six, so we can concentrate now just on the attributes which identify him mythographically as the son in the family of the four festivals. The zodiacal constellation at Beltane is Taurus – perfectly appropriate, since the bull (as in many other early religions) is the totem of the young male god and the virility he represents. A bull sacrifice is depicted on the Iron Age silver cauldron found at Gundestrup, in Jutland. Many bull figurines and statues have been found at Celtic archaeological sites, including Hallstatt. Perseus is the constellation above the ecliptic, and its appropriateness was mentioned earlier in the chapter.

Ancient heroes

Bel's counterparts in the vernacular texts are the great heroes. The most interesting of these are Ferghus mac Roich, the hero of the *Tain Bo Cuailnge*; Finn mac Cumhaill, the hero of the Fionn Cycle, the group of legends relating to the Fianna, a warrior band; and Cu Chulainn, mentioned already, who was Ferghus's foster-son, and, more than any other, represents the ideal and epitome of the Celtic warrior. Ferghus, Finn and Cu Chulainn are all Goidelic; there are counterpart heroes in the Brythonic tales, including Manawydan, who marries Rhiannon after Pwyll's death, but the British heroes look pale by comparison with the Irish.

Finn, or Fionn, derives his name from 'fionn', meaning white or fair-haired. His name is the same as the Brythonic Gwyn, although he is a god or hero of a different type. The Fianna, or warrior bands, gave their name in more recent times to the Fianna Eireann, a national insurrectionary scout body, and to the political party Fianna Fail (Warriors Together). The word 'fianna' was also used to describe the pieces, or soldiers, on the chess-like game board (see page 81) used by the early Celts: they were called 'fianna fichille'. The name Ferghus is related to 'fearchu', which means 'man-dog' literally, but it was used metaphorically to mean fierce warrior. Cu Chulainn also took his name from a dog (he is 'Culainn's hound'), as was mentioned on page 62.

There is no need to repeat the exercise with Rhiannon in full, but a few details from the tales of any one of these heroes will illustrate the underlying mythographic attributions.

Ferghus, for example, is so virile that it normally takes seven women to satisfy him. This is obviously the incarnation or counterpart of Bel, the young male god. He is the lover of Queen Medb as well as the husband of Flidais, goddess of deer and cattle. Not only did he require seven women, he also consumed seven pigs, seven deer, seven cows and seven vats of liquor at a sitting. Not surprisingly, he had the strength of 700 men. After a long and complicated story, too involved to repeat here, he meets his end at the hands of Medb's husband, who kills him while he is bathing in a pool with the queen. The pool, of course, is the lustral bath, the 'vat of water' we last saw with Lleu Llaw Gyffes balanced on its edge, about to receive Gronw's spear. (By this stage in the story, Ferghus has become the father-king. His successor to the role of son-king is his foster-son, Cu Chulainn.)

Cu Chulainn himself is the son of so many different father-god representatives that we are spoiled for choice. His father is Lugh (the archetype), or Conchobar by an incestuous liaison with his sister Deichtine (unusual birth circumstances, including incest, are often associated with Celtic heroes), or the human Sualtaimh (who seems to have been a Viking – obviously a late interpolation to the legend – since the related 'Sualainnis' means Swedish). Whoever his real father was, his birth was accompanied by the mysterious birth of two foals which later become his chariot horses, the Grey of Macha and the Black of Saingliu – this is an obvious parallel to the Brythonic story of Pryderi. In battle, Cu Chulainn is prone to a unique and terrifying madness during which his body undergoes terrible transformations and generates fierce heat. He has a number of bizarre attributes: his hair is in three colours; he has seven pupils in each eye, seven fingers on each hand and seven toes on each foot. Seven was clearly the number of the hero, perhaps of the god Bel himself. Like Pwyll, Cu Chulainn travels to the other world. He finally dies at the river ford (as we would expect) of Magh Muirtheimne. Instead of bathing in a lustral bath, we find an interesting variant: an unknown person (it is the goddess, of course) washes his armour in the river, as if washing clothes, which is the necessary ritual before his death.

Finn is reared by a Druidess (representative of the mother-goddess.) His weapons are kept in a bag made of craneskin. The crane was a totem of the goddess as crone (a crone-crane!) and the craneskin bag represents the womb (or anti-womb) to which men return at their death. The bard Finnegas (an obviously invented name) gives Finn a salmon to cook; Finn burns his finger on the hot fish, licks it, and is granted knowledge of all things, just like Gwion (i.e., Taliesin) in the Brythonic tale. As already described, it is Finn who holds the sharp spear against his cheek to resist the enchanting harp music of the goblin Aillen, thus saving the royal palace of Tara. Even with no knowledge of the story, the reader can probably guess where Finn dies: he attempts to leap across the River Boyne and fails in the attempt because he has broken a 'geis' against him.

A mythographic pattern?

There seems then to be a reasonably credible mythographic pattern of attributions to the four major festivals and their associated deities and constellations (see the illustration on page 188).

If the mythographic pattern of the four cross-quarter festivals is as described above, despite the few anomalies, then the mythographic attributions appropriate to the remaining four stations of the year, namely the solstices and equinoxes, are to some extent predetermined. We have far more evidence for the possible attributions at midsummer and midwinter, but it seems likely that the equinoxes were also recognized and celebrated in some fashion. The pattern described below does make mythographic sense, and the little information we have, particularly about midsummer and midwinter celebrations, seems to fit the pattern well enough.

Midsummer seems to have marked the transition from the old king to the new, a celebration of the transfer of divine power from the old god to the new. In human terms, the passage celebrated is the transition from boyhood to manhood. Similarly, midwinter appears to have celebrated the rebirth of the goddess as mother. Unlike the male god, who is repeatedly killed and replaced by his own son – a simple paradigm of generation succeeding generation in the endless round of life – the goddess is always the same, unchanging, eternal,

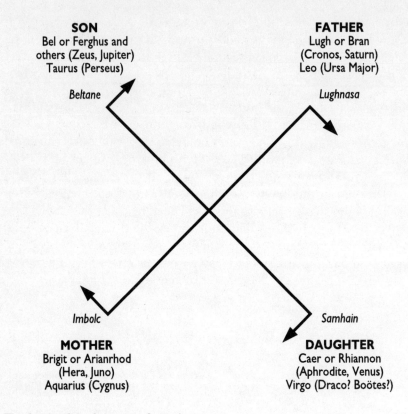

SON
Bel or Ferghus and
others (Zeus, Jupiter)
Taurus (Perseus)

Beltane

FATHER
Lugh or Bran
(Cronos, Saturn)
Leo (Ursa Major)

Lughnasa

Imbolc

MOTHER
Brigit or Arianrhod
(Hera, Juno)
Aquarius (Cygnus)

Samhain

DAUGHTER
Caer or Rhiannon
(Aphrodite, Venus)
Virgo (Draco? Boötes?)

The family of the four great festivals.

but manifest in different forms, especially in the three easily recognized forms of maiden, mother and crone. The midwinter festival, with its holy lights and sacred fires, seems to have celebrated the rekindling of motherhood in the goddess. In human terms, the passage celebrated is the menarche. Both stations may have been marked by appropriate initiation and puberty rites.

The equinoxes are not associated with any named festival, or hero, or even legend. The mythographic sense of each is implied by what lies either side. The autumn equinox lies between the celebration of the old father-god at Lughnasa and the celebration of the virgin goddess at Samhain. The mythographic import, therefore, should be about siring, about passing down characteristics; in the broadest sense about depositing a legacy which is unchanging, and which we might refer to as fate. By contrast, the spring equinox should be about bearing, about bringing forth into the world, and about

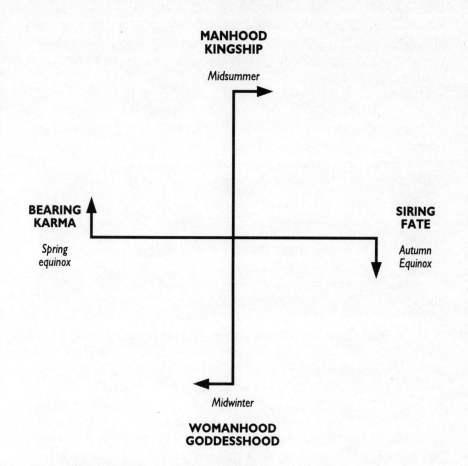

The attributions of the solstices and equinoxes.

exactly the opposite of fate – heroism, or the ability to bring about change by correct utterance and noble deeds. This makes good mythographic sense. As the year moves to its dead halfway point, midwinter, that which is fated, predetermined and invincible predominates. After midwinter, when the mystery of girl becomes woman becomes mother becomes goddess has taken place, the new son can be born, and he can challenge what is predetermined and, by his noble action, change it. He can grow through Beltane towards midsummer, at which point his strength will be sufficient to topple the old king and the whole cycle can begin again. The essence of the religious thought behind the pattern – however crude or alien it may seem – is that the mystery of motherhood in the goddess, a mystery that has its place in the most dead part of the year at midwinter, allows the child to be born, and in the child is the hope of eternity, of escaping the endless karmic cycle and entering the blessed orchard of Avallon.

However, honesty demands acknowledgment that, elegant and poetic (and truthful) as all this may be, there is very little hard evidence to support any of it, at least evidence in the modern, scientific sense. Nevertheless, let us follow the old advice, 'If the fool would persist in his folly, he would become wise', and summarize the solstitial and equinoctial attributions as shown in the illustration on page 189.

Start and finish of the Celtic year

Now we can return to the question: When did the Celtic year begin and end? The Roman year ended at midwinter, with the old father-god Saturn being celebrated at the Saturnalia, before the son-god (and sun-god) Jupiter took his father's place. If the Celts reckoned the New Year from the same place, it would be placing the male transition immediately between two major festivals dedicated to female aspects of the deity. That does not seem very likely. Why did the Romans choose that time of year, then? Partly, the answer resides in the Roman attitude towards death and the afterworld; death led to darkness, to the realms guarded by Pluto, to a sterile, fearful black Hell. Midwinter (which was comparatively mild in Rome by British standards) would still have seemed the appropriate time for the old god to die. To the Celts, however, the afterlife was lived in a permanent summer, a Land of the Ever Young, an apple orchard where the trees were always in fruit, so midsummer would be far more appropriate.

More importantly, placing the beginning and end of the year at midsummer puts it between the two great festivals dedicated to the son-god and the father-god, which seems a far more suitable place. Every midsummer, the old god (or king) dies and goes to reside in the permanent midsummer of the other world. His son takes his place and becomes the father-god (or king) in his stead. The marriage of the eternal to the diurnal, the kingdom to the king, is renewed. The year falls into two halves, each working towards the other and, indeed, bringing it about.

It seems certain that the Celtic year was divided into two halves

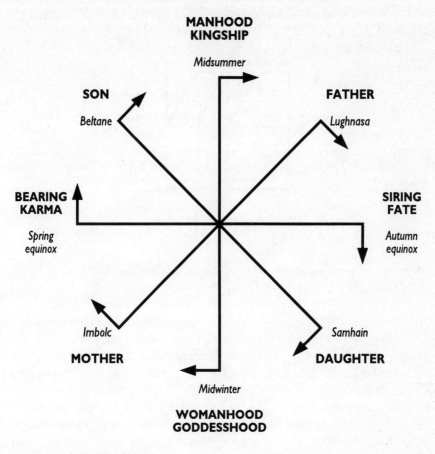

The cycle of the eight stations.

and it was reckoned either from midsummer to midsummer, or midwinter to midwinter. Samhain, now very widely presumed as the Celtic New Year by neo-pagan groups, seems a very implausible candidate for the position.

If we now combine the two sets of attributions discussed so far, we arrive at the complete cycle illustrated above.

Even if these mythographic attributions are not entirely correct, the basic pattern of the eight stations of celebration in the ancient Celtic year is well attested. The number itself is significant. The Pythagoreans (and, I believe, the Druids) were well aware that in three-dimensional reality, any three intersecting planes divide space into eight regions as shown on page 192.

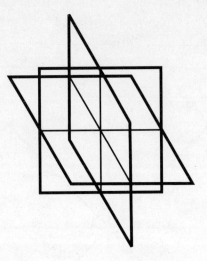

Any three intersecting planes in three dimensions divide the affected space into eight segments.

In other words, the dimensions of living reality, represented by the sacred number 3, the first real number, are encompassed in the number eight. It would be fitting for the year to be encompassed in the same number.

The question remaining is: if the pattern of eight stations or festivals is correct, how did the Druids reconcile it with the 365 days (plus a quarter) of the whole year? That is the topic of the next chapter.

Notes

1. Bromwich, R., *Trioedd Ynys Prydein; The Welsh Triads.*
2. Robert Graves, *The White Goddess.*
3. & 4. Kathy Jones, *The Ancient British Goddess.*

CHAPTER NINE

THE THIRTEEN MONTHS OF THE YEAR

OUR PRESENT WESTERN CALENDAR has now been adopted as standard throughout most of the world, at least for commercial purposes, although many nations and religions still maintain their own calendar traditions. The Western calendar was devised by Sosigenes, a Greek astronomer, and instituted by Julius Caesar. The year originally began with March, the month dedicated to Mars, the god of war, and the fifth and sixth months were known as Quintilis and Sextilis; but they were subsequently dedicated to Julius Caesar and Augustus Caesar, from which we obtain the modern July and August. It was Julius Caesar who adopted the suggestion, made centuries earlier by Eudoxus, that every fourth year should have an extra day to accommodate that awkward lump of a few hours which trailed behind the 365 full days. The system has worked passably well ever since, despite the turmoil over the loss of 11 days brought about by the change to the Gregorian calendar, mentioned on page 143, and the minor problem of remembering whether the year which turns the century is counted as a leap year or not (it is not, unless it is divisible by 400 as well as 100). The Gregorian calendar does have two disadvantages. The first is that different months have different lengths and we have to learn mnemonic rhymes to remember which are 30 days in length and which 31 (or 28 or 29). The second is that it is not perfectly accurate: every 3,320 years it generates one day too many, as was noted earlier.

Other significant calendar systems in the modern world are the Russian, the Muslim and the Jewish. The Russian calendar is a solar calendar, but it is more accurate than the Gregorian. The Russians designate all years as 365 days, apart from years which, when divided by 9, leave 2 or 6 as a remainder – these are 366 days in length. This complex but ingenious calendar generates an extra day only once in every 45,000 years. The Muslim calendar has 12 months of 29 days and 30 days alternately, making a year of 354 days – the Muslim New Year therefore 'retreats' 11 days in the Western calendar each year. The Jewish calendar attempts to reconcile lunar and solar months. Like the Muslim calendar, it has 12 months of alternate lengths, 29 days and 30 days. However, when the 'missing' solar days have accumulated sufficiently, a thirteenth month is added. This is very similar to the ancient Babylonian system.

There is no inherent reason why a year should have 12 months, apart from the obvious one that a year has 12 lunations. Once it has been decided that lunations are just too complicated for the purpose of maintaining an annual calendar (and by no means all nations have so decided, even yet), then any system which accurately groups and numbers solar days will suffice. Staying close to the observed 12 periods of lunation would be a bonus, but not strictly necessary. There could be 16 months in a year, or 6. The Paris revolutionaries of 1793 introduced a new calendar in which every week had 10 days (the tenth day was a day of rest) and four 10-day weeks made a month. Robespierre was executed on 9 Thermidor, Year 1 of the Revolution, by their calendar (28 July 1794 by ours). But even a year comprising 36 weeks (i.e., 9 months), with 10 days in each week, still leaves some days and hours to juggle with. There is no easy arithmetical solution to the problem.

It seems highly likely that the Druids chose 13 as the number to work with. It comes immediately after 8 in the Fibonacci series, and it is the sum of 8 and 5, both of which seem to have been especially important numbers: 8 because of the eight regions of three-dimensional space and the cycle of eight festivals, 5 because it was the number of the goddess herself, of the marriage of female (two) and male (three), and the number of the sacred pentagram within which the Golden Ratio or Divine Proportion is to be found. The ratio of months to stations of the year, or festivals, would be $13 \div 8$, in other words a simple approximation of the Golden Ratio itself. As we shall examine in the next chapter, it is also possible to deduce the mystic 19, the number of the Golden Year, from a 13-month calendar.

The most exhaustive and impressive account of the ancient Druidic calendar is to be found in Robert Graves's *The White Goddess*, which has already appeared frequently in the Notes of this book, and from which much of the material of this chapter is summarized. Graves's book is, as the Faber fly-note describes it: 'a prodigious, monstrous, stupefying, indescribable book . . . the outcome of vast reading and curious researches'. Put more simply, it is tough going for the average reader. Nevertheless, it is as important to our present topic as all the rest of the Bibliography put together, and the earnest reader who has not yet read the book, but remains in good wind for the present argument, should certainly attempt it. Graves gives immensely detailed and elaborate parcels of interlocking evidence to support his descriptions, which there is not space enough to repeat or summarize here, even if I were the man fit for the task, which I am not.

Graves describes two ancient Druidic alphabets, the Boibel-Loth and the Beth-Luis-Nion. The alphabets are not simply letters. Each letter signifies a tree or shrub, and each tree or shrub is associated with an array of mythological attributions. Moreover, the letters in their sequence represent or symbolize portions of time ('months') in the calendar.

The earliest alphabet, the Boibel-Loth, sometimes also known as the Babel-Lota, has fifteen consonants and five vowels, as follows:

B L F SS N H D T C CC M G NG Y R   A O U E I

Beth-Luis-Nion alphabet

The Beth-Luis-Nion, named after its first three letters, just as we call our modern alphabet the ABC, has only thirteen consonants, in a slightly different order, and the same five vowels, as follows:

B L N F S H D T C M G P R   A O U E I

After a long and densely argued explanation, Graves restores the Beth-Luis-Nion to fifteen consonants and adds a further two vowels, as follows:

B L N F S SS H D T C CC M G P R   AA A O U E I II

The four added letters are 'doubles' of their accompanying letter: SS (or Z) follows S, CC (or Q) follows C, AA (or long O) precedes A, and II (or Y) follows I. As will become clear in a moment, it is important that these added letters do not occupy space of their own; they sit in the places of their partner letters (or calendar dates) because their attributions apply to the same calendar period.

The significance of the Beth-Luis-Nion alphabet is that it contains within it a series of references which would only be known to the initiated (specifically Druidic initiates.) These references are of interest to our present purpose: firstly, because they adumbrate the mythological attributions we have already discussed and, secondly, because they clearly imply a calendar sequence of thirteen months. Graves's account pursues the cryptic references in prodigious detail, and then sets specific calendar dates for each of the letters (months). Greatly simplified, the references and allusions he identifies are as follows.

B is the letter Beth (all these letter names are Goidelic words), which means birch. It is identified as the tree of inception. Roman *lictors* carried birch rods at the installation of a new consul, which took place shortly after midwinter. Moreover, there were 12 lictors assigned to each consul, making 13 in all. In Scandinavia, birch trees coming into leaf signalled the start of the agricultural year.

L is the letter Luis, meaning rowan, also known as quickbeam, quicken and mountain ash. In Ireland, Druids lit fires of rowan wood to summon the spirits of the dead to assist warriors in battle. In the Irish romance of Fraoth, magical rowan berries healed and sustained the wounded and prolonged life. In the romance of Diarmuid and Grainne, the rowan berry, apple and red nut are all described as 'food of the gods', suggesting that there may have been a taboo against eating them, or that they were reserved for the Druidic priesthood themselves. The rowan berry, or more likely a cluster of rowan berries, is a possible contender for the role of *anguinum*, or serpent's egg, described in some detail in Chapter 4, pages 98–9.

N is the letter Nion, meaning ash. We have already discussed the importance to the Celts of ash for making spears and chariots, and in other construction. Supple but very strong, ash was also used for the frames of coracles and rowing oars. In Greece, the tree was sacred to Poseidon, god of the sea. In Ireland, timber from the sacred ash of Killura was carried as a charm against drowning. The great sacred tree of Norse mythology is the ash, Yggdrasill, closely associated with Woden (Wotan, Odin), whose British counterpart is the magician-god Gwydion. In British folklore, the ash is a tree of rebirth and regeneration: Gilbert White describes in his *History of Selborne* the practice of passing children through cleft pollard ashes as a cure for congenital hernia or rupture.

F is Fearn, meaning alder, the sacred tree of the Blessed Bran. The Brythonic spelling of Fearn is Gwern, a name which actually appears as a mythological character, Gwern, who is described as Bran's nephew. The tree was held in high regard by the Celts for the charcoal it produced. It was also used for conduits and pipes to channel water, being especially resistant to decay. For the same reason, it was used for the piles on which the earliest European houses were built, usually at the edge of lakes. This explains the description of Bran, that 'no house could contain him' – no house can contain the piles on which it is built. Twice Bran lays himself across stretches of water so that his armies may march over on his back: he is the epitome of piles and bridges made of alder timber. The tree stains reddish when cut, reminiscent of the shedding of blood. It also yields three important dye colours: red from the bark, green from the flowers and brown from the twigs. Graves suggests that Orpheus, the Greek totem god of the Orphic initiation undergone by Pythagoras, may have derived his name from the Greek *orphruoeis*, meaning growing on the river-bank, i.e., alder.

S is for Saille, meaning willow, or osier. It is dedicated to the goddess in her death aspect, as represented by Hecate, Circe, Persephone and others in Greece, and by Cerridwen, Morgana and others in British mythology. The willow is traditionally associated with witchcraft; so strongly in fact, that the words wicker (meaning willow reed or osier), wicked and witch are all etymologically related. Called *helice* in Greek, it gave its name to Helicon, the abode of the Muses. 'Helygenn' is the Cornish for willow, found in the widespread Cornish personal name Penhaligon. The Goidelic 'saille' is related to the Latin name *salix*. The alleged Druidical fire sacrifices, which Strabo and Caesar both describe, were supposed to have imprisoned their victims in a huge figure, or *kolosson*, made of wickerwork. Pliny tells us that a willow tree grew outside the Cretan cave where Zeus was born. Traditional British folklore, as in the well-known song 'All around my hat I will wear the green willow', commemorates willow's ancient significance as a symbol of the rejected or disappointed lover – it was originally intended as a charm and invocation to the goddess. Its leaves and bark yield salicylic acid, a principal constituent of aspirin, and they were infused since earliest times to relieve cramps, especially menstrual cramps, and other pain. The tree was sacred to poets, as well as to the death goddess.

H is for (H) uath, the hawthorn, also called whitethorn and may. It is an unlucky tree. In the Irish Brehon laws it is also called 'sceith', which seems related to the Indo-European root 'skeud-', from which shoot, shut and scathe are derived. In Old Norse, *skuta* meant shooting words, i.e., mockery or satire, from which is derived the word shout.[1] The Greek goddess Maia, after whom the month of May is named, was the 'maia', meaning grandmother or dame, whose son Hermes led souls to Hell. May was a purification month in Rome, when temples were swept and images refurbished. It was considered unlucky to marry in May. In the British myths, the hawthorn is also associated with chastity. It appears personified as Yspaddaden Pencawr ('cawr' means giant), the father of Olwen, whose name means white track. In other words, hawthorn is associated with the father-god of the daughter-virgin-goddess, who presents every obstacle he can to his daughter's loss of virginity. In the romance of Culhwch and Olwen, Yspaddaden sets Culhwch 13 impossible treasures to be secured as dowry, including the comb from the back of Twrch Trwyth, the magical sacred boar.

D is Duir, meaning oak. The word is very similar in Goidelic and Brythonic, and the word Druid is almost certainly derived from it (see Chapter One, page 32). It is the totem tree of the son-god, the maker of thunder, in all his manifestations – Zeus (and Herakles) in Greece, Jupiter (and Hercules) in Rome, Thor in Scandinavia, Bel (and a legion of heroes, including Finn, Ferghus and Cu Chulainn) in Britain and Gaul. It is common knowledge that the oak was specially venerated by the early Celts. There were also oak cults in ancient Greece and Libya. Graves suggests that the oak cult came to Britain via the Baltic somewhere between 1600 and 1400 BC, (i.e., at least 500 years before the earliest Celtic incursions). In other words, the Celts inherited the oak cult; they did not devise it.

T stands for Tinne, meaning holly. The Brythonic word is 'kelynn'. It is the totem tree of the oak-god's twin (or father), the holly-god or Green Knight, represented by Bran in the British tradition and by Cronos in Greece and Saturn in Rome. He is the god of the waning half of the year, while his brother-son Bel is the god of the waxing half of the year. When Christian mythology began subsuming aspects of earlier pagan mythology, St John the Baptist (beheaded at midsummer, the day of transition between the oak-king and holly-king) became identified with the oak, which in turn led to the identification of Jesus with the oak's successor, holly – this is the origin of the line of the carol 'The Holly and the Ivy':

Of all the trees that are in the wood,
The Holly bears the crown.

In Middle English, the word for holly was spelled 'holi', derived from Old English 'holen'. The word for holy was also spelled 'holi', derived from Old English 'halig'. There has been an association of holly with holy ever since. A further association with Jesus is the shape of the letter itself. The Hebrew *Tav* (last letter of that alphabet), the Greek *Tau* and our letter T all graphically represent the cross of the Crucifixion.

C is for Coll, meaning hazel. In Celtic mythology it is always associated with wisdom. Over Connla's Well, near Tipperary, hung the nine hazels of poetic art – their nuts fed salmon swimming in the pool (the salmon also being associated with wisdom, or, more precisely, 'gnosis', or mystic wisdom). Then as now, hazel was the favoured wood for making divining rods. The letter was used by the Bards to signify the number 9, a highly regarded number because it was sacred three times three.[2] Keating's *History of Ireland* gives the names of the three brother gods who first ruled Ireland as Mac Ceacht (son of the plough), Mac Greine (son of the sun) and Mac Coll or Mac Cool (son of the hazel).[3] White hazel wands were carried by Druids as symbols of their authority. Fionn uses a shield made of hazel which gives off poisonous vapours and kills thousands of the enemy; it represents the power of the Druidic curse or satiric utterance. The tree was also called 'bile ratha' in Irish, meaning 'tree of the rath' – the 'rath' was the sacred abode of the 'sidhe', or spirits.

M is the letter called Muin, meaning vine. The vine is not native to Britain, but it was important in Mediterranean mythology, principally because it is the source of wine. The vine does figure in British art of the Bronze Age onward, which suggests that its mythology was understood, and to some extent subsumed, in Druidic culture. Wine was imported from earliest times, stored in large clay jars, or *amphorae*. Graves suggests that the blackberry took the vine's place in the British context: he cites Breton and Welsh taboos against eating blackberries, despite the fact that the fruit is very sweet and nourishing. A folk superstition persists in Devon and Cornwall that blackberries are unfit to eat after September because 'the Devil is in them'. Blackberries contain so much natural sugar that they ferment spontaneously, and they make a potent and convincing red wine.

G is for Gort, meaning ivy. The vine and the ivy share the characteristic of growing spirally. Both are associated with resurrection. Ivy leaves, which are toxic, may have been chewed for their hallucinatory effects. Both holly and ivy are associated with the holly-god, Bran, Cronos or Saturn, whose demise was celebrated by the Romans at the Saturnalia, or midwinter festival. His club is made of holly, and his sacred bird the gold-crested wren, nests in ivy, which explains why they are linked in the carol 'The Holly and the Ivy', mentioned earlier.

P is for Peith, meaning water-elder, also called whitten or guelder-rose. Peith is not the original letter. It was substituted for NG (the nasal g at the back of the throat, as in the French *sang*, or the sound in a German's pronunciation of finger). The name of the letter is Ngetal, which means reed. In Egyptian and Mediterranean mythology, the reed symbolized royalty. A reed was pushed in Jesus's hand when he was mockingly robed in purple. The substitution of P is Brythonic in origin. The sounds represented by p and b are very similar, and the letters are often confused in Welsh and Cornish medieval texts, as in the word for son, which may be found written as 'mab', 'map', 'ab' or 'ap'. The sounds of p, b, f and v are produced by very similar positions in the mouth and are confused in many languages, not just the Brythonic. P and ng are quite different sounds, however, so this was a deliberate substitution, not an accident of pronunciation. Graves does not explain the substitution, other than to say that the original NG was 'of no literary use to the Brythons'. It does, however, represent a sound found commonly in Welsh, particularly as a result of the process (common to all the Celtic languages) of initial consonantal mutation. Cat, for example, is 'cath' in Welsh, but my cat is 'fy nghath'.

The thirteenth and last consonant is R for Ruis, which means elder. Although the flowers and bark of the elder yield therapeutic substances, and elder flowers and elder berries make good wine, the tree has a reputation for evil. It is associated with witchcraft and death, along with the yew, cypress and nightshade. In Langland's *Piers Plowman*, it is an elder tree on which Judas Iscariot hangs himself. The superstition that the number 13 is unlucky is supposedly derived from the presence of thirteen people at the Last Supper, the thirteenth being Christ's betrayer, but it may also be related to the thirteenth letter or tree, the evil elder.

Before moving on to the vowels, we need to go back to the 'doubled' consonants, SS or Z and CC or Q. S stands for Saille, or the willow, wicker or osier. Its double, SS or Z, represents the blackthorn, or sloe. The tree was called *bellicum* by the Romans, which seems to be related to *bellum*, meaning war. There is a long-held belief that blackthorn was the stock timber for the Irish 'shillelagh', or fighting club, although Graves suggests that these were more usually made of oak. The fruit or sloe, after which the whole tree is sometimes named, is small and very sour. It is used nowadays to flavour gin, but it would have been comparatively useless nutritionally or medicinally to the early Celts. The words sloe and slay are etymologically related, and the blackthorn became associated in English folklore with the crown of thorns placed on Christ's head at the Crucifixion – a good deal of the tree's supposed evil may derive from this attribution.

The double of C for Coll, is CC or Q for Quert, meaning apple. The Brythonic languages do not use the letter Q, and the double CC might better be represented as CW or KW, which are the combinations used (in Welsh and Cornish or Breton respectively) to convey the intended sound. The apple is greatly significant in Celtic mythology. Above all, it symbolizes eternal life, since paradise or the other world is an apple orchard, called Avallon ('aval' is the Brythonic for apple). The fruit simultaneously quenches thirst and satisfies hunger. Even though the fruit would have been smaller and more sour in the early Celtic period, at least by comparison with the highly developed fruit we now take for granted in our supermarkets, it was still very highly regarded. A meal of hazel nuts and apple would have been satisfying nutritionally, aesthetically and spiritually to the early Celts. There may have been a partial taboo against eating the fruit, which may have been reserved for royalty, or for the priesthood. Eating too many apples too quickly, as most children discover at some stage, can lead to a very unpleasant stomach-ache, which would make reinforcing such a taboo an easy matter. However, apples appear in such abundance, are so easily stored and dried, and could so easily have been cooked and sweetened with honey or berries, that it seems equally possible that they formed a major part of the diet for the whole tribe, their religious significance notwithstanding. Some varieties of apple deliver fruit very late in the autumn or early winter – indeed, some varieties actually soften and improve their flavour after a sharp frost – so the timing of their addition to the food store would have been very propitious. As a child, I helped my father pick Cox's Pippins from the tree in our garden in October or even November, to put away ready for Christmas. We wrapped each apple in paper individually, then stored them away from the light in wooden drawers. Although one or two went bad, the bulk of the crop lasted well into February or even March, and the longer they stayed in storage, the sweeter and fuller was their flavour, despite a little shrinkage and wrinkling of the skin. Apple ferments very easily, and the long tradition of cider drinking in the west of England, particularly Devon and Somerset, and in Cornwall, perhaps suggests that cider was popular with the early Celts, too.

The five vowels (seven in the complete restoration) are also associated with trees. Moreover, the vowels are charged with special significance: they emerge from the body without (apparent) modification by the mouth, and therefore seem closer to whatever truth lies within. In many religions, including Judaism, the mystic and ineffable name of God is formed solely from vowels. None of the consonants has any significance until it is combined with one or more vowels. Some languages omit vowels in writing.

A in the Druidic alphabet stands for Ailm, which means silver fir. In Greece, the tree was sacred to Artemis. Throughout northern Europe, it is associated with childbirth. The same Old Irish word 'ailm' was also used for palm, which is the Middle Eastern tree also associated with childbirth – revered in Egypt, Babylonia and throughout Arabia, it also gave its name, through the epithet *phoenix*, meaning bloody, to Phoenicia, and to the mythical creature, the phoenix, which dies in a conflagration of palm leaves and is born again of its own ashes, symbolizing rebirth or resurrection. 'Ailm' is the Tree of Life in the story of the Garden of Eden. The Hebrew name is *Tamar*, which is found in Britain as the name of the river which now separates Cornwall from Devon, supposedly named after a Brythonic goddess, Tamara. The famous Trojan horse was made of the timber of the silver fir, since it was dedicated to Athene, and because it was in the sacred form of the mother-goddess as a horse, represented in Britain and Gaul by the goddess Epona.

O stands for Onn, which means furze or gorse. Known in Brythonic as 'eythin', this prickly bush with its bright golden flowers typifies the sun at the vernal equinox. A Gaulish goddess, Onniona, takes her name from Onn (gorse) and Nion (the ash tree). Gorse was highly regarded by the early Celts for its practical value in controlling livestock. Old, hardy plants make an impenetrable hedge. Even full-grown cattle will not venture through thick gorse. It is still widely planted (or allowed to grow) on top of Cornish stone walls (called 'hedges'). The timber burns with a ferocious flame, and it was the standard fuel for baking ovens for centuries. In Wales, one variety was known as 'eithen ffrennig', or French gorse, which may have been an imported variety from very early times – it is apparently better and more tender fodder for animals, but less hardy than native British gorse. When the plants are burned in the field, they recover and send out new growth very quickly – sheep are very fond of these new shoots. The flower is a brilliant, full yellow in colour, and gives off a faint but pleasant scent, a little like coconut. They are often the first flowers visited by bees, and honey from gorse-fed bees is lighter, sweeter and more delicate than clover honey. In Wales, a sprig of gorse is considered 'good against witches', and in Cornwall, the gorse is almost a national emblem – only *Erica vagans*, the Cornish heather, is more important.

Heather is the plant of the third vowel, U or Ura. It also is associated with bees, and with midsummer. It was sacred to the Roman goddess Venus Erycina, the second part of her name being derived from the Greek name for heather, *ereice*. Another double-barrelled Gaulish goddess is Uroica, whose name seems to have been formed from Ura and the Latinized *erica*.

E is Eadha, meaning aspen, also known as white poplar. It is the tree of old age. Its leaves are distinctively lighter on the underside than above – in a breeze, it 'turns white'.

I is for Idho, meaning yew. In all European cultures, the yew is the tree of death. When black bulls were sacrificed to Hecate in Rome, they were wreathed with yew. A Breton legend is that the roots of yews planted in churchyards seek out the mouths of the dead buried there. The toxicity of the tree is disputed. The Latin name *taxus* seems related to Greek *toxicon*, the poison smeared on arrows (*toxon* is Greek for bow), but John Evelyn in his *Silva* (1662) claimed that horses and cattle could nibble yew leaves without ill effect. It is poison from the yew which Claudius pours into the elder Hamlet's ear while he sleeps. Yew matures very slowly, but it is immensely durable when seasoned and polished.

The mythology of the sequence of vowels is very obvious. It runs around the year from birth to death, starting at the point of the female mystery, namely midwinter (see the illustration on page 204).

The two doubled or additional vowels are AA and II. Graves gives a very long and detailed explanation of the significance of these extra vowels, which is related to the sacred name of God. He identifies the sequence AA A O U E I II with the Roman letter sequence J I E V O A O which leads in turn to J E H U O V A O and the mystic name, the 'holy unspeakable name of God', Jehovah, with all its associated

Ura; heather;
high summer
U
Midsummer

Onn; gorse;
spring
O

Eadha; aspen;
old age
E

Midwinter

A
Ailm; silver fir;
birth

I
Idho; yew;
death

The round of vowels.

derivations and connotations.[4] The revised vowel sequence is seven letters long, which Graves relates to the days of the week. The trees assigned to these double letters are the palm for AA (already mentioned) and the mistletoe, already discussed, for II. The AA is also long O, or Omega in Greek, which, although it is the last letter of that alphabet, is often associated with the first letter, Alpha. The doubled I is II, or J, pronounced Y. It is fairly widely known that a single character stood for I and J in both Latin and Greek.

The doubled letters SS and CC mark the upper 'corners' of the alphabet (or year) as it would be written in the secret Ogham script. AA and II would occupy the corresponding lower corners, but they do not have Ogham equivalents. Ogham was known and used by the Druids. It is a very simple script, formed by cutting straight or angled incisions across the corner of a surface – it is especially convenient for marking cut timber or square-hewn stone. Graves's reconstruction of the Ogham alphabet is shown in the illustration on page 205.

Now we can begin to see the cycle of the year represented figuratively in the alphabet. The vowels, as explained above, do not occupy spaces, or 'months', of their own: they form a pentangle which encompasses the whole year. Similarly, the doubled letters SS and CC, although they have Ogham equivalents, are reduplications of their initial letter and they are ascribed to the same month.

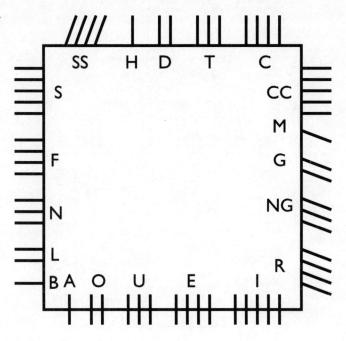

The Ogham alphabet.

Graves assumes midwinter as the beginning of the year (or very close to it; he calls 24 December the first day). Each letter represents a month of 28 days. There are, therefore, 13 months, ending on 22 December. The day between the end of the year and the beginning of the next is 23 December, the 'day' of the 'year and a day'. Graves correlates the mythographic attributions of each of the letter months with the seasons of the year, as they fall in sequence, and we shall see shortly that many of the attributions agree exactly with what I postulated in the previous chapters. Some of the attributions, however, seem to be quite clearly misplaced, and realigning those will be the subject matter of our final chapter. In the meantime, the Beth-Luis-Nion alphabet year, with the dates ascribed by Graves, is illustrated on page 206.

With that sequence visually established, it would be simpler to recapitulate the progression of months in tabular form (see the table on page 207) to check off the correspondence between the mythological associations ascribed by Graves to the letter months.

If we begin by looking at the four major festivals discussed at length in Chapters Six and Eight, we see some correspondences

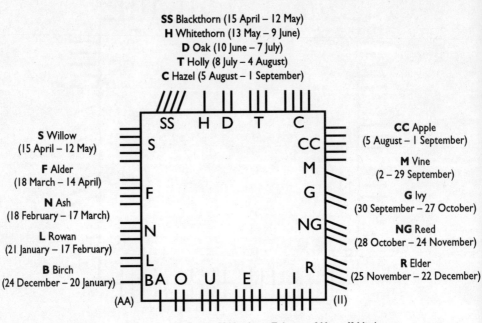

The Beth-Luis-Nion alphabet year, according to Robert Graves.

which apparently make good sense for at least three of them: Beltane, Lughnasa and Samhain.

According to Graves's allocation of the months, Beltane falls in the *S* and *SS* month, ascribed to Saille the willow and to Straif the blackthorn. Although the willow is principally associated with the goddess in her death aspect, it is also associated with poets, aspirants to divine knowledge, acolytes in general – it is a fitting tree for Bel the virgin son aspiring to knowledge of his mother-goddess. Even more appropriate is the association with blackthorn, the tree of SS or Z. It is the warrior's tree.

Lughnasa falls in the holly month, which, again, seems absolutely appropriate. Lugh, or Lleu Llaw Gyffes, or Bendigeidfran, or Bran the Blessed, are all representations of the holly-god, Bel's brother and father, who, like Cronos and Saturn in classical mythology, yields to his conquering son and is commemorated in death.

Samhain falls in Ngetal, the reed month, also called Peith, or the month of the water-elder. The association with Rhiannon, the virgin goddess, is difficult to discern, but there is a correspondence between

The Beth-Luis-Nion calendar correspondences, according to Robert Graves.

24 December – 20 January	B	Birch	
21 January – 17 February	L	Rowan	Imbolc
18 February – 17 March	N	Ash	
18 March – 14 April	F	Alder	Spring equinox
15 April – 12 May	S	Willow	Beltane
	SS	Blackthorn	
13 May – 9 June	H	Whitethorn	
10 June – 7 July	D	Oak	Midsummer solstice
8 July – 4 August	T	Holly	Lughnasa
5 August – 1 September	C	Hazel	
	CC	Apple	
2 September – 29 September	M	Vine	Autumn equinox
30 September – 27 October	G	Ivy	
28 October – 24 November	NG	Reed	Samhain
25 November – 22 December	R	Elder	Midwinter solstice
23 December		'and a day'	

the warning sound of roaring waters, which Graves describes as represented by Ngetal, the dismal whistling of the wind through winter reed-beds, and the hooting of Rhiannon's bird, the owl, often associated with death. In Ireland, the roaring of the sea was held to be prophetic of a royal death. In *The Romance of Taliesin*, a complex and highly allusive Welsh poem which Graves reconstructs as part of his argument to explain the Beth-Luis-Nion, he translates the Ngetal line as 'I have been a wave breaking on the beach', or 'I am a threatening noise of the sea.'

For the festival of Imbolc, however, Graves's allocation of dates seems to produce a correspondence which is clearly wrong. We would expect a tree associated with motherhood, child-bearing, general fecundity in nature. Instead, we are given Luis for L, or the rowan tree, which is clearly associated with the dead. It was rowan wood which was burned to summon the spirits of the dead to battle. Its berries were reputed to heal wounds and sustain life, but the correspondence with what we have already understood Imbolc to represent, the festival of mother's milk, seems very doubtful.

When we look at the other four stations, the solstices and the equinoxes, other anomalies appear. Midsummer falls right in the middle of the oak month, which would put Bel in sole charge of the transition and leave Bran no role to play. The autumn equinox would be dedicated to Muin, or the vine (probably the blackberry in the British context), which seems roughly appropriate in terms of the right fruit for the right season, but it does not generate any more specifically appropriate correspondences. The real midwinter solstice would fall in Ruis, for elder, the month of evil and death, with no correspondence to the menarche and the female mystery, although Graves presumably means us to take 23 December as midwinter, despite its being two days adrift. The spring equinox falls in Fearn month, the month of the alder, a tree very closely identified with Bran. Why Bran should appear at all in this half of the year is not entirely clear. Fearn month does immediately precede Saille month, the month of Bel's birth – perhaps Bran is a ghost prefiguring his son's appearance. If Bel is conceived at Imbolc and born at Beltane, or born at Imbolc and brought to maturity at Beltane – either way makes no difference – it is not wholly inappropriate that the image of his father should intercede between the two events.

But the anomalies remain. The attempt to resolve them, and in so doing to describe the Golden Year and draw together the different mythographic elements we have already discussed, is the subject of the next and final chapter.

Notes

1. Calvert Watkins, 'Indo-European Roots', appendix to *The American Heritage Dictionary of the English Language*, third edition, 1992.
2. The Hebrew alphabet similarly represents numbers as well as letters.
3. This name should not be confused with Mac Cumhail, as in Finn Mac Cumhail, which is pronounced very similarly.
4. Chapter Sixteen of *The White Goddess*, especially pp 285–288.

CHAPTER TEN

THE GOLDEN YEAR

AS ALREADY MENTIONED in Chapter One, it was a contemporary of Pythagoras, the sixth-century BC historian Hecateus, who described the Hyperboreans (i.e., Britons) living on an island beyond the North Wind, 'of a happy temperature, rich in soil and fruitful in everything, yielding its produce twice in the year.' Hecateus wrote about the 'remarkable temple, of a round form, adorned with many consecrated gifts', which we reasonably assume must indicate Stonehenge. He discussed the close association between the natives of the island and the Greeks, telling us that the Greek philosophers visited Britain and, in return, one Abaris (presumably a Druid or Archdruid) visited Greece. Finally, 500 years before Caesar mentioned the 19 years of study required to become a Druid, he wrote this:

> It is also said that in this island the Moon appears very near to the Earth, that certain eminences of a terrestrial form are plainly seen in it, that Apollo visits the island once in a course of nineteen years, in which period the stars complete their revolutions, and that for this reason the Greeks distinguish the cycle of nineteen years by the name of the 'great year'. During the season of his appearance the god plays upon the harp and dances every night, from the vernal equinox until the rising of the Pleiades, pleased with his own success.[1]

The case for closely identifying Druidism with Pythagoreanism was presented in Chapter Seven. As Graves points out, the 19-year cycle was not understood and adopted in Greece until at least a century after Hecateus's time. If the quotation is accepted as of genuine provenance, then Hecateus is describing something which was a great and esoteric mystery in his own time. Moreover, he is confirming our earlier suggestion that number mystery was central to Druidism as well as to Pythagoreanism; indeed that one was learned from the other.

The number 19 is prime, and therefore would have had special significance to Pythagoreans. All prime numbers were specially venerated, and much of Pythagorean mathematics is concerned with calculating primes and their relationships. Indivisible (other than by themselves and one), prime numbers are the paradigm of the early Greek notion of the *atoma*, or indivisible entity, from which our word atom is derived. The eighteenth-century mathematician, Leonhard Euler, devised the formula $n^2 + n + 41$ for generating prime numbers. It works splendidly for a while: $0^2 + 0 + 41 = 41$; $1^2 + 1 + 41 = 43$; $2^2 + 2 + 41 = 47$; etc. In fact it reaches $39^2 + 39 + 41 = 1,601$ (which is prime), but with 40 the formula suddenly fails, since $40^2 + 40 + 41 = 1,681$, which is not prime. Prime numbers are still used today as the basis for the sophisticated encoding and decoding used in military and secret service operations.[2]

The number 19 was certainly important to the Celts. Almost all the stone circles in Cornwall have 19 stones. The number is so easily generated from the 13-month calendar that it is almost evidence in itself that the Druids must have calculated the year in that way: 13 letter days for each month, plus the unnamed eternal day at midsummer (or midwinter, according to Graves), plus the five vowels sacred to the goddess and stationed around the year, equals 19. (The two sets of doubled consonants and doubled vowels take up no calendar space and do not affect the calculation.) The stone circles and alignments erected by the Celts' predecessors were not always built to astronomical alignments; several were clearly aligned with mountains, outlying stones or other features of local topography. However, some – notably Stonehenge – were clearly designed with astronomical observation in mind. We have every reason to believe that the Celts absorbed knowledge not only from the Greeks (and perhaps the Persians and Egyptians, too), but also from the peoples who preceded them in Gaul and, especially, in Britain.

Aubrey Burl, beginning with a description of earliest neolithic burials in wedge-graves and ending with the great stone ring of Cashelkeelty 3,000 years later, eloquently describes the continuity forward into the Celtic period and beyond:

> Even with the abandonment of the uplands as the climate worsened and when the megalithic tradition had faded some of the customs endured. The occasions of the Celtic festivals demanded the keeping of a calendar. And, in the iron age, temples and shrines at Heathrow, Brigstock, Winchester and Danebury faced eastwards. At South

Cadbury the porched shrine also faced east and outside its verandah pits with offerings of sacrificed animals lay in line with the equinoctial sunrise . . .. Visitors to these ancient places today often sense the mysteries contained within the stones but it is our ignorance, not the forgotten powers of a psychic world, that causes our feeling of loss. From the first neolithic tomb to the last iron age temple the stones were not mysteries to the people who raised them.[3]

The astronomical cycle represented by the frequent reference to the period of 19 years is the time period required for the apparent motions of the sun and stars and the sequence of lunations to coincide: in other words the period of time it takes for the solar calendar and lunar calendar to become reconciled momentarily, before diverging again. The exact period is 18.61 years, or 6,797 days.

So far, we have consistently used 21 March, 21 June, 21 September and 21 December as the dates of the vernal equinox, midsummer solstice, autumnal equinox and midwinter solstice, respectively. In fact, the Earth does not necessarily reach these solstitial and equinoctial points precisely on these dates, because the eccentricity of the Earth's orbit and the angle of 10° between the line of the solstices and the major axis of the Earth's orbital ellipse generate slightly different periods of time between each transit: in the Northern Hemisphere, spring is 92.9 days, summer 93.7 days, autumn 89.6 days and winter 89 days.[4] So, the spring equinox may happen to fall on 20 March or 21 March, midsummer on 21 June or 22 June, and so on.

I think it is reasonable to assume that the smallest unit of time known to the early tribal Celts was the day, meaning a night followed by a day. There are many ancient forms of clock, using candles, dripping water or other devices to divide the day into hours or shorter periods, but there is no evidence to suggest that the early Celts were as sophisticated in their timekeeping. Therefore, we can probably assume that the Celts (in fact, the Druids, who probably performed such calculations) were not concerned with the small time differences on which modern calendars and ephemerides are based. Where we would place an 11.59 pm equinox on 20 March and a 12.01 am equinox on 21 March, the Druids would presumably have had no instruments precise enough to know the difference, and so they would have stuck with 21 March (or the twenty-first day of the month of alder).

That accuracy would have been sufficient for observation of the difference in extreme risings of the southern full moon over the 18.61 period of the Golden Year. The risings would be observable against features of topography, like hills or rocks, or they could be marked by standing stones. The careful and very patient observer would see, after almost 19 years, a complete cycle in which the midwinter full moon would appear to rise each year from a point slightly further north on the horizon than its rising point the previous year. After almost nine years, the most northerly, or minor, point of this cycle would be reached. For the next nine years or so, the midwinter full moon would appear to rise at progressively more southerly points, until, after almost 19 years, it would reach the most southerly, or major, point and the cycle would begin again (see the illustration below).

As Aubrey Burl points out, it would have taken years of observations, possibly lasting over several generations, for the cycle to be observed fully and accurately. Such dedication would have required a strong sense of purpose, almost certainly related to a religious perception of the cosmos, coupled with a highly disciplined and effective system of learning and transmitting information from generation to generation. We associate both qualities very strongly

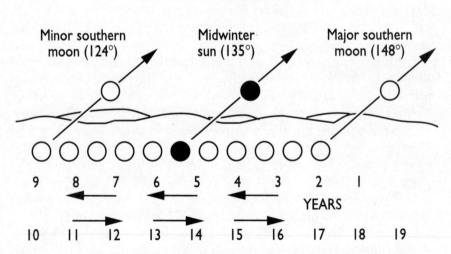

South-eastern horizon at 55° north

Minor southern moon (124°) Midwinter sun (135°) Major southern moon (148°)

YEARS

The 18.61-year lunar cycle (adapted from Aubrey Burl, *Prehistoric Astronomy and Ritual*).

with Druidic practice. The question remains moot concerning the extent to which, and the mechanisms by which, the knowledge accrued by the megalith builders who preceded the Celts in Britain may or may not have been handed down to them.

The system of reckoning 13 months of 28 days each also comes very close to yielding an accurate estimation of the Golden Year. If we reckon the period as 18.61 years in our calendar, and 18 years and 8 months in our suggested Celtic calendar, we find that the calculations are accurate to within three days:

Modern reckoning		Suggested early Celtic reckoning	
18 times 365 =	6570	18 times 13 times 28 =	6552
0.61 times 365 =	223	18 midsummer days =	18
Leap year days =	4	8 months of 28 days =	224
Total	6797		6794

There are many even finer astronomical observations available to us today – for example, the steady progress of the celestial pole as the Earth's axis moves, which takes about 26,000 years to complete – but observation of the Golden Year is still a delicate and sophisticated astronomical skill. The Pythagorean and Druidic reverence for the number 19, and specifically the requirement of 19 years' training for the Druidic priesthood, suggest strongly that not only did the Druids observe and recognize the Golden Year, but that they also held it representative of some great cosmic cycle to which their own studies and mysteries should be attuned.

The Coligny Calendar (described on pages 141–2) is the only hard evidence we have that the early tribal Celts had any kind of calendar at all. But, as Graves suggests, it seems a crude and possibly unrepresentative artefact. As I hope is now more clear, there is an abundance of inferential evidence to be drawn from Celtic history, art and mythology, as well as the classical and vernacular sources, which suggests that the Druids maintained effective astronomical observations and a sophisticated, esoteric calendar, both of the year and the greater cycle of the Golden Year, and that this knowledge was passed down orally from generation to generation, to survive in variously bowdlerized forms in the legends and mystery tales written down in the Middle Ages.

At the finish of the last chapter, we were left with the loose ends of some anomalies in the mythological attributions associated with the

13 letter months of the Beth-Luis-Nion alphabet calendar. There is a possible solution to these anomalies. It is not a perfect solution, but it does produce some more clearly recognizable correspondences. It is based on the simple principle, suggested earlier, that we should reckon the beginning and end of the Celtic year as midsummer, not midwinter. That idea is also not entirely an invention. Pliny tells us quite clearly that the Celtic year began in his time in the month of July. Perhaps we may be allowed to interpret Pliny's meaning rather flexibly as 'high summer', so 21 June would not be too far off.

If, as I have already suggested, we take midsummer as the beginning of the year, rather than midwinter, and count our months of 28 days from midsummer to midsummer (but without changing the letter order), we arrive at this slightly different table of correspondences (see below).

The author's Beth-Luis-Nion calendar correspondences

7 December – 3 January	B	Birch	Midwinter solstice
4 January – 31 January	L	Rowan	
1 February – 28 February	N	Ash	Imbolc
1 March – 28 March	F	Alder	Spring equinox
29 March – 25 April	S	Willow	
	SS	Blackthorn	
26 April – 23 May	H	Whitethorn	Beltane
24 May – 20 June	D	Oak	
21 June	'and a day'		Midsummer solstice
22 June – 19 July	T	Holly	
20 July – 16 August	C	Hazel	Lughnasa
	CC	Apple	
17 August – 13 September	M	Vine	
14 September – 11 October	G	Ivy	Autumn equinox
12 October – 8 November	NG	Reed	Samhain
9 November – 6 December	R	Elder	

The changes are small but significant. They may be set out as follows:

- The midwinter solstice moves from Ruis, the unlucky elder month, to Beth, the birch month.
- Imbolc moves from Luis, the month of rowan, the death tree, into Nion, the ash month.
- Beltane moves from Saille or willow month into Huath, the month of whitethorn.

214

- The midsummer solstice moves out of Bel's oak-king month of Duir, and now stands as the 'day out of time' at the transition point between the oak-king and the holly-king.
- Lughnasa moves from Tinne, the holly month, to the month of Coll and Quert, the hazel and the apple.
- The autumn equinox moves from Muin, the vine, to Gort, the ivy month.

The two festivals which keep their original stations are the spring equinox, which is still in Bran's month of Fearn or the alder tree, and Samhain, which remains in the month of Ngetal or reed month, also called Peith or water-elder month.

Midwinter was ill-placed in Ruis: the associations with misfortune and death do not accord with my earlier mythographic attribution of the female mystery, the transition from girl to woman, at this important station in the calendar. In Beth, the month of the birch, midwinter is far better placed. The birch is the tree of inception, of new beginnings. The new broom which sweeps all clean is a birch besom. The Romans may well have adopted the tree as the proper timber for *lictors'* rods because it was identified earlier by the Greeks with inception. It is a far more appropriate tree than elder for the mystery of the menarche, the inception of menstruation and womanhood.

By Graves's chronology, we found Imbolc, the festival associated with lambing ewes, first lactation and motherhood generally, in the wholly inappropriate month of Luis, the rowan or mountain ash burned to summon the spirits of the dead to battle and widely associated with death. Imbolc now moves into Nion, the ash month. Ash was used for weapons and chariots, but it was also used to build coracles and oars, almost certainly in housing, and quite possibly for cradles. In British folklore, ash is still associated with rebirth and regeneration. Gilbert White's description in the *History of Selborne* of children being passed through pollarded ash trees to cure their congenital afflictions, especially hernias, is evidence of the long-standing belief that the ash has curative powers. This may be Nordic, rather than Celtic, in origin, since the ash is represented by Askr Yggr-drasill, or Yggdrasill, which means the ash tree that is the horse of Yggr, the enchanted ash whose roots and branches extend through the whole universe. However, the ash is also associated with the Celtic goddess Ana or Danu, the great mother-goddess from whom sprang the Tuatha de Danaan, or people of Danu. The Irish legend of

Trefuilngid Tre Eochair (the triple bearer of the triple key) mentions two great ash trees, the Tree of Tortu and the Branching Tree of Dathi, which are purportedly representative of the Brythonic and Danish (i.e., Nordic) ash-cults respectively. It, therefore, seems more appropriate for the festival of the goddess as the mother in milk to occur in the month of the ash, the tree of rebirth and regeneration associated with the mother-goddess.

Beltane seemed well placed in Saille, the willow month. Although the willow is principally associated with the goddess in her death aspect, and has become even more closely associated with witchcraft subsequently, it is also the tree of the aspiring poet or acolyte. The accompanying double-letter month, SS or Z for blackthorn, also had the appropriate association with the god as hero or warrior. However, I believe Huath for whitethorn, Beltane's new location by my allocation of dates, is even more appropriate. The whitethorn is the tree associated with the Celtic myth of Yspaddaden Pencawr, the giant (father-god, or Bran) who sets impossible tasks for his daughter Olwen's suitor, Culhwch. Culhwch is the perfect Brythonic embodiment of the hero, the aspiring god, Bel in other words. Culhwch (his name means pig run) hunts Twrch Trwyth, the magical sacred boar. He is first cousin to Arthur, and, like all the Celtic heroes, he is born in peculiar circumstances: his mother, Goleudydd, finds herself near a swinery, gives birth, then flees in terror from the pigs, abandoning the child to the care of a swineherd, who gives him his fitting name. Hawthorn, flower of chastity and tree of the warrior hero Culhwch, would be very appropriate for Beltane.

The 'day out of time', the day of 'a year and a day', is now midsummer itself. The day celebrates the mystery of son succeeding father succeeding son succeeding father through all the ages of time. It clearly separates the oak-god from the holly-god and stands precisely between them, set to precipitate the boy, the aspiring king or god, into manhood and the man, the vanquished king or god, into decline and death. It stands at the high point of summer, when all things are plentiful and good, the locus of the Celtic paradise, or Avallon. All references to the life after death in Celtic mythology are realized in a summer context – even when a term like Annwn (godless place) is used, and usually translated as Hell in English, it is clear that the place described is rich in meat, fish, fruit, vegetables and other crops; pleasantly mild, bright and sunny. It is a welcome place, where heroes are justly rewarded for their valour and mingle freely with gods and demi-gods. Movement to and from the other world is easy, and it may be undertaken in different guises, including shapeshifting into animal form. The day without a letter, representing the moment of eternity, or nirvana, when the endless cycle of generation succeeding generation is momentarily suspended, is midsummer's day.

Lughnasa seemed perfectly placed in Graves's scheme: the holly-god was celebrated in Tinne, the holly month. However, Coll and Quert, hazel and apple, are also mighty trees with which Bran could associate himself. MacColl or MacCool, (son of hazel), in Irish mythology one of the three brother gods who first ruled Ireland, is a fitting counterpart for Bran or Cronos, the first-father god. The fact that white hazel wands were carried by the Druids as symbols of their authority may indicate a connection with the godhead worshipped at Lughnasa. In 'The Romance of Lleu Llaw Gyffes', in *The Mabinogion*, Dylan (the son of the wave) is born mysteriously when his mother Arianrhod, daughter of Don, steps over a magic wand laid down by Gwydion, son of Don. The magic wand is made of hazel wood, of course. Lleu, or Lugh, visits the Castle of Arianrhod, the revolving crystal palace in which Arianrhod (Silver Wheel) holds court, in a coracle made of rushes on a frame of hazel twigs. Lugh is killed at midsummer and commemorated at Lughnasa; his resurrection comes at midwinter, when he passes through the holed stone which represents the womb of the mother-goddess – and he is led to the holed stone by divining rods, which are hazel wands. Apple, the sacred fruit, the fruit of Avallon the eternal orchard, would also be the fruit of the father-god. After death, he dwells for ever in the orchard, feasting on salmon baked in honey, with hazelnuts and sweet apples. His drink is the old man's drink of apple-cider.

Finally, the autumn equinox moves by my reckoning from Muin, month of the vine, to Gort, the ivy month. Ivy is more closely associated with Bran, or at least with his counterpart, Saturn, than vine or blackberry, the British substitute for the Mediterranean tree. Ivy and holly share the honours at the Saturnalia. Neither the spring equinox nor the autumn equinox is associated with any particular Celtic festival, although it seems certain that they were recognized for calendrical purposes and probably celebrated in some way. According to my allocation, both would be closely associated with Bran, the father-god: the vernal equinox falling in the month of Bran's totemic tree, the water-resistant alder, and the autumnal equinox falling in the month of the ivy, also associated with him. Perhaps that reflects a fair allocation. Bel dominates midsummer because it marks the transition point when he succeeds to the throne and becomes Bran. He also dominates midwinter because he is the child who will be born of the female mystery between Samhain and Imbolc, when the virgin becomes the mother. If Bel has the solstices, Bran has the equinoxes.

The complete map of the mythographic cycle of the Celtic year can thus be represented in the illustration below.

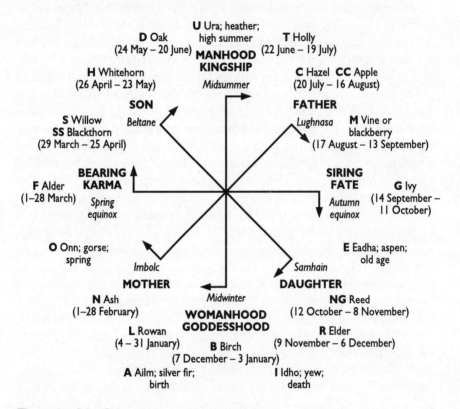

The cycle of the Celtic year.

Conclusion

Druidism is an ancient Western religion, with many apparent similarities to Persian religions, including the worship of Ahura Mazda, to the Medean priest-cult of the Magi, to the religion of ancient Egypt, and possibly to the religion of the ancient Phoenicians. There are certainly many parallels between early Greek thought and Druidism. Especially significant is the apparently close relationship between Pythagoreanism and Druidism. Hecateus specifically describes contacts between Greeks and Hyperboreans, or Britons, during the time of Pythagoras, who was his contemporary. The doctrine of metempsychosis, best known by the Eastern term karma, is central to Pythagoreanism, and it seems closely related to the Celtic conceptions of an other world out of time which is earned by noble thoughts and actions, and of shapeshifting, in which the spirit of a human, demi-god or god can be transformed temporarily into the body of an animal. The calendrical and mathematical skill of the Druids, their great reverence for learning, their deep passion for religious and speculative thought, their reverence for natural law, and, above all, the high status accorded to women in early Celtic tribal society, all combine to support the notion of direct exchange of ideas between Pythagoreanism and Druidism, although the means remain unclear.

The original provenance of the Celts is shrouded in the mists of time. The horse was first tamed some time around 3000 BC in central Europe, and the Celts have been renowned horsemen since earliest times. There was also a vigorous Celtic horse-cult, with the great goddess represented as a mare and worshipped under the name of Epona. Archaeological finds of Celtic artefacts date from around 700 BC, the period known as Hallstatt, from the site of the finds. A new cultural phase, known as the La Tène period, dates from around 500 BC, about the same time as Pythagoras. The artwork of this period shows immense sophistication, an obvious preoccupation with mathematical and geometric figures, and a rare ease in moving from the concrete to the abstract, suggestive of a philosophical and speculative attitude towards reality. There is no clear date for the first Celtic invasions of the British Isles, but any date earlier than around 900 BC seems unlikely. From around 280 BC, Celtic tribes began incursions against the empire of Alexander the Great – it is from the Greek name *keltoi* that the name Celt is derived. From about the same period until the middle of the fifth century AD, the history of the Celts is intimately related to the history of the Romans. In Gaul, and later in Britain, Roman influence was very powerful, but Druidism appears to have survived, at least in some form, up to and beyond the Christianization of Britain. The Druidic tradition was oral, and the laws and mythology of Celtic society were not recorded in written form until the early Middle Ages, by which time they were already centuries old. For the same reason, most of our written accounts of the Celts are not by Celts, but by Greek and Roman authors, who naturally tended to exaggerate the barbaric and bellicose characteristics of their enemy. Some elements of the Druidic tradition were transmogrified and incorporated in the great wealth of legend about the sixth-century military leader, Arthur, developed in the later Middle Ages into a body of literature known as the Matter of Britain, in which Arthur's rank is elevated to king. As an active, widespread participatory religion, Druidism had all but disappeared by the time of the Norman Conquest in the eleventh century.

Early Celtic society was tribal and hierarchical, with Druids occupying positions of high rank. The Celts were renowned for their battle valour, their vanity, and their elegant and sophisticated appearance and personal effects. Religion played an important part in the daily lives of all members of Celtic society. Law was held in very high regard, with the principles of 'fair play' and 'the fitness of things' highly honoured. Some of these legal and moral precepts survived into the medieval chivalric code, which has greatly influenced Western moral philosophy. Religious worship appears to have been conducted mainly outdoors, with the sacred grove, usually known by the Greek word *nemeton*, frequently attested. The cave or tunnel known by the Cornish word 'fogou' may also have been used for religious purposes, although the evidence is very unclear. Some larger, rectangular buildings and plots of land seem to have been used for religious rites on occasion, but evidence here is even more speculative. Principal tribes tended to remain limited in size and restricted to certain geographical areas. Individual rocks, mountains, wells, springs, even single trees, were specially revered and associated with tribal gods and goddesses. The general pattern was for tribes to move their herds and flocks within the tribal area, rather than build elaborate and permanent settlements. Raids against other tribes to steal cattle and other livestock were frequent. Tribal loyalties were established and maintained by a system of royal inheritance and lineage, which might be matrilinear or patrilinear, by clientship, and by the widespread practice of fosterage, which had a greatly stabilizing influence. The early tribal Celts were highly competitive, and enjoyed many games and sports, often warlike in character.

Druids operated with retinues. Some of the retained men would be warriors, although evidence of Druids actually participating in battle is extremely rare. The two principal functions of the ranks below full Druid were the composition and declamation of poetry, probably including satires, by poets called Bards, and divination or prophecy, by seers know as Vates, Ovates or the Irish term 'filid'. It is apparent that there must have been some overlap in function, and the evidence

220

suggests that the position of Bard and Ovate were occupied as part of the 19-year training period required for full induction into the priesthood. All the teaching was conducted orally, and classical authors inform us that a Bard or prospective Druid might have to learn over 20,000 verses by heart during a training period lasting nine years. Priestesses are mentioned in the classical texts, and there are occasional references to Druidesses, which, coupled with our knowledge of the important roles often taken by women in Celtic society, including generalship in battle, suggests that Druids may have been female as well as male. One of the principal Druidic functions was the composition and utterance of satire. True utterance was held to have great magical power, and a properly and fairly composed satire was deemed sufficiently powerful to cause disfigurement and even death. Another principal role was the administration of religious ceremonies, although some of the classical evidence for what constituted those ceremonies seems unreliable, notably the famous description by Pliny of the cutting of the sacred mistletoe. There is plausible evidence that the religious practices did include human sacrifice, but the gruesome and barbaric depictions by Caesar and Strabo may have been exaggerated for political reasons. A very important Druidic function was the giving of judgement. The Druids acted as ambassadors and arbiters in disputes, especially in war or over territory and inheritance. They were judges and lawmakers, and were probably involved in domestic law, including marriage, divorce, fosterage, clientship and contractual arrangements, as well as the more religious ceremonies of birth, initiation and death.

The lives of the early Celts were closely bound to an agricultural cycle based on hunting, fishing and mixed pastoral and arable farming. The winter was a hard and lean time. Salt was a valuable commodity because it preserved meat. Many of the Druidic practices would have been related to agricultural events. One attested festival, Beltane, is specifically agricultural, involving the blessing and purification of livestock by driving the animals between two ritual fires, probably as a prophylactic measure. Food was abundant in high summer, but winter survival depended on careful use of stored cereals, especially barley and oats, supplemented by dried meat. Pork was highly regarded as meat, but the foods most frequently mentioned in the vernacular tales as having high status are salmon, hazelnuts and apple. Plants and herbs were gathered for medicinal purposes. Leather was used for clothing, for boats, and possibly for armour, although archaeological evidence of any kind of personal armour is rare. Sheep were raised for their wool as well as their meat, and Celtic woollen cloaks were of such quality that they were imported into Rome.

The stations of the agricultural cycle, indeed of the whole year, were marked by religious festivals. The four principal festivals, well attested in many texts, were: Beltane, the festival of purification dedicated to Bel, a sun god; Lughnasa, a commemorative festival dedicated to a first-father god, similar to the Greek Cronos or Roman Saturn, known as Lugh in Ireland, Llew Llaw Gyffes in Britain, and frequently as Bran (Crow) or Bendigeidfran (Blessed Crow), and many other names; Samhain, a festival associated with the dead but also with the virgin goddess Rhiannon, also known as Caer and by many other names; and lastly, Imbolc, a pastoral festival associated with lambing, ewes' milk and motherhood, whose principal associated deity is the goddess Brigit, later Christianized as St Brigid, or Bride.

Midwinter and midsummer seem also to have been celebrated, along with the vernal and autumnal equinoxes, thus making eight festival stations fairly evenly spaced throughout the year. Most of our evidence for the beliefs and practices associated with these festivals is derived or inferred from surviving folklore relating to each time of year. A frequently repeated and varied pattern of religious belief seems to emerge from Celtic folklore and mythology: it is the pattern of an eternal and primal goddess, who appears in three main aspects, virgin, mother and crone, who gives birth to a son, who grows to become a father and eventually dies, to be succeeded in turn by his son, and so on, down through countless generations. Midwinter and midsummer seem to be important transitions in the mythography of this pattern, with midsummer representing the transition from boyhood to manhood, or from manhood to kingship, or from hero-god to father-god, and midwinter representing the transition from girlhood to womanhood, or virgin to mother.

The only archaeological evidence that the early Celts had a calendar system to record the agricultural cycle and the religious festivals of the year is an engraved calendar found at Coligny, dating from the first century; but the calendar seems crude and may be unrepresentative, made after a Roman pattern to please Roman overlords. It is obvious, however, that carefully stationed religious festivals would have required a calendar of some kind. The mathematics of Pythagoreanism is surprisingly sophisticated considering how ancient it is, and there are many striking parallels between

Pythagorean number attributes and Celtic lore surrounding particular numbers – again suggestive of intellectual commerce between Celts and Greeks* at some stage. Some numbers highly regarded by Pythagoreans were also especially important to the Celts, including the numbers 3, 5, 8, 13, 19 and 28. Many of the stone circles, chamber tombs and standing stones in Ireland, Britain and France have clear astronomical alignments (although most were built before the arrival of the Celts), and it is possible that the Celts continued the astronomical observation associated with them. The esoteric calendar lore of the Celts, deeply concealed in the mythographic attributions of the ancient Beth-Luis-Nion tree-alphabet, is open to various interpretations in its unravelling, but there is at least some evidence that the Celts may have reckoned the year as 13 months of 28 days followed by a single unnamed day, from which the frequently used phrase 'a year and a day' appears to be derived. This phrase often conveys a legal or contractual implication, which would accord with what we already know about Druidic functions. The most likely days for the 'extra' day seem to be either Midsummer's Day or Midwinter's Day, and it is probable that the months were calculated forward from whichever day it was. For some reason, Samhain has also been proposed as the beginning of the Celtic year, although evidence for the attribution is unclear. Pliny describes the Celtic year as being divided in two halves and beginning in July, which, along with other important mythographic evidence, suggests that the months were reckoned from midsummer.

From all this evidence, inference and conjecture emerges a picture of a Celtic cosmogony consistent within itself, rich in mythological legend and pattern, closely related to the reality of the agricultural and biological cycle, yet rooted in a profound reverence for a truth beyond the immediately apparent and a deep faith in a real active afterlife beyond empirical observation. The full detail of this religion and its accompanying mythology and ceremonial practice will always escape us, because our sources are either limited or biased. However, the merest glimpses which do emerge convincingly are sufficient to tell us that the early Celtic tribal way of life and the Druidic religion, so closely woven into its fabric, were something quite out of the ordinary in the ancient world.

Plainly, we should not automatically underestimate cultures apparently more barbaric than our own. If we can suspend cultural judgement, we may observe highly sophisticated beliefs and practices where we might not have anticipated finding them. In an age when the world's cultures are very sharply divided between so-called advanced and so-called primitive, it remains a useful and practical exercise for us to approach cultures other than our own with a cool-headed generosity.

The powerful survival of much of the Druidic tradition by oral transmission alone reminds us forcibly of the strength of the spoken word. If we want the best of our own culture (whatever that is) to survive, the lesson seems to be that we must talk as well as write. We must tell our tales to our children using our own well-chosen words; we must ask our students to use their minds, and their ears and their voices, and apply them to learning, and in so doing honour the obligation upon us to send our truth cascading down the ages, as best we can. When Pwyll speaks without thinking, Rhiannon tells him, 'Never was there a man made feebler use of his wits than thou hast.' We allow much of our talking to be done by others, supposedly on our behalf, in modern Western society. Perhaps we should think more carefully about the power of true utterance, and make a more concerted effort to keep our own wits about us and speak with our own tongues.

Notes

1. The description is actually given by the later historian, Diodorus Siculus, as a quotation from Hecateus.
2. Paul Hoffman, *Archimedes' Revenge: The Joys and Perils of Mathematics*.
3. Aubrey Burl, *Prehistoric Astronomy and Ritual*.
4. Lucien Rudaux and G. de Vaucouleurs, *Larousse Encyclopaedia of Astronomy*.

FULL NAMES OF CLASSICAL AUTHORS

Full proper names of the classical authors mentioned in the text are as follows:

Ammianus   Ammianus Marcellinus, Roman historian of the Christian era
Aristotle   Aristoteles, Greek philosopher, *c*.385–322 BC
Caesar   Caius Julius Caesar, Roman general and historian, 100–44 BC
Cato   Marcus Porcius Cato, Roman orator, historian, 235–149 BC
Catullus   Caius Valerius Catullus, Roman poet, *c*. 84–54 BC
Cicero   Marcus Titus Cicero, Roman philosopher and orator, *c*.107–43 BC
Clement   Called Clemens Alexandrinus (Clement of Alexandria) in Rome, Greek philosopher and historian, *fl.* AD 206
Diodorus   Diodorus Siculus (the Sicilian), Roman historian, *fl.* 44 BC
Dio, Dion   Dio Cassius, also Graecized as Dion, Roman historian, *fl. c.* AD 230
Dion   Dion Chrysostom, Christian historian, AD 353–407
Eudoxus   Eudoxes, Greek geometer and astronomer 405–352 BC
Hecataeus   Hecates, also spelled Hecateus, Greek historian, *fl. c.*520 BC
Hirtius   Aulus Hirtius, Roman historian, died 43 BC
Livy   Titus Livius, Roman historian, BC 59–AD 17
Lucian   Lucianus, Roman philosopher and writer, AD 90–180
Lucretius   Titus Lucretius Carus, Roman poet and philosopher, 95–55 BC
Lucullus   Lucullus Lucius Licinius, Roman general and philosopher, *fl.* 85 BC
Mela   Pomponius Mela, Spanish (Roman) geographer, *fl.* AD 45
Plato   Originally Aristocles, epithet Plato means big-shouldered, Greek philosopher, *c*.429–348 BC
Pliny   Caius Plinius Secundus (Pliny the Elder), Roman writer on natural history, *c*. AD 23–79
Pliny   Caius Plinius Caecilius Secundus (Pliny the Younger), Roman letter writer, *c*. AD 62–113

Polybius   Polybius of Megalopolis, Greek historian, 206–124 BC

Posidonius   Posidonius Apameae, Roman philosopher, *fl.c.* 50 BC

Pythagoras   Pythagoras, Greek philosopher, died *c.* 497 BC

Strabo   (Roman slang for squint-eyed), Greek geographer, died AD 25

Suetonius   Suetonius Caius Paulinus, Roman general, governor of Britain from *c.* AD 110 to 130.

Suetonius   Suetonius Caius Tranquillus, Roman historian, secretary to Hadrian, *fl.* AD 110

Tacitus   Caius Cornelius Tacitus, Roman historian, *c.* AD 55–11

Timagenes   (Called Timageneus in Rome), Greek historian, *fl.* 54 BC

Vopiscus   Native of Syracuse, historian, *fl. c.* AD 303

BIBLIOGRAPHY

Classical texts

Many of the classical authors cited appear in various editions of *The Loeb Classical Library* series. This series was published by Heinemann in London and the Macmillan Co. in New York in the first decades of this century, with reprints of the more popular titles through the 1920s and 1930s. The Loeb edition format places the Latin text on the left-hand page and an English translation on the right.

A smaller series, in a different format, is *The Roman World Series*, published and reprinted through the 1940s and 1950s by Allen & Unwin Ltd., in London. These editions contain useful biographical notes on the authors, vocabularies and explanatory paragraphs, as well as selected passages of original text from the different authors and poets represented, but they are not translations – the reader needs to know some Latin to be able to use them.

There are grounds for recommending each series, depending on the reader's needs. To take Pliny (the letter writer) as an example: the Loeb series gives us a two-volume edition, called *Pliny's Letters*, based on William Melmoth's translation of 1746, revised for publication by W.M.L. Hutchinson in 1915, reprinted through the 1920s and 1930s. The advantage of this edition is its completeness and its academic authority. The comparative text from the Roman World series is *Pliny, Selections from the Letters*, edited by C.E. Robinson, first published in 1939 and reprinted through the 1940s and 1950s. While this edition contains far less of the original Latin material, it does give us a great deal of historical background and explanatory introduction to the selections, as well as maps and photographs.

A recent reprint of a well-known book is very useful to the general reader. It is *Latin Selections/Florilegium Latinum*, edited by Moses Hadas and Thomas Suits, originally published 30 years ago, but reprinted by Dover Publications Inc., New York, in 1992. The text follows the dual-language format, and the translations are clear, accurate and elegant. The text includes extracts from Caesar's *De Bello Gallico* and from Tacitus's *Annals* and *On the Life of Julius Agricola*.

Graves, R., *Suetonius, The Twelve Caesars*, Harmondsworth: Penguin Books, 1957

Lemprière, J., *A Classical Dictionary*, London: Routledge, n.d.

Scott-Kilvert, I., *Plutarch, The Makers of Rome, Nine Lives by Plutarch*, Harmondsworth: Penguin, 1965

Selincourt, A. de, *Livy, The History of Rome from its Foundation, Books I–V*, Harmondsworth: Penguin, 1960

Selincourt, A. de, *Livy, The History of Rome from its Foundation, Books XXI–XXX*, Harmondsworth: Penguin, 1965

Classical quotations are also given in:

Chadwick, N.K., *The Druids*, Cardiff and Connecticut: 1966

Kendrick, T.D., *The Druids: A Study in Keltic Prehistory*, London, 1927, repub. 1966, New York

Tierney, J.J., 'The Celtic Ethnography of Posidonius', *Proceedings Royal Irish Academy*, LX (C), 1960, 189–275

Zwicker, J., *Fontes Historiae Religioni Celticae*, Berlin, 1934

Vernacular texts

Broome, D., *Fairy Tales from the Isle of Man*, Helsinki: Norris Modern Press, 1951, repub. 1953

Bromwich, R., *Trioedd Ynys Prydein: The Welsh Triads*, Cardiff, 1961

Dunn. J., *Tain Bo Cualgne*, Dublin, 1914

Gantz, J., *The Mabinogion*, London: Penguin, 1976

Gantz, J., *Early Irish Myths and Sagas*, London: Penguin, 1981

Gwynn, E., *The Metrical Dindschenchas*, Dublin, 1913

Jones, G. & Jones, T., *The Mabinogion*, London: Dent, 1948, revised 1974

Kinsella, T., *The Tain*, Dublin: Oxford University Press, 1969

Knott, E., *Togail Bruidne Da Derga*, Dublin, 1936

Luzel, F.M., *Celtic Folk-Tales from Armorica*, trans. Bryce, D., Lampeter: Llanerch Enterprises, 1985

O'Faolain, E., *Irish Sagas and Folk Tales*, Oxford, 1954

Scott, M., *Irish Folk and Fairy Tales*, (two volumes), London: Sphere Books, 1983

Smith, A.S.D. (Caradar) & Hooper, E.G.R. (Talek), *An Mabinogion yn Kernewek*, Falmouth: Kesva an Taves Kernewek/The Cornish Language Board, 1975

Williams, I., *Pedair Keinc y Mabinogi*, Cardiff, 1930

Celtic language

Anwyl, J.B., *Spurrell's English-Welsh, Welsh-English Dictionary*, Carmarthen: Spurrell, 1934

Bhaldraithe, T. de, *English-Irish Dictionary*, Dublin: Oifig an Solathair/Office of Procurement, 1959

Brown, W. (Crenner), *A Grammar of Modern Cornish*, Saltash: Kesva an Taves Kernewek/The Cornish Language Board, 1984

O Donaill, N. (ed.), *Gearrfhocloir Gaeilge-Bearla*, Dublin: An Roinn Oideachais/Department of Education, 1981

Gell, G., *Conversational Manx*, Port Erin: Yn Cheshaght Ghailckagh/The Manx Society, 1973

George, K. (Profus an Mortyd), *The Pronunciation and Spelling of Revived Cornish*, Seaton: Kesva an Taves Kernewek/The Cornish Language Board, 1986

George, K. (Profus an Mortyd), *Gerlyver Kernewek Kemmyn*, Seaton: Kesva an Taves Kernewek/The Cornish Language Board, 1993

Gillies, H.C., *The Elements of Gaelic Grammar*, London: D. Nutt, 1902

Gregor, D.B., *Celtic – A Comparative Study*, Cambridge and New York: Oleander Press, 1980

Hedd Wynn, *Cerddi'r Bugail*, Cardiff: J.J. Williams, 1918

Hemon, R., *Marvailhou ar Vretoned*, Brest: Gwalarn, 1941

Hemon, R., *Nouveau Dictionnaire Breton-Français*, Brest: Al Liamm, 1978

Holmes, J., *1000 Cornish Place-Names Explained*, Redruth: Dyllansow Truran/Truran Publications, 1983

Kneen, J.J., *English-Manx Pronouncing Dictionary*, first published 1938 by Mona's Herald, Douglas: Yn Cheshaght Ghailckagh/The Manx Society, 1970

Lewis, H., *Welsh Dictionary*, London and Glasgow: Collins, 1960, re-edited 1969

MacFarlane, M., *Gaelic-English Dictionary*, Stirling: Eneas Mackay, 1953

Morton Nance, R. (Mordon), *Cornish-English* (1955), *English-Cornish* (1952) *Dictionary*, Penzance: originally published by the Federation of Old Cornwall Societies, subsequently republished by Kesva an Taves Kernewek/The Cornish Language Board in one volume, 1978

Padel, O.J., *A Popular Dictionary of Cornish Place-Names*, Penzance: Alison Hodge, 1988

Richards, M., *Cystrawen y Ffrawddeg Gymraeg*, Cardiff, 1938

O Siadhail, M., *Learning Irish*, Dublin: Dublin Institute for Advanced Studies, 1980

Stowell, B., *Gaelg Trooid Jalooghyn*, Douglas: Yn Cheshaght Ghailckagh/The Manx Society, 1947

Strachan, J., *An Introduction to Early Welsh*, Manchester, 1937

William, U., *A Short Welsh Grammar*, Llandybie: Christopher Davies, 1960
Williams, R., *Llawlyfr Gramadeg Cymraeg, Gyda Gwersi*, Wrexham: Hughes a'i Fab/Hughes & Son, 1923

General

Ashbee, P., *The Ancient British: A Social–Archaeological Narrative*, Norwich: Geo Abstracts, Ltd., 1978
Ashe, G., *The Quest for Arthur's Britain*, London: Pall Mall Press, 1968
Baillie Reynolds, P.K., *Chysauster*, London: Department of the Environment pamphlet, 1978
Bain, G., *Celtic Art – the Methods of Construction*, London: William Maclellan, 1951
Berresford Ellis, P., *A Dictionary of Irish Mythology*, London: Routledge & Kegan Paul, 1987
Bertrand, A., *Archéologie Celtique et Gauloise*, Paris, 1954
Bertrand, A., *La Religion des Gaulois*, Paris, 1897
Bessy, M., *Histoire en 1000 images de la magie*, Paris, 1961, trans. Crosland, M. & Dave, A., *A Pictorial History of Magic and the Supernatural*, London: Spring Books, 1964
Boardman, J., *Greek Art*, London: Thames and Hudson, 1973
Bord, J. & C., *A Guide to Ancient Sites in Britain*, London: Latimer New Dimensions, Ltd., 1978
Bouquet, A.C., *Sacred Books of the World*, London: Penguin, 1954
Branston, B., *The Lost Gods of England*, London: Thames & Hudson, 1957
Breffny, B. de, (ed.), *The Irish World*, London and New York: Abrams, 1978
Broadhurst, P., *Secret Shrines – in Search of the Old Holy Wells of Cornwall*, Launceston: Broadhurst, 1988
Bronowski, J., *The Ascent of Man*, London: BBC Publications, 1973
Burl, A., *The Stone Circles of the British Isles*, London and Yale: Yale University Press, 1976
Burl, A., *Prehistoric Avebury*, London and Yale: Yale University Press, 1979
Burl, A., *Prehistoric Astronomy and Ritual*, Princes Risborough: Shire Publications, 1983
Campbell, J., *The Hero with a Thousand Faces*, Princeton: Princeton University Press, 1949
Campbell, N., *Pageant of Saints*, Oxford: Mowbray, 1963
Cavendish, R., *King Arthur and the Grail*, London: Weidenfeld & Nicolson, 1978
Chippindale, C., *Stonehenge Complete*, London: Thames & Hudson, 1983
Clark, G. and Piggott, S., *Prehistoric Societies*, New York: Knopf, 1965

Clarke, G.H., *Selections from Hellenistic Philosophy*, New York: Appleton-Century-Crofts, 1940

Clayton, P., *Archaeological Sites of Britain*, London: Weidenfeld & Nicolson, 1976

Cone, P. (ed.), *Treasures of Early Irish Art*, New York: Metropolitan Museum of Art, 1977

Crowley, V., *Wicca – the Old Religion in the New Age*, Wellingborough: Aquarian Press, 1989

Cunliffe, B.W., *The Celtic World*, London, 1979

Delaney, F., *Legends of the Celts*, London, 1989

Devereux, P., *Places of Power*, London: Blandford, 1990

Drake-Carnell, F.J., *Old English Customs and Ceremonies*, London: Batsford, 1938

Drinkwater, J., *Roman Gaul*, London, 1983

Duckett, E., *The Wandering Saints of the Early Middle Ages*, London and Glasgow: W.W. Norton, 1959

Duval, P.-M., *Les dieux de la Gaule*, Paris, 1976

Dyer, J., *Ancient Britain*, London, 1990

Evans, J.G., *The Environment of Early Man in the British Isles*, Cardiff: Paul Elek, 1975

Falkus, M. & Gillingham, J. (eds.), *Historical Atlas of Britain*, London: Kingfisher Books, 1981

Ferguson, G., *Signs & Symbols in Christian Art*, Oxford: Oxford University Press, 1954

Fox, C., *A Find of the Early Iron Age from Llyn Cerrig Bach, Anglesey*, Cardiff, 1946

Frazer, J.G., *The Golden Bough*, London: Macmillan, 1992

Garner, A., *The Owl Service*, London: Collins, 1967

Gimbutas, M., *The Language of the Goddess*, London: Thames & Hudson, 1990

Ginzburg, C., *Ecstasies – Deciphering the Witches' Sabbath*, trans. Rosenthal, R., New York: Pantheon Books, 1991

Graubard, M., *Astrology and Alchemy – Two Fossil Sciences*, New York: Philosophical Library Inc., 1953

Graves, R., *The White Goddess*, London: Faber, 1948, revised 1961, and New York: Farrar, Straus and Giroux, 1966

Graves, R., *The Greek Myths*, (two volumes), Harmondsworth: Penguin, 1955

Green, M.J., *Symbol and Image in Celtic Religious Art*, London and New York, 1989

Green, M.J., *Dictionary of Celtic Myth and Legend*, London: Thames & Hudson, 1992

Green, V.J., *Festivals and Saints' Days*, Poole, Dorset: Blandford, 1978

Gruffydd, W.-J., 'Mabon ab Modron', *Revue celtique*, 33, 1912, 452–61

Guthrie, W.K.C., *The Greek Philosophers from Thales to Aristotle*, New York: Harper Torchbooks, 1950

Hadingham, E., *Early Man and the Cosmos*, London: Heinemann, 1983

Harbison, P., *Pre-Christian Ireland*, London, 1988

Hartley, C., *The Western Mystery Tradition*, 1968

Hawkins, G.S., collab. White, J.B., *Stonehenge Decoded*, London: Souvenir Press, 1965

Heggie, D.C. (ed.), *Archaeoastronomy in the Old World*, Cambridge: Cambridge University Press, 1982

Hendricks, R.A. & Shapiro, M.S (ed.), *Mythologies of the World: A Concise Encyclopedia*, New York: Doubleday, retitled *A Dictionary of Mythologies*, London: Granada Publishing, 1979

Henig, M., *Religion in Roman Britain*, London, 1984

Herm, G., *The Celts*, trans. 1976, London: Weidenfeld & Nicolson, 1975

Hill Elder, I. (Merch o Lundain Derri), *Joseph of Arimathea*, pamphlet, Glastonbury, 1982

Hitching, F., *Earth Magic*, New York: Marrow, 1977

Hoffman, P., *Archimedes' Revenge: the Joys and Perils of Mathematics*, New York: Ballantine Books, 1988

O'Curry, E., *The Manners and Customs of the Ancient Irish*, 1954

O'Hogain, D., *The Encyclopaedia of Irish Folklore, Legend and Romance*, London, 1990

Hole, C., *English Folklore*, London, 1940

Hole, C., *Witchcraft in England*, London and New York: Collier-Macmillan, 1947

Hole, C., *Saints in Folklore*, New York: Barrows & Co., Inc., 1965

Hole, C., *A Dictionary of British Folk Customs*, London: Granada, 1976

Humphreys, C., *A Popular Dictionary of Buddhism*, London: Arco Publications, 1962

Ions, V., *Egyptian Mythology*, London and New York: Hamlyn, 1965

Ivimy, J., *The Sphinx and the Megaliths*, London: Turnstone Books, 1974

James, T.G.H., *Myths and Legends of Ancient Egypt*, New York: Gosset & Dunlap, 1969

Jenkins, E., *The Mystery of King Arthur*, London: Michael Joseph, 1975

Jones, K., *The Ancient British Goddess*, Glastonbury: Ariadne Publications, 1991

Jung, C.G., (ed., posthumously) & Von Franz, M.-L., (ed.), *Man and his Symbols*, London: Aldus Books, 1964

Keller, W., *The Etruscans*, trans. Henderson, A. & E., London: Cape, 1970

Koch, R., *The Book of Signs*, 1930 (in translation), repub. New York: Dover Publications

Lacey, R., *A Dictionary of Philosophy*, London: Routledge & Kegan Paul, 1976

Leek, S. & S., *A Ring of Magic Islands*, New York: American Photographic Book Publishing Co. Inc., 1976

LeRoux, F. & Guyonvarc'h, C.J., *Les druides*, Rennes, 1978

Lynch, F., *Prehistoric Anglesey*, Anglesey, 1970

Mac Cana, P., *Celtic Mythology*, London, 1983

MacManus, S., *The Story of the Irish Race*, New York: The Devin-Adair Co., 1921

MacNeill, M., *The Festival of Lughnasa*, Oxford, 1962

Masson, G., *A Concise History of Republican Rome*, London: Thames & Hudson, 1973

Maurice, *Ancient History of Hindoostan*, 1904

McLeish, J., *Number – The History of Numbers and How They Shape Our Lives*, New York: Fawcett Columbine, 1991

Michell, J., *A Little History of Astro-Archaeology*, London: Thames & Hudson, 1977

Miller, H., & Broadhurst, P., *The Sun and the Serpent*, Launceston: Pendragon Press, 1989

Miners, H. (Den Toll), *Gorseth Kernow – the first 50 years*, Penzance: Gorseth Kernow, 1978

Moran, Cardinal, *Irish Saints in Great Britain*, Callan: Sisters of Mercy, 1903

Nahm, M.C., *Selections from Early Greek Philosophy*, New York: Appleton-Century-Crofts, 1964

Nordenfolk C., *Celtic and Anglo-Saxon Painting*, New York: George Braziller, 1977

Owen, A.L., *The Famous Druids*, 1962

Pennick, N. & Devereux, P., *Lines on the Landscape – Leys and Other Linear Enigmas*, London: Hale, 1989

Peterson, I., *Islands of Truth – A Mathematical Mystery Cruise*, New York: W.H. Freeman & Co., 1990

Piggott, S., *Ancient Europe*, Edinburgh: Edinburgh University Press and Chicago: Aldine Publishing Co., 1965

Piggott, S., *The Druids*, London: Thames & Hudson, 1968

Pool, P.A.S. (Gwas Galva), *Antiquities of Penwith – the Land's End Peninsula*, Penzance: Penwith District Council, n.d.

Powell, T.G.E., *The Celts*, London: Thames & Hudson, 1958

Powell, T.G.E., *Prehistoric Art*, London: Thames & Hudson, 1966

O'Rahilly, T.F., *Early Irish History and Mythology*, Dublin, 1946

Rees, A. & B., *Celtic Heritage – Ancient Tradition in Ireland and Wales*, London: Thames & Hudson, 1961

Reik, T., *Pagan Rites in Judaism*, New York: Gramercy Publishing Co., 1964

Ross, A., *Everyday Life of the Pagan Celts*, London: Batsford, 1970

Ross, A., *The Pagan Celts*, London, 1986

Rudaux, L. & Vaucouleurs, G. de, *Larousse Astronomie*, Paris, 1959, repub. *Larousse Encyclopedia of Astronomy*, London: Hamlyn, 1967

Russell, B., *History of Western Philosophy*, London: Allen & Unwin, 1946

Scott-Moncrieff, P.D., *Paganism and Christianity in Egypt*, Cambridge: Cambridge University Press, 1913

Scullard, H.H., *Roman Britain – Outpost of the Empire*, London: Thames & Hudson, 1979

Sharma, C., *Indian Philosophy: A Critical Survey*, London, 1960, repub. New York: Barnes and Noble, 1962

Silver, D.J., *A History of Judaism*, New York: Basic Books, 1974

Smith, D.E., *Number Stories of Long Ago*, London: Ginn, 1919

Squire, C., *Celtic Myth and Legend, Poetry and Romance*, New York: Bell, 1979

Straffon, C., *The Earth Mysteries Guide to Ancient Sites in West Penwith*, Penzance: Meyn Mamvro Publications, 1992

Stuart, M., (ed.), *The Encyclopedia of Herbs and Herbalism*, London: Macdonald & Co, 1979

Thom, A., *Megalithic Sites in Britain*, Oxford: Oxford University Press, 1967

Thom, A., *Megalithic Lunar Observatories*, Oxford: Oxford University Press, 1971

Thom, A. and A.S. and Burl, A., *Megalithic Rings: Plans and Data for 229 Sites*, British Archaeological Reports 81, 1980

Thomas, C., *Exploration of a Drowned Landscape – Archaeology and History of the Isles of Scilly*, London: Batsford Ltd, 1985

Tolstoy, N., *The Quest for Merlin*, London: Hodder & Stoughton Ltd, 1985

Treharne, R.F. (ed., posthumously) and Fullard, H., (ed.), *Muir's Historical Atlas, Ancient and Classical*, London, 1938

Waite, A.E., *The Holy Kabbalah*, New York: Samuel Weister (first published 1899), 1960

Waring, P., *A Dictionary of Omens and Superstitions*, London: Souvenir Press, 1978

Wells, D., *The Penguin Dictionary of Curious and Interesting Numbers*, London: Penguin, 1986

Wright, D., *Druidism – the Ancient Faith of Britain*, Wakefield: EP Publishing Ltd and Totowa, NJ: Rowman and Littlefield, 1974

INDEX

Page numbers in *italic* refer to illustrations.